The Psychiatric Witness in Court

The Psychiatric Witness in Court

What Mental Health Professionals Need to Know

Calvin A. Colarusso

ROWMAN & LITTLEFIELD
Lanham • Boulder • New York • London

Published by Rowman & Littlefield
A wholly owned subsidiary of The Rowman & Littlefield Publishing Group, Inc.
4501 Forbes Boulevard, Suite 200, Lanham, Maryland 20706
www.rowman.com

16 Carlisle Street, London W1D 3BT, United Kingdom

British Library Cataloguing in Publication Information Available

Library of Congress Cataloging-in-Publication Data

Colarusso, Calvin A., author.
Psychiatric witness in court : what mental health professionals need to know / Calvin A. Colarusso.
p. cm.
Includes bibliographical references and index.
ISBN 978-1-4422-3039-2 (cloth : alk. paper)—ISBN 978-1-4422-3040-8 (electronic)
I. Title. [DNLM: 1. Expert Testimony. 2. Forensic Psychiatry. W 740]
RA1148
614'.15—dc23

2014032565

∞™ The paper used in this publication meets the minimum requirements of American National Standard for Information Sciences Permanence of Paper for Printed Library Materials, ANSI/NISO Z39.48-1992.

Printed in the United States of America

No lawyer jokes here, I dedicate this book to the legal profession because of the absolutely essential role they play in the life of their clients and in the maintenance of our free society. There are all too many examples around the world of countries where the courts are agents of repression and slavery rather than the freedom of the individual.

Contents

Acknowledgments

As I mention in the introduction, I never would have become involved in expert testimony work if I had not been approached, out of the blue, by Attorney Vincent Bartolotta, who asked me why teenagers climb telephone poles. His client was a teenager who had done that and was severely injured as a result. As a child psychiatrist and child analyst I had always been interested in normal development, not only in childhood but adulthood as well; so without realizing what I was getting myself into, I agree to become an expert witness in the lawsuit.

Actually, the experience was wonderful. I was fascinated with my new understanding of how the law worked and appearing in court. And so a new career began.

Over the years I have worked with literally hundreds of lawyers, too many to mention, but I must acknowledge a few of those who have had a great effect on me because of their intelligence, dedication to their clients, and integrity. Anyone familiar with the legal scene in San Diego will immediately recognize these names: Dennis Schoville, Milton Silverman, Joseph George, and more recently, Mike Bomberger and Steve Estey. I apologize to the many, many outstanding lawyers whom I have not mentioned by name.

I'd also like to thank Al Adler M.D., Clark Clipson PhD, Don Houts M.D., Reid Meloy PhD and Robert Stieber PhD for their assistance and advice.

As any author of a professional book knows, a fine editor is indispensible to a finished product. I'd like to thank Amy King of Jason Aronson for her outstanding understanding and assistance.

And of course, as any married person knows, the most important supporter (some would say sufferer) I've had is my wife of fifty-four years, Jean Colarusso. She missed out on many hours of companionship as I labored in my cave to finish this book.

Cal Colarusso
May 2014

Introduction

In the course of serving as a psychiatric expert witness in over one thousand civil cases over more than thirty years, I have been asked many questions about the experience by lawyers and mental health professional alike.

Lawyers ask about what psychiatrists and psychologists do and how they are different in their training and capabilities. They want to be educated about the psychological issues in the case at hand. Many are not familiar with DSM-V, *The Diagnostic and Statistical Manual of Mental Disorders* of the American Psychiatric Association, the only widely used diagnostic nomenclature in the field, used by every mental health professional in and out of court. They want to know what makes an expert witness "good" or "bad."

Although I will use the term psychiatric expert witness throughout the book, I am using the term to include *both* psychiatrists and psychologists because, with the exceptions of psychological testing and medication issues, both perform the same functions as experts.

Most psychiatrists and psychologists want nothing to do with the legal system. They are terrified of having their deposition taken or above all appearing in court. They do not understand, or respect, the adversarial nature of plaintiff versus defense and expect lawyers to abuse them, which sometimes they try to do.

Those mental health professionals who have an interest in serving as an expert witness will hopefully find this book useful because it is based on an understanding that the adversarial nature of the legal system is intended to educate the jury so that they can make an informed decision. The mental health expert witness plays an important role in that process.

There are many comprehensive textbooks about psychiatric experts and the law. The two I find most outstanding are *Psychological Evaluations for the Courts* by Gary Melton, John Petrila, Norman Poythress, and Christopher Slobogin (3rd ed., 2007) and *Testifying in Court: Guidelines and Maxims for the Expert Witness* by Stanley Brodsky (1991). Both are very comprehensive and detailed and describe legal theory and case law. I do not intend to duplicate their efforts. Instead, in this book, in a straightforward manner, using plain English, I attempt to explain to mental health professionals, particularly those considering becoming expert witnesses, (1) the nuts and bolts of choosing/being chosen as an expert witness, (2) the diagnostic/reporting process, and (3) the experience of being deposed and testifying in court. I provide examples of all of the forms needed to function and examples of reports. In other words, the *practical* information you need to know in order to succeed as an expert. In addition, I attempt to describe some of the practical wisdom that I have acquired over the past thirty-five years of serving as a psychiatric expert witness.

One of the unique features of this book is the presentation of a single case from the initial phone call through cross-examination in court. Of course, the material has been disguised in regard to names and location and unessential information, etc., but otherwise the data, including the deposition transcript and the direct and cross-examination in court, although altered to protect confidentiality, is presented in detail to provide the reader with as realistic a sense as possible of the experience of a mental health expert in the court system.

At various points in the book, particularly in the midst of the deposition, direct testimony, and the cross-examination of the case of Robert Rose, which is presented from initial phone call through cross-examination and a jury verdict; and the case of Evan Doe, which is presented from initial phone call through the deposition; I will convey my thoughts at the time and use italic print to distinguish from my thinking at the time from the actual questions and answers which were being asked by the attorney and answered by me.

I admire lawyers, particularly the good ones. I like and respect them. I admire the litigators ability to absorb huge amounts of information about subjects previously unknown in order to fulfill their roles as advocate or defendant, or as one fine lawyer told me, to "empty the bathtub" full of information about a particular case, only to begin to fill it again with a totally different body of knowledge as he proceeded to the next case. Mental health expert witnesses must do the same thing.

I did not seek out a career in forensic psychiatry. I was happily engaged in the private practice of adult and child psychiatry and psychoanalysis, teaching child and adult psychiatric residents at the University of California at San Diego, and writing and lecturing.

One day in the late 1970s I got a phone call from a then young, now very prominent, San Diego lawyer, Vincent Bartolotta, who asked me out of the blue, "Why do teenagers climb telephone poles?" His adolescent client had done just that and suffered severe electrical burns and injuries. My knowledge of normal development in adolescence became the foundation of my testimony. After I testified the phone began to ring and without stopping my work with patients, my teaching, and writing, I managed to serve as an expert more than one thousand times up to and including today. I still find the work stimulating and exciting.

Working within the best legal system in the world, lawyers and mental health professionals provide invaluable services to people in need. We need more psychiatrists and psychologists to serve as experts. In particular we need more *women* who are willing to serve as experts. Hopefully, this book will diminish the fear and misconceptions of the courtroom and our particular role in the court system.

Now on to the nuts and bolts.

ONE

Accepting the Role

"Expert Witness"
A witness who, by virtue of specialized knowledge or skill, can provide the fact finder with facts and inferences drawn from those facts that will assist the fact finder in reaching a conclusion on the issues addressed by the witness.

—Melton et al., 2007, p. 695

THE INITIAL CONTACT

The process usually begins with a phone call. Either a paralegal or Lawyer Jones will tell you that he or she is looking for a psychiatrist (or psychologist) to serve as an expert witness on a case. From now on I'll just use the pronoun he to refer to both sexes. Very often the request to find someone like you came from a senior member of the firm who is busy elsewhere and assigned the job to the paralegal or junior partner. In a calm friendly voice, even if it's your first time and you are shaking in your boots, ask about the particulars of the case, taking notes as you do. People sue for various reasons. For the purpose of our discussion let's assume that Lawyer Jones tells you that a client of his was in an automobile accident and suffered several broken ribs and a fractured leg (not your area of expertise, he will have an orthopedic surgeon discuss that) and is having nightmares and is afraid to drive. Are you interested? You begin to think PTSD.

After you express an interest in learning more he may ask you about past forensic experience. State it matter-of-factly—everyone has to start sometime! He probably got your name from someone who recommended you because of your personality or knowledge of a particular field of psychiatry. I've often referred younger colleagues to lawyers when I was either unavailable or lacked the expertise needed for a particular case.

He may or may not ask you what your fee is for expert testimony work. We'll discuss fees later but again, assuming that you are a beginner or someone fairly new at this game, tell him matter-of-factly that it is $300 per hour. You heard me correctly, $300 an hour! He won't be shocked. If he has had any experience he will know that that's a relatively low expert fee for a psychiatrist or psychologist expert witness. Psychiatric expert witness fees range anywhere from $300 an hour up to $600 or $700 or more in San Diego where I practice. Inquire about psychiatric expert fees in your area. They may differ. Medical expert witnesses in other fields often charge more, sometimes into the thousands. Describe what you are willing to do and give a brief description of your diagnostic evaluation procedure. Also ask about deadlines. Many lawyers wait till the last minute before calling because of the hope or expectation that the lawsuit will settle, thus eliminating the considerable additional expense of involving you. Be sure that you have sufficient time both in your schedule and within the time frame he gives you to review records, do an evaluation, get psychological testing, and write a report. An incomplete or rushed evaluation leaves you vulnerable at deposition or trial. If you and he come to a decision to proceed, he will then ask you to send him via e-mail a current curriculum vitae and a fee schedule.

Before the conversation ends be sure to get the proper spelling of his name, whether he is a paralegal or a lawyer, the name of the plaintiff and defendant involved in the case (e.g., John Thomas v. Marjorie Johnson) to be sure you do not know the individuals and have no conflict of interests, the individual's e-mail address, and the name of the partner or lawyer who will have the major responsibility for the case.

You are over the first hurdle.

THE CASE OF ROBERT ROSE

This case will be presented from the initial phone call through the cross-examination. The initial phone call follows immediately. Each succeeding aspect of the case is presented in the chapter dedicated to a discussion of that subject. The evaluation and report are presented in chapter 3, the deposition in chapter 5, the direct examination in chapter 6, and the cross-examination in chapter 7.

A child case, that of Evan Doe, from initial phone call through the deposition, will be presented in its entirety in chapter 8.

INITIAL PHONE CALL

The initial phone call came from a very experienced lawyer with whom I had worked before. He described the experience of a man in his forties who was waiting for his car outside of a restaurant when the valet driver put a car in forward instead of reverse and slammed Mr. Rose against the wall of the restaurant building. The plaintiff's pelvis was crushed and he had significant neurologic, sexual, and emotional issues.

I agreed to serve as an expert on the case. Because we had worked together before I did not need to explain the diagnostic process, including the employment of a psychologist to do psychological testing. I e-mailed my curriculum vitae, and fee agreement. Both were returned promptly with the retainer, medical records, and the police report. Other records would follow as they became available.

RESPONDING TO THE LAWYER'S REQUEST FOR INFORMATION

Your response to the paralegal or lawyer should include a curriculum vitae and fee schedule. Depending on your experience (and the lawyers) and the particulars of the case you may want to include a legal record and an outline of the diagnostic procedures you will follow. Examples of each follow.

I'm sure you already have a *curriculum vitae*. Be sure it is up to date. You may have to alter it some for forensic work. In addition to the usual information about education and training, list board certifications (certification in adult and/or child psychiatry is very important), university affiliations, teaching experience, and publications.

Your e-mail should always include a *fee schedule*. This not only informs the lawyer about the hourly cost of your services and retainer but also includes information on billing for missed appointment and psychological testing. As you can see from the form that follows the fee schedule may also serves as a contract between you and the law firm. Some lawyers will want a more formal agreement that they will draft.

Schedule of Fees for Expert Testimony Services

Your name
Your address
Your phone number
Your fax number
Your e-mail address
Nonrefundable retainer for services: (A fee of $1,500 to $3,000 is acceptable. The retainer is applied toward work done on the case.)

All fee rates in the book are based on practice in San Diego, California, for the years 2013–2015.

Your name may not be used as the designated expert witness until the signed fee agreement and nonrefundable retainer have been returned to your office.

Evaluations and consultations:

For all diagnostic interviews, review of records, report presentations, meeting, and discussions: (Your fee per hour.)

Testimony:

Deposition testimony: (Your fee per hour. Most experts charge the same, or more, than their fee for reviewing records and doing diagnostic interviews.)

Trial testimony: Half day—($1,500 and up)

Full day—($3,000 and up)

Travel: $250 per hour (to and from court locally or out of town).

Information:

Independent medical examinations (the term often used for forensic psychiatric evaluations) usually take three to four hours to complete.

Psychological testing will be arranged by (your name) with a psychologist of your choice. This evaluation, which usually takes from four to six hours to complete and costs approximately $3,000–$3,500, including a report, will be billed directly by the psychologist who sets the fee. The psychologist is an independent contractor and is not connected with (your name) office.

NOTICE OF CANCELLATION of independent medical evaluations is required at least three working days in advance of the scheduled time. Notice of cancellation of depositions and court appearances must occur within two working days. Cancelled depositions, court appearances, and missed diagnostic appointments will be billed at (your fee) per hour.

Contracts for consultation or expert testimony will not be made on a lien basis.

Services will be billed monthly. Payment is due within 30 days.

Insurance adjuster (in defense cases) or

Attorney signature and date

Your signature and date

TAX IDENTIFICATION (your social security or corporation number)

Please sign and return the fee agreement to fax number or mail to the above address.

One of the less studied areas in the literature is what to charge for travel. I base my figure of $250 on an approximation of what I would be earning if I were seeing patients during the time traveled. But the cost involved in traveling across town or to a nearby city to testify will obviously be quite different if you have to travel by plane or spend a night in a hotel. Deciding how much to charge for different situations present dilemmas. One study found that as the complexity of the travel situation increases, a tendency toward redundant billing emerges (Gutheil, Slater, Commons and Goodheart, 1998, pp. 21–26).

Expert Report

If you have been doing expert testimony work for a while and have a history of involvement in cases, no matter how brief, include what I call an *expert report* that lists the cases you were involved in in the past. Once you gain more experience your legal records should cover at least the past five years. Here is a brief example of a legal record. The actual names of plaintiffs and defendants have not been used.

Expert report of (your name)
Your address

Deposition and trial experience
2007–2013

2007

Deposition, January 10, *Trembly v. Chrysler Motor Company*, John Williby, Superior Court of California, County of San Diego, GIC 943871

Trial, May 15, *Lawrence Watkins v. Juan Petro*, Superior Court of California, County of San Diego, Northern Division, GIC 680573

2008

Trial, June 15, *Wayne Simpson v. USA*, U. S. District Court, Southern District of California #86LV2496F

Deposition, November 11, *Veronica Lewis v. Oceanview Townhouses HOA*, Superior Court of California, County of San Diego, North County Division, 369-0507

The expert report would continue from year to year to the present.

Forensic Psychiatric Evaluation

Outline of Procedures

I include this when I'm approached by a lawyer or firm that I have not worked with before. The intent is to acquaint the lawyer with the details of a psychiatric evaluation since many have no idea what a mental health evaluation consists of and also to demonstrate that I will do a thorough assessment. Since I am a child psychiatrist and frequently serve as an expert in cases involving children, I describe the differences between the procedures for evaluating children as well as adults.

My outline of procedures is contained in chapters 4 and 5 but you will certainly have your own or may find one in any psychiatric textbook of your choosing.

After receiving your information packet the lawyer may call with questions about your credential, fees, etc. Make no apologies for your fees and answer calmly and directly. Many lawyers, particularly if they have not worked with you before, will want a face-to-face meeting before deciding to hire you. I always try to arrange to have those meetings in my office. I want the lawyer to see that I work in a setting that is both professional and comfortable. In Southern California a coat and tie are rarely necessary, except for deposition or trial, but an attractive dress, business suit, or coat and tie are always acceptable.

DECIDING WHETHER OR NOT TO TAKE A CASE

This decision is not always easy but the principle used to determine the decision is easy to articulate. *Do not agree to serve as an expert on a case that is beyond your experience or outside your area of expertise.*

For instance, I have not worked at an inpatient unit since completing residency training, therefore, I do not consider myself qualified to serve as an expert on cases that involve inpatient issues. If I were to be foolish enough to accept such an assignment let me tell you how the lawyer for the opposing side would tear me to shreds at deposition or trial. Lawyer: "Dr. Colarusso, I see that your credentials are in order and that you are well trained but I don't see any evidence that you ever worked in a psychiatric hospital setting after your residency, and that was more than thirty years ago wasn't it? Dr. C: "Yes." Lawyer: "Doctor, do you mean to tell me that you are as qualified to provide expert opinion on the treatment of this hospitalized patient as Dr. Newman [defense expert] who has been doing inpatient work for more than ten years?" You get the idea. Things will go downhill from there.

I'm not attempting to frighten you away from serving as an expert witness, quite the opposite. If you do a thorough evaluation and stick to your areas of expertise there is little that an attorney can do to you on cross-examination. A well-prepared expert always has the upper hand because you know more about psychiatry and the bases for your opinion than he does. We'll deal with cross-examination in detail in chapter 7.

Let me give you another example of a type of case that I always turn down. Medication has never been a particular interest of mine and almost all of the patients that I work with, adult or child, are candidates for psychotherapy or psychoanalysis. When I do prescribe medication for my patients I do not hesitate to get a consult from one of my more knowledgeable colleagues. Thus, if the main issue is the use or misuse of a particular medication and its effects, I decline and refer the lawyer to a colleague who is expert in these matters.

So what does that leave me with—actually most of the cases which come my way. Among the most commonly referred cases are wrongful termination, personal injury, childhood sexual abuse, automobile accidents, sexual assaults, custody disputes, and malpractice, to name just a few.

DECIDING WHAT TO CHARGE

Much of what you need to know has already been covered in the comments that I added to the sample fee agreement. The best way to determine a reasonable fee, particularly when you are starting out, is to inquire about what others in the community are charging. There will likely be a range of several hundred dollars per hour between those starting out and the most experienced experts. As you gain more expertise and begin to build a network of referring attorneys your fee can gradually increase.

Billing practices of experts have been studied. Deciding what to bill is based on numerous factors such as experience, feelings about a particular case and the complexity of the case. A study found that experts tended to bill more reasonably when a case was considered to be simple, (Gutheil, Commons and Miller, 2001, pp. 202–206).

Do not do any work on plaintiff cases until you have received the signed fee agreement and retainer. If you do you may not get paid for those hours because the case may suddenly settle or the lawyer has decided that he doesn't need a psychiatric expert, or has found one more suited to the situation as he determines it.

The situation is different when working for the defense because insurance companies pay your retainer and fee and usually several weeks pass before a check arrives. However, the statement about not doing any work until a signed fee agreement arrives stands. That is your contract, your guarantee that you will be paid for your time.

Remember: *You do not have a doctor-patient relationship with the plaintiff or defendant. Your relationship is with the retaining attorney who asked you to serve as an expert.* If the case does not go well and the plaintiff and the attorney lose, the lawyer may have to dig into his own pocket to pay you because there are no funds forthcoming from the defense. This usually happens when an attorney is in solo practice or working for a small firm. Large firms do not expect to win every case and have resources to pay you regardless of the verdict.

In the course of my more than thirty years doing this work I have only been stuck a handful of times, and always by plaintiff lawyers. Insurance companies pay the cost of defending a client and will pay you, sooner or later, more often later than sooner.

Do not work on a lien. The reason is obvious. The other side will accuse you of coming to conclusions that will increase the likelihood that you will be paid rather than making determinations on the basis of your evaluation.

Let's move on. In chapter 2 I'll discuss the nature of the relationship between expert and retaining attorney. Chapter 2 also contains samples of case reports.

TWO

Professional and Personal Relationships with Lawyers

Three Sample Reports

Relationships between lawyers and experts are complicated to say the least. A statement by Melton et al. from their 2007 comprehensive textbook on the subject of psychiatry and the law provides a foundation on which to build your understanding of the nature of such relationships. The authors speak of "an uneasy alliance" between mental health professionals and the law. There are inherent conflicts in perspective because of disciplinary differences in conceptualizing and finding facts. The level of certainty that the mental health professions can bring to the law is far below that the law would like. On the other hand, the knowledge about human behavior that mental health professionals bring to the legal system can result in more informed judgments on many issues. "Our primary admonition to mental health professionals and to lawyers who would consult them is that both aspects of this theme should be kept in mind. Mental health professionals who exaggerate the state of knowledge (either their own as individuals or that of the field as a whole), or who ignore problems in translating the behavioral sciences into legal findings, do the law no service. At the same time, lawyers who ignore the behavioral sciences or, conversely, who swallow whole the conclusions of mental health professionals fail to exercise proper diligence in generating the facts necessary for the pursuit of justice" (p. 24).

So, with this conceptual framework let's proceed to a discussion of how to manage this "uneasy alliance."

Be friendly with the lawyers who use you as an expert, but do not become social friends. I have often been asked at deposition or trial if I have a social relationship with the lawyer who retained me. The reason is obvious. If you go out to dinner or play tennis together you give the impression that your opinions are more likely to be slanted in his direction. Even if that is not the case consciously, if may be so unconsciously.

Reputable lawyers want a realistic, honest appraisal from you. Others will pressure you into providing opinions that strongly support their case. Your practice as an expert witness will grow by leaps and bounds if you do a thorough evaluation, come to your own conclusions, and present them clearly and concisely in your report and at deposition and trial.

Your integrity is your greatest asset!

Gutheil and Simon (1999, pp. 546–553) described the early warning signs that should alert you to attempts by attorneys to manipulate your objectivity and opinions. They describe the natural tension that exists between retaining attorney and an expert witness. "The goals and ethical mandates of the psychiatric expert witness and of the retaining attorney differ in essential ways: these differences always create an enduring tension between the parties. The attorney is ethically obligated to embark on zealous, vigorous, and partisan advocacy on behalf of the client. While objectivity may govern case selection, the attorney need not be objective in presenting the case in court. In contrast, the expert is committed to honesty and to striving for objectivity throughout even when those goals are accomplished at the cost of disappointment the retaining attorney by, in essence, failing to be sufficiently partisan" (p. 546). These tensions can significantly compromise the attorney-expert relationship when the attorney attempts to exploit the expert financially or compromise the expert's honesty and striving for objectivity.

Early warning signs of such behavior on the part of the retaining attorney include the **Assumed Opinion**, **Selected Data**, **Applied Parsimony**, **Cry Poverty**, and the **Client May Balk**, among others.

The **Assumed Opinion** refers to an attorney's attempt, during the initial phone conversation, to convey, sometimes firmly, the fact that the attorney anticipates what the expert's opinion will be before the expert has seen any records or conducted an evaluation. In my experience, if this early warning sign is met head on with a declaration that you can only express an expert opinion after your evaluation is complete and that you cannot guarantee that your opinion will match the attorney's expectation, you may decide to proceed, albeit with caution. If you remain uncomfortable after such a discussion, as the author of this chapter suggest, the case should probably be turned down.

Selected Data refers to an attorney's attempt to influence your opinion by only presenting you with selected data. As described in chapter 1, an honest attorney will provide you with all the vital data in a case and will respond to your requests for additional information that became known to you during the diagnostic interviews. *Always insist that you have* *reviewed everything that the mental health expert on the other side has seen or you will be vulnerable to not being as prepared as he on the stand.*

Applied Parsimony and **Cry Poverty** refer to an attorney's attempt to limit your access to important data by express concerns about the costs. "Some attorneys have no idea of the time required to assess a forensic case and, hence, are surprised and dismayed at the appropriate costs thereof" (p. 548). Others know full well how much time and effort is required for an expert to be fully prepared but use cost as a reason to control your access to the material that they want you to see. This is why I recommend that you do no work on a case until a significant retainer has been received. This insistence will eliminate involvement in cases in which receiving compensation for your work will be difficult or impossible.

The **Client May Balk** is an attempt to ignore the absolutely essential idea that the contractual relationship is *always* between the retaining attorney and the expert, never between the expert and the client. This aspect of the lawyer-expert relationship needs to be completely clear before your work begins.

Even when the contractual relationship is clear an attorney may attempt to influence your testimony by *subtle extortion*, namely withholding payment. I send out my bills monthly and expect to be paid within thirty to forty-five days, at the latest. If payment is not received within that time framework, I contact the attorney directly and ask for payment and refuse to do further work until the bill is paid. Do not agree to appear for a deposition or to testify in court until your current bill has been paid in full.

Gutheil and Simon also describe what they call the "quasi-countertransferential dynamics that may enter into the expert's side of the equation" (1991, p. 551). They describe the **Desperate Expert**, the **Beginning or New Expert**, the **Expert Who Needs to Be Loved**, and the **Expert on a Mission**.

They also give a fine description of the **Venal Expert**. "The venal expert, or 'hired gun' constitutes the *bête noire* of forensic work. Such experts 'sell out' by charging for testimony rather than for time. The attorneys who hire such experts can be assured of getting the testimony they want. Hence, for this group of experts, the entire concept of early warning signs is irrelevant: both parties usually know what they are getting" (p. 552).

The **Beginning Expert** may lose his objectivity because of uncertainty about his worth and abilities. The **Expert Who Needs to Be Loved** often loses his objectivity. "The relationship between expert and retaining attorney works best when it represents a business relationship based on mutual respect rather than a mutual admiration society based on the expert's need for relational or narcissistic gratification" (p. 552). The **Expert on a Mission** puts a personal or political agenda ahead of a search for the truth. He becomes a trier of fact, a job designated for the jury or judge.

If as a case progresses you are being subjected to increased pressure to change your opinion to ones preferred by the retaining attorney or you feel that attorney is incompetent and is proceeding in a manner that is harmful to his client, or to you, you may withdraw from the case. An expert's decision to withdraw from a case at a late stage in its progression, for instance at the time or deposition of even at the time of trial, is a serious step that has forensic and ethical consequences but may become necessary.

The mutual right to terminate the relationship between expert witness and lawyer at will is an essential component of the contract between you and the retaining lawyer that helps immunize the expert from threats to objectivity and independence (Gutheil, Bursztajn, Hilliard, and Brodsky, 2004).

GETTING THE INFORMATION YOU NEED TO COMPLETE YOUR EVALUATION

In addition to conducting the diagnostic interview or interviews (in almost all instances when serving as an expert for the defense you are only allowed to see the plaintiff once, and on occasion the length of the interview may be dictated by the court), and getting psychological testing (the length of which may also be limited by the court in regard to length of time and which tests may be given) you will need to review *all* relevant records. It is your responsibility to ask for any records not provided to you prior to seeing the plaintiff or defendant that concern areas of importance that become apparent during the diagnostic interview (e.g., certain medical or psychiatric records, school records, police investigations of automobile accidents, etc).

It is also your responsibility to ask the retaining lawyer to be sure that you are provided *all* of the records reviewed by the opposing expert, as previously emphasized—otherwise your opinions will appear to be based on an incomplete data base, and you can be sure that this will be pointed out on cross-examination.

In your initial conversation with the retaining lawyer be sure to ask for the complaint because it summarizes the basis for the lawsuit and the details of the behavior (e.g., sexual harassment by a boss) or experience (e.g., an auto accident) that led to the lawsuit, thus allowing you to organize your thinking for the evaluation.

PROVIDING HONEST OPINIONS

The best way to build and maintain an expert witness practice is to do a thorough evaluation and give an honest summary of your diagnosis, treatment recommendations, and prognosis regardless of whether or not your conclusions support the position of the retaining lawyer. A good lawyers will use your opinions to determine how to proceed with his case. A few will de-designate you as an expert if they do not like your opinions. The "venal expert" is also referred to as a "bought expert" (Brodsky, 1991, p. 5) or as a "defense expert" or a "plaintiff expert"; in plainer English "a hack" whose opinion is for sale.

STAYING IN TOUCH DURING THE EVALUATION

I always make it a point to contact the lawyer who hired me after a diagnostic interview to inform him that the individual showed up and to provide him with an initial impression. Frequent communication goes a long way toward building rapport and increasing the likelihood that you will be approached about other cases in the future.

COOPERATING WITH THE LAWYER IN THE PRESENTATION OF YOUR OPINIONS

Once you have completed your evaluation and *independently* arrived at your opinions in regard to diagnosis, treatment, prognosis, discussion, and critique of the opposing expert's report and conclusions, the next step is to work with the retaining lawyer to organize your opinions in the best possible manner to contribute to his presentation of the case. Usually, but not always, a report will be requested. Other lawyers may want an abbreviated form of a written document that I call a diagnostic summary. The reasons behind the lawyer's preference are his assessment of how much of your opinion he wishes to reveal to the other side prior to deposition or trial.

An example of a plaintiff and defense report and a diagnostic summary are presented at the end of this chapter. All information has been thoroughly disguised to protect confidentiality.

If you are not asked to put anything in writing it is still essential to do the mental work required to organize your conclusions so that you can clearly and concisely express them at deposition or trial. As you gain experience it is often in your, and the lawyer's, best interest in terms of clarity of presentation if you express a preference among the choices of a formal report, diagnostic summary, or nothing written. Of course, the final decision about how to present your independently arrived at opinions is up to the lawyer.

INTERACTIONS WITH THE LAWYERS ON THE OPPOSING SIDE

You will rarely, if ever, have any contact with opposing lawyers prior to deposition or trial. If you receive this type of communication, consult with the retaining lawyer before responding. However, it is not unusual for secretaries or paralegals to contact you for tax identification so that a check may be prepared for payment to you at your deposition. All other fees for service are paid by the retaining lawyer.

We will discuss the interaction between you and the lawyer taking your deposition in detail in chapter 5. The main point I wish to make now is to treat the opposing lawyer with utmost consideration. His job is to undermine your opinions as much as he can. Your job is to respond directly to his questions with calmness, civility, and a firm determination to present your opinions and the basis for them. When you present yourself in this manner, often, when the case is over, you will get a call from the opposing lawyer asking you to serve as an expert witness for his firm. Lawyers are always looking for excellent experts and know one when they see one.

Brodsky (1991) described the efforts of lawyers on the opposing side to influence your testimony or gain information outside of when you are testifying under oath during a deposition or trial in the following manner: "Some attorneys approach witnesses in the corridors or during breaks with such an easy, enthusiastic style that the witnesses want to talk at length to these charming folks. Don't! I speak readily about the weather, I suppose, but I monitor my words with care and say nothing about any aspect of the case. That closed-mouth attitude extends to not talking about other witnesses, about other trials in which I have testified, or how long I have been involved in the present case. As politely as possible, I explain that we need to hold off just now on talking business. They understand" (p. 88).

DIFFERENCES IN WORKING WITH PLAINTIFF AND DEFENSE LAWYERS

In terms of your process of arriving at your independently derived opinions there is no difference. Your integrity is not for sale. However, the financial arrangements do differ. Plaintiff firms pay you out of their resources. Remember, your relationship is with the law firm, not their client. This is not a doctor-patient evaluation. Do not do *any* work until you have received a signed fee agreement and retainer.

There is a third party involved when you work for the defense, namely the insurance company that pays the law firm for your time and expertise. Although you have greater certainty of being paid, payment is not always timely. As with plaintiff cases, do not begin work without a signed fee agreement but do recognize that in many instances your retainer check may not arrive until weeks later. Monthly bills may not always be paid within thirty to forty-five days, a reasonable amount of time to expect payment from plaintiff firms—but they will eventually be paid.

Usually defense lawyers are more likely to provide you with all relevant records in a more timely fashion than some plaintiff lawyers who are trying to conserve funds. There is little or no difference when dealing with large, well-established plaintiff firms.

WORKING WITH OTHER EXPERTS

You may request, or be asked, to contact other experts in the case. For example, recently in a plaintiff case involving a severely physically injured child the lawyer arranged a conference call in which all of the experts—surgeons, pain managers, internists, and urologists, among others—shared our opinions and had the opportunity to ask each other questions. The task in such a conference is to enhance the other specialist's knowledge of the child's mental and emotional needs.

Whenever a life care plan is involved (a computation of present and future needs and costs) a telephone call or meeting with the life care specialist is almost always requested so that you can describe your estimate of present and future psychiatric care which will be turned into a dollar figure by the life care planner.

AN EXAMPLE OF A PLAINTIFF EVALUATION REPORT PREPARED FOR APPEARANCE IN FEDERAL COURT

There is a specific format required for reports in federal cases as opposed to state civil cases. Legal record (court appearances) and an up-to-date CV are integral parts of the report.

Calvin A. Colarusso M.D.
1020 Prospect St., Suite 415
La Jolla, California 92037

Date

Introduction

This is a report of a psychiatric evaluation of Arnold Johnson of [address]; by Calvin A. Colarusso, M.D., Board Certified Adult and Child Psychiatrist practicing at the above address; at the request of [attorney's name and address].

The opinions expressed herein are based on a 2-hour-and-15-minute diagnostic interview with Mr. Johnson, [date]; psychological testing performed at my request by [psychologist's name and address]; and a review of records.

The following records were reviewed:

Third Amended Complaint
Fourth Amended Complaint
Deposition Transcript of Arnold Johnson Volumes I and II
Deposition Transcript of Bruce Revolyn, M.D.
Deposition Transcript of William Shector, M.D.
Deposition Transcript of Gale Johnson
Deposition Transcript of Steven Rolls
Deposition Transcript of Jack Ocean
Plaintiff's Documents (JOHNSON 00001-JOHNSON 01567)
Employer Documents (SSD000001-SSDO002510)
Documents from Mary Williams
Medical Records Subpoenaed from SCPMG

Legal Record

Name and board certification and academic appointment followed by a statement of publications and legal history. For example, "The author of 3 professional books and approximately 25 professional articles and book reviews, he has served as an expert in more than 750 civil suits for both the plaintiff and the defense. His legal record and curriculum vitae accompanies this document."

Fees

[Name], fee per hour for all work related to performing as an expert witness in this case.

Diagnostic Interview

No one else was present during the diagnostic interview with Mr. Johnson. He was informed that unlike the usual doctor-patient relationship there was no confidentiality since I was serving as an expert witness and not as his physician. All of the information described from the diagnostic interview was obtained from Mr. Johnson, directly.

Identifying Information:

Arnold Johnson, born February 4, 1959, is a truck driver.

Mr. Johnson has been divorced three times.

First wife—Estelle Evans. The couple was married for approximately one and one half years when Mr. Johnson was 19 or 20 years of age. "We were too young."

Second wife—Karen Thimble. The couple was married when Mr. Johnson was age 23. The marriage lasted nine years and broke up because they grew apart.

Third Wife—Sissy Larue. The couple married in 1992 when Mr. Johnson was 33 years of age. The marriage lasted for 11 years. It ended when Mrs. Johnson had an affair.

Mr. Johnson has a daughter from his first wife. She is 25 years of age and lives near her father.

Mr. Johnson has two sons from his second wife. They are in their 20s and live in another state. Mr. Johnson sees them often.

The Problems Leading to the Law Suit:

Mr. Johnson gave the following detailed history that eventually led to his filing a lawsuit.

He began to work for a food market during January 1990. The company was eventually purchased by a larger company. Mr. Johnson became one of nearly 50 employees who were asked to move and be retained by the larger company. It was a "downhill slide with (the company) since then." The local drivers didn't like those who came from out of town.

Mr. Johnson was a route driver. He also ran extra shuttles and eventually became a shop steward. In 2006, while driving a 43-foot trailer that carried 43,000 pounds, as Mr. Johnson climbed into the trailer and lifted product over his head, he sprained his back and arm. When he called his supervisor to report the injury he was told that there was no one to help him at that time. Mr. Johnson decided to finish the day and worked for the following three weeks in this condition, helping other drivers. Then, a few weeks later, Mr. Johnson's arm "gave out." He went to the routing office where he was told to call in and report his injury.

At the emergency room x-rays revealed that there was a possible rotator cuff injury. Mr. Johnson was told to go to his family doctor. Soon afterward, Mr. Johnson filled out workers' comp forms with his boss. When he returned to the clinic, a physician worked on his shoulder but not his back. When he was asked to lift a 50-pound crate to determine if he was fit to return to work he could not do so without pain. Mr. Johnson was upset when the physician placed him on permanent disability. He was not yet 50 years of age. Surgery was mentioned as a possibility. Eventually, Mr. Johnson was sent to an orthopedic surgeon.

On a visit to his medical provider soon after, a co-worker informed Mr. Johnson that he was told to be careful about what he said to Mr. Johnson because he was filing a law suit against the company. When Mr. Johnson approached the doctor, the physician told him that there was a letter to the effect that he had filed a suit from an insurance company. The physician agreed to show the letter to Mr. Johnson but couldn't find it.

A MRI revealed rotator cuff damage. Surgery was set for the late fall of 2006. A caseworker for the employer's insurance company made appointments for Mr. Johnson and accompanied him on most visits. She denied that she knew about a letter indicating that Mr. Johnson was suing his employer. She told Mr. Johnson to write a letter requesting that a certain doctor become his primary physician. Mr. Johnson complied. Nothing had been done about his sore back up to this point.

His employer had not yet placed Mr. Johnson on workers' comp. He felt that the company was using his FMLA leave and sick and vacation time to pay him. He had asked for light duty but the employer put him to work caring for equipment. This started in September 2006 and lasted for one year. It was humiliating. The employer knew Mr. Johnson had restrictions on lifting but he was on his hands and knees painting much of the time. It was "a spectacle." At this point Mr. Johnson was unable to speak for approximately 60 seconds. With tears in his eyes he said, "It humbled me." Mr. Johnson was very hot as he worked outdoors during the summer. He requested a shade cover because his ears were becoming sunburned. He had to fill out more forms and was initially refused. After further complaining he was given salve to apply to his ears.

The company representative said that the employer did not want Mr. Johnson to use his current HMO. He had too many primary physicians there and was sent from doctor to doctor. Mr. Johnson told the company representative that he wanted his arm and back fixed so that he could return to work. The representative said that he had to write a second letter requesting a change of physician. Mr. Johnson chose Dr. B., a back specialist. After doing tests the specialist said it looked like a strain. He was not an arm specialist. Mr. Johnson was sent to another doctor who did another MRI and performed surgery in the spring of 2007.

After going six months without workers' comp pay Mr. Johnson called the state and was placed on disability. He was told that his employer hadn't gotten the paperwork in on time so the workers' comp claim was dismissed.

After the 2007 surgery Mr. Johnson did well and was released by the surgeon for full duty on a trial basis. He could drive but not lift heavy objects. Later in 2007 his employer told Mr. Johnson that he had a problem with his back. The doctor who had seen him at the company's request had declared him permanent and stationary. The company refused to send Mr. Johnson for a reexamination. He wanted to be transferred to a position that did not require heavy lifting. The company refused, saying that other employees at that position might outbid him, even though he was fifth in seniority.

Because he had not worked for 18 months, despite the fact that he had been ready to work and had medical approval to do so, the employer terminated Mr. Johnson in the winter of 2009. After that Mr. Johnson filed a lawsuit.

Symptoms:

As just described, Mr. Johnson had shoulder and back problems. His shoulder is now fine. His back still hurts. Mr. Johnson is currently employed as a driver by another company. It is difficult work that often strains his back but he is able to do it.

Mr. Johnson described the following psychological symptoms: low self-esteem, problems sleeping, headaches, lack of energy, anger, and feelings of uselessness.

The low self-esteem was most severe from the time he was terminated until approximately four to five months ago when Mr. Johnson began to go out more and do home projects. He also began to play softball with his son.

Mr. Johnson had problems falling asleep. "My brain wouldn't shut down. . . . I had nightmares arguing with [his employer] about work." The nightmares would wake him up. The sleeping problems began approximately six to twelve months before he was terminated and were most severe after he was fired. Now he still has problems sleeping but does get approximately four to five hours per night. He did not have problems sleeping before the problems at work began.

Mr. Johnson's headaches start in the temples and radiate to the back of the head. They began before he was fired and were most severe in the months after being fired. At that time the headaches occurred three to four times per week. Currently, they occur twice per week. Mr. Johnson did not have any significant difficulty with headaches before being fired. He took Excedrin and other over-the-counter remedies for the headaches.

Beginning during the months before being fired and continuing for a year or more afterward, Mr. Johnson had little or no energy. Now his energy is "picking up."

He reported being "very depressed" before being fired and for at least a year afterward. This affect was accompanied by thoughts of worthlessness, embarrassment, and fear. Mr. Johnson did not have suicidal thoughts and had never been clinically depressed before. "I'm 52 and I have to live with my mother. She was helping pay my bills. I felt destitute. If it wasn't for her I could have ended on the street. They took my dignity away."

"I spent a lot of time in my room . . . staying away from everybody. I didn't want to have people see me be down . . . I cried a lot. I wanted to be like a hermit."

When Mr. Johnson was working for his employer he weighed 190 pounds. During the first year after being fired his weight increased to 230 pounds. "That made the depression worse. I felt like a slob. Then I started to starve myself." His current weight is 200 pounds.

Since being terminated Mr. Johnson was unemployed until recently.

Mental Status Examination:

The mental status examination is the standard procedure by which a mental health professional assesses an individual's mental and emotional state; assessing appearance and behavior, speech, affect or feeling tone, thinking and orientation and memory.

Mr. Johnson presented as an overweight, adult male. He did not demonstrate any unusual mannerisms and was sad and serious as he talked, demonstrating a good command of English. Affect ranged from anger to sadness and depression as he talked about his experiences at work. At one point he stopped talking for about a minute and cried. At other times his affect was euthymic (within the normal range). Thinking was logical and goal directed. There was no evidence of delusions and hallucinations. Mr. Johnson was oriented as to time, person, and place, did calculations easily, and interpreted a proverb abstractly.

Developmental History:

The developmental history traces an individual's life from birth to the chronological present and allows the diagnostician to trace this person's life course against a large body of knowledge on normal and pathological development.

Father—died at age 54 of a heart attack. He had retired from the military.

Mother—is a retired government worker.

The couple was married for more than 30 years when father died.

Mr. Johnson is an only child.

He was born and raised primarily in Southern California. Mr. Johnson "idolized" his father. His parents "were the best in the world." Mr. Ruiz was an adult when his father died.

Ages 0–6: Although Mr. Johnson was born two months premature, there were no significant problems with the pregnancy, labor, or delivery. Mother was at home as the primary caretaker throughout the early years of his life. Father was often on overseas tours of duty. Mr. Johnson was not a bed wetter and described himself as an outgoing, happy child.

Ages 6–12: During the elementary school years Mr. Johnson made good grades, was well behaved, and had lots of friends. He was very interested in all sports. The family went camping, to the beach, and to the zoo.

Ages 12–20: Puberty occurred at ages 12/13. Mr. Johnson began to date when he was 16/17 years of age. His sexual orientation is heterosexual. He graduated high school with a GPA of about 3.0. During adolescence he did not use drugs and had no significant problems with the law. Mr. Johnson played on high school teams. After high school he worked at various jobs for approximately two years and then began to drive a truck at age 20. He was married for the first time when he was 19 and divorced more than a year later. His daughter was a product of this union.

Ages 20–30: During this decade Mr. Johnson drove a truck and married for the second time. His sons were born during this decade. Mr. Johnson worked for two different companies during his twenties.

Ages 30–40: Mr. Johnson began working for his employer when he was 30 years of age and continued with the company until he was 51. He was married for the third time when he was 33 years of age. The marriage ended about eight years later.

Ages 40–present: Mr. Johnson was working for his employer during this decade until he was fired. Hobbies included fishing, surfing, auto racing, and taking his children to the beach and on trips. Most of these pleasurable activities were diminished in frequency after he was fired.

Mr. Johnson did not have any significant emotional problems in his life prior to being fired and has never been in therapy.

Records

The medical records from the four physicians who saw and treated Mr. Johnson confirm, as indicated by Mr. Johnson, that he was treated for shoulder and back problems by these physicians when he was an employee.

The history of his difficulties at work and symptoms resulting from the work stresses and termination in Mr. Johnson's deposition transcript is essentially the same as he provided to me during the Independent Medical Examination.

Psychological Testing

A forensic psychiatrist, at my request, administered a complete battery of psychological tests. His complete report accompanies this document. A summary of some of his findings follows. In addition to a clinical interview and mental status examination, the psychologist administered a Shipley 2, Mini-Mental State Examination, 2nd Edition, Expanded Version (MMSE-2EV), Beck Depression Inventory, 2nd Edition (BDI-II), Minnesota Multiphasic Personality Inventory, 2nd Edition (MMPI-2), and a Rorschach Inkblot Test.

On his mental status examination the psychologist described Mr. Johnson's affect as depressed and labile during the interview. When asked to describe his usual mood during the past month Mr. Johnson replied, "I picked up after getting this job. I still get down at times. I try to stay active." He reported having recent symptoms of depression. He denied suicidal ideation.

The Shipley 2 is a brief measure of cognitive functioning and impairment. Mr. Johnson scored in the well below average range of intellectual functioning. "His test performance suggests low average functioning in acquired information, long-term memory storage, speed of information processing, working memory, and attention. His measured level of intelligence is somewhat lower than would be expected given his academic and occupational history."

On the MMSE-2EV, a brief, quantitative measure of cognitive functioning Mr. Johnson scored in the average range.

"Overall, Mr. Johnson is best considered as being of low average to average intellectual ability and to be free of any significant cognitive deficits."

"The BDI-II is a self-report measure of the symptoms of depression. Mr. Johnson's responses place him in the mild range of depression. While he reports having several depressive symptoms, he denies having any symptoms of greater than mild severity. He denies suicidal ideation on this measure."

Mr. Johnson's responses to the Rorschach Inkblot Test suggest the presence of depressive symptoms, although he does not appear to be in any immediate or significant distress. He attributes his current predicament to the unfair and insensitive treatment of others. He is prone to worry and feel sad and tired. He also harbors feelings of inferiority, is preoccupied with his aches and pains, and tends to feel mistreated and victimized. He is highly alert to what is going on around him, and tends to be on guard for any perceived attempt to take advantage of him."

Using DSM-IV, *The Diagnostic and Statistical Manual of Mental Disorders* of the American Psychiatric Association, 4th Edition, the psychologist suggested the following diagnostic possibility supported by psychological testing:

Axis I: Dysthymic Disorder (300.4). This is a diagnosis of depression. Symptoms were rated in the mild range of severity.

Summary and Discussion:

"Mr. Johnson is a 52-year-old man of low average to average intelligence who appears free of any significant cognitive impairment. Test results would support a diagnostic impression of dysthymic disorder. Final diagnostic conclusions and other opinions and recommendations will be left to [the forensic psychiatrist] who has the benefit of additional historical and clinical information."

Diagnosis

The Diagnostic and Statistical Manual of Mental Disorders of the American Psychiatric Association, 4th Edition, is the only widely used diagnostic nomenclature in the field. When using it the diagnostician is asked to divide his or her diagnostic impressions into five subdivisions, called Axes. Using that framework, which was the latest edition of the DSM at the time, I made the following diagnosis.

Axis I: Dysthymic Disorder 300.4. Mr. Johnson met the criteria required in the Manual for this diagnosis because of the presence of depressed mood for most of the day, for more days than not; and the presence, while depressed, of overeating, insomnia, low energy, low self-esteem, poor concentration, and feelings of hopelessness.

Occupational Problem V62.2. "This category can be used when the focus of clinical attention is an occupational problem that is not due to a mental disorder."

Axis II: Character disorders, long-standing patterns of maladaptive behavior are to be described here. None were present.

Axis III: Any medical conditions that directly relate to the diagnosis on Axis I are listed here. The shoulder and back injuries that Mr. Johnson developed on the job are directly, causally related to the development of the Dysthymic Disorder.

Axis IV: Psychosocial and Environmental Problems: from a list provided in the Manual the diagnostician is asked to describe any psychosocial and environmental problems which add to an understanding of the diagnosis on Axis I.

Problems with primary support group—unable to visit children due to inadequate finances.

Problems related to the social environment—significant withdrawal from friends and activities.

Occupational problems—unemployment, threat of job loss, stressful work schedule, difficult work conditions, job dissatisfaction, and job change.

Economic problems—inadequate finances.

Problems related to interaction with the legal system/crime—litigation is specifically listed as a stressor.

Axis V: Global Assessment of Functioning Scale: on a scale from 1, profound, to 100, superior functioning, the diagnostician is asked to rate the severity of the patient's symptoms. During the last year or two of employment and the first year afterward, I rated Mr. Johnson's symptoms in the 51–60 moderate ranges. At the time of the evaluation I rated them in the 61–70 mild ranges.

Treatment

Mr. Johnson would benefit from one year of once per week, individual psychotherapy to help him deal with the depression, shame, anger, and embarrassment that he still feels as a result of his treatment by his employer and the loss of his job. An experienced psychiatrist in Southern California would charge $225–$250 per 45-minute session.

Prognosis

The prognosis, with the treatment outlined above, is good.

Discussion

Mr. Johnson is an individual who had no history of mental illness or significant problems with the law prior to developing a depression as a result of the experience with his employer of many years. Married and divorced three times, his most consistent emotional ties have been centered on his children and his mother. A somewhat reserved individual, his career was a very important part of his identity and stability. As a result of feeling mistreated by his employer after being injured on the job Mr. Johnson developed a recognizable psychiatric illness, a Dysthymic Disorder. He has not received any treatment for his depression and is in need of a relatively brief course of individual psychotherapy to help him work through the emotional pain related to his dismissal and return to his premorbid mental and emotional state.

Calvin A. Colarusso, M.D.
Clinical Professor of Psychiatry
University of California at San Diego

AN EXAMPLE OF A DEFENSE EXPERT WITNESS REPORT

Calvin A. Colarusso, M.D.
1020 Prospect St., Suite 415
La Jolla, California 92037

Date

Introduction

This is a report of a psychiatric evaluation of William Forest of [address], by [name, board certification, and address], at the request of [name and address of the retaining attorney].

The opinions expressed in this report are based on a two hour and twenty minute diagnostic interview with Mr. Forest held in my office on [date]; psychological testing performed at my request by [name], and a review of the following records:

Complaint
Deposition and medical records of [medical doctor]
Medical records of [medical doctor]
Medical records of [medical doctor]
Deposition of William Forest, Volumes I and II
First set of interrogatories and responses
Forest's supplemental responses to first set of interrogatories
Second set of interrogatories and responses
Supplemental responses

Third set of request for production of documents and responses
Medical records, Dr. [medical doctor]
Medical records, Dr. [medical doctor]
Medical records, Dr. [medical doctor]
Deposition, [psychologist], Volumes I and II

Diagnostic Interview

When working for a defense firm, rarely is the diagnostician allowed more than one interview with the plaintiff.

Mr. Forest was evaluated on [date], in my office. All of the information gathered during the interview was provided by Mr. Forest. No one else was present. Mr. Forest was informed that due to the fact that this was a diagnostic evaluation being conducted in conjunction with his lawsuit the usual doctor-patient confidentiality did not apply. My chart would be available to the lawyers on both sides of the case.

Identifying Information:

Mark Forest was born in 1953. Mr. Forest was an educator.

Wife: [Name], in her early 50s. Mrs. Forest was a retired businesswoman.

The Forests had three children in their late 20s and early 30s.

The Issues Leading to the Law Suit:

Mr. Forest reported that his boss harassed him. This had never happened before in his more than 20 years with the company. Jokes were made about his age and he was threatened with the loss of his job. Efforts to move to a different division were blocked. Mr. Forest appealed to headquarters but eventually he was terminated.

A top salesman in a large company, he had always been treated fairly and gotten along well with earlier managers prior to his difficulties with Ms. Jay, his last manager. Ms. Jay would talk of the need to get rid of some of the staff "low hanging fruit," and would point fingers at Mr. Forest. He didn't know why she harassed him. When Mr. Forest was honored at a ceremony after being with the company for 25 years, Ms. Jay did not even smile. He worked hard and had great relationships with the clients that he serviced. Mr. Forest had to report to other managers as well. "I had seven bosses." He felt that Ms. Jay and the others were focused on him for unknown reasons.

A client who had made a request for money for educational presentations made a complaint against Mr. Forest over their communication about the amount of money requested. Mr. Forest felt that his bosses did not listen to his side of the story.

He was suddenly fired. Two managers met Mr. Forest at his locker, accompanied him to his home, and took possession of the company car, computer, and electronics. "I was the same over 25 years. My efforts didn't change."

Symptoms:

Mr. Forest was asked to describe any physical and or psychological symptoms that he felt were job related.

Physical Symptoms:

Stomach distress: Described as a churning discomfort, the stomach distress began during the last year at the company. The symptoms disappeared after Mr. Forest was fired. He did not take medication or seek treatment for this distress.

Clinching of teeth: This also began during the last year at work when Mr. Forest felt that he had been put on the spot and was helpless. This symptom is still present to some extent when Mr. Forest is under stress.

Heart palpitations and feelings of being ill at ease: These symptoms were present during the last six months at work. They occurred occasionally after he was fired. "The thought was what do I do now?"

Headaches: Described as a dull ache, the headaches occurred during the few months both before and after being fired. Mr. Forest took Excedrin for the headaches. He was prone to having migraine headaches approximately once to twice a year prior to the difficulties at work.

None of the physical symptoms described above had been present before the difficulties at work began.

Psychological Symptoms:

Anxiety: Anxiousness began in the last two years of employment and gradually increased. The anxiety was most severe three to six months before being terminated. Afterward, the anxiety diminished during the day but continued at night when Mr. Forest would think of his situation and worry about bills and the future. Significant anxiety had not been present prior to the difficulties at work.

Depressed state: Mr. Forest described this as "something sitting on my chest, a need to cry, a sense of despair." These feelings began during the last two years at work. The day he was fired Mr. Forest had the sense that a weight was lifted off of him but the depressed feelings returned soon afterward. They continue occasionally to the present. Mr. Forest had been taking an antidepressant before the difficulty with Ms. Jay and continues to do so to the present. He and his wife had been seeing a counselor because of concerns about their children. Mr. Forest plans to continue using medication until he feels more settled.

Financial and personal concerns: Mr. Forest was animated as he talked about how much he loves teaching, his new occupation. However, he has financial concerns since he is making less than his former income. His wife's pension is of some help. Without this income the couple would not be able to pay their bills. The couple is losing money on a house they built for speculation. There are no buyers at present. Mr. Forest thinks that he and his wife owe over $1 million for mortgages and equity lines of credit.

Rumination: This began about six months before Mr. Forest was let go and was most severe during the first few years afterward. The rumination continues to the present, but less frequently and less intensely. "I've become more negative and less patient. I was always a positive person."

Mental Status Examination:

The mental status examination is the standard method by which a mental health professional assesses an individual's mental and emotional state, evaluating appearance and behavior, characteristics of speech, affect or feeling tone, thinking, and orientation and memory.

Mr. Forest presented as a well-dressed, middle-aged man. He was cooperative and friendly. He had a fine vocabulary and spoke easily. Affect or feeling tone was bright, particularly when talking about teaching. He expressed concern and annoyance when discussing his work situation. There was no evidence of significant depression or anxiety. Thinking was logical and goal directed. There was no evidence of delusions or hallucinations. Mr. Forest was oriented as to time, person, and place and had no memory impairment. No abnormalities were noted on this mental status examination.

Developmental History:

The developmental history traces an individual's life from birth to the chronological present and allows the diagnostician to compare this person's experience against a large body of knowledge of normal and pathological development.

Mr. Forest's father died several years ago. He had retired from his employment of more than 30 years.

His mother is in her 80s and comfortably retired.

The couple was married for more than 30 years, the only marriage for both.

Mr. Forest has four siblings. He and his siblings were raised in a very loving home. Mr. Forest never experienced any physical or sexual abuse.

Ages 0–6: There were no difficulties with mother's pregnancy, labor, or delivery. Mr. Forest was bottle fed and mother was at home as the full time provider of care. There were no significant separations from either parent during these years. Mr. Forest was a healthy child who did not have any serious illnesses or operations during childhood.

Ages 6–12: During the elementary school years Mr. Forest was a very good student, had friends, and was well liked by his teachers. Hobbies included outdoor activities and traveling with the family. Mr. Forest was part of a large, extended family. He did not experience any significant deaths during his childhood.

Ages 12–20: Puberty occurred at age 11. Mr. Forest began to date at age 16 and became sexually active in late adolescence. He did not have any problems with the police or use drugs or alcohol during adolescence. He graduated from high school with a GPA of 3.8. He did not participate in organized sports.

After high school Mr. Forest attended college and graduated after four years.

Ages 20–30: Mr. Forest married in his early 20s to a woman who had significant emotional problems. They had one child and divorced after several years.

Mr. Forest began to work for his long-time employer in his early 20s.

Ages 30–40: Mr. Forest remarried in his early thirties. Together, he and his wife raised his and her children from previous marriages. Despite difficulties in raising a blended family, the marriage continues to be a good one.

Age 40–present: Mr. Forest was fired when he was in his early 50s. He began to teach soon after and has been attempting to begin a small business.

Record Review with Mr. Forest:

During this section of the interview I asked Mr. Forest questions based on the records I had reviewed.

Medical Doctor: Dr. [name] prescribed the Wellbutrin. She was a hypnotist and "absolutely worthless in my book." He saw her for the stress of everyday life. He used the Wellbutrin as a "mood stabilizer."

Medical Doctor: A helpful, primary care physician who prescribed Wellbutrin.

Psychologist: Mr. Forest saw [name] because of the stress at work. He needed someone to talk to. [Name] was very helpful. He continues to see [name] about every four to six weeks to continue to try and resolve his feelings of anxiety and depression.

Medical Doctor: Mr. Forest saw [name] at his therapist's suggestion for one year, for medication management.

Mr. Forest's Deposition: Mr. Forest spoke to the regional director about promotions and other positions without success. He has dreams about the company that he described as flashbacks. Mr. Forest worked for another company for a few months after he was fired. It was a good company but the work was not for him.

Psychological Testing

Dr. B., a clinical psychologist, evaluated Mr. Forest, at my request. After conducting a clinical interview Dr. B. did a mental status examination and administered the following psychological tests: Mini-Mental Status Examination; Ruff Neurobehavioral Inventory; Beck Depression Inventory, 2nd Edition; Personality Assessment Inventory; Million Clinical Multiaxial Inventory; Rorschach Inkblot and Thematic Apperception Test.

Findings from the test results will be summarized here.

There was no evidence of cognitive impairment.

"While he perceives the overall quality of his life as negatively affected by his termination, the discrepancy between his pre- and post-morbid functioning in this domain is not significant. He reports no significant discrepancies in the cognitive, emotional or physical domains."

On the Beck Depression Inventory, 2nd Edition II test, a self-report measure of the symptoms of depression in adults, Mr. Forest scored in the "minimal" range of depression. "He endorses only symptoms related to pessimism and irritability."

On the Personality Assessment Inventory test, a self-report measure of psychiatric symptoms and personality functioning, Dr. B. notes that "He tends to be blindly uncritical of his own behavior and insensitive to the negative consequences associated with his behavior, so that he minimizes the negative impact that his behavior has on others as well as himself. . . . He appears to have little motivation for any type of psychological intervention, as he reports experiencing little distress and appears to be satisfied with himself as he is."

Rorschach test: "When confronted with even ordinary amounts of stress, he is likely to become overly distressed with limited tolerance for frustration and poor impulse control. Typically emotionally constricted, when under stress the plaintiff is more likely to act out his anger and resentment . . . he demonstrates low self-esteem and a tendency to compare himself unfavorable to others. . . . He tends to become overly involved in figuring out the underlying significance of events or sorting out his feelings about them. As a result, he tends to make things more complicated than they are. This tendency to make a big production out of a small matter may be wearing both to him and to others around him."

Thematic Apperception test: "There is no evidence of depressed mood or feelings of hopelessness or despair in his responses to this instrument. He appears to value love and hard work as a means to success and happiness."

Review of Records

The following are excerpts from the records that I reviewed that add to an understanding of Mr. Forest and my conclusions.

Psychologist: Dr. [name] is Mr. Forest's psychotherapist. She saw him approximately 50 times. In a treatment summary, using *The Diagnostic and Statistical Manual of Mental Disorders* of the American Psychiatric Association, 4th Edition, Dr. [name] made the following diagnoses:

Axis I: Major Depressive Disorder, chronic, currently controlled with psychotropic medications. She also made a diagnosis of chronic Dysthymia.

Axis II: Histrionic Personality Features.

Axis IV: Wife disabled. Litigation continues with former employer, financial strain.

She described the outcome of treatment as fair/good. "Patient is able to function at a high level at work despite significant Axis IV stressors. Monthly meetings, medications, and rest were planned.

A treatment summary described the Major Depressive Disorder as resolved. The treatment outcome was good. "Improved significantly with therapy and antidepressant meds."

The psychologist-therapist administered two Minnesota Multiphasic Personality Inventory tests, one year apart. In the second report some stress was indicated. There was evidence of a hysteroid adjustment and a tendency to be demanding, immature, egocentric, selfish, and generally narcissistic. A Pollyannaish attitude prevented acknowledgement of life's difficulties. Ineffective resolution of feelings resulted in physical complaints. The possibility of a psychophysiological reaction and hypochondria was noted.

Medical Doctor: Is a psychiatrist who prescribed the medications for Mr. Forest. He made a diagnosis of Major Depressive Disorder, single episode, and rated his symptoms in the moderate range.

Medical Doctor: Mr. Forest saw [name] who utilized biofeedback and medication. She noted that Mr. Forest was interviewing for a job opening with another company. She reported the following comment from Mr. Forest. "I'm stuck with limited choices [career]. I love my job but hate my job."

Medical Group: Mr. Forest was seen at various times over the course of four years. The only mention of work occurs in a note in which anxiety and sleep deprivation was related to stress on the job. Mr. Forest had chest pains from anxiety. He described losing control because of his boss and wanted a referral to a psychiatrist. His boss had her feet on his head. Medication was prescribed.

Diagnosis

Using *The Diagnostic and Statistical Manual of Mental Disorders* of the American Psychiatric Association, 4th Edition, the only widely accepted diagnostic nomenclature in the field, I made the following diagnostic conclusions:

Axis I: Major diagnoses are to be listed here.

At the time of my evaluation no psychiatric diagnosis was indicated on Axis I.

During the year before termination from his job and during the first 6 to 12 months afterward, a diagnosis of Adjustment Disorder with Depression, chronic (indicating that it lasted more than six months), was present. 309.0.

Axis II: Character disorders, long-standing patterns of maladaptive behavior are to be listed here. Multiple psychological testing results indicate the presence of histrionic personality traits. The use of the term traits implies that the psychologist does not think the behavior characteristics are severe enough to warrant a full diagnosis of a character disorder. DSM-IV describes histrionic personality disorder as "a pervasive pattern of excessive emotionality and attention seeking . . . as indicated by five (or more) of the following: 1. Is uncomfortable in situations in which he or she is not the center of attention. 2. Interaction with others is often characterized by inappropriate sexually seductive or provocative behavior. 3. Displays rapidly shifting and shallow expression of emotions. 4. Consistently uses physical appearance to draw attention to self. 5. Has a style of speech that is excessively impressionistic and lacking in detail. 6. Shows self-dramatization, theatricality, and exaggerated expression of emotion. 7. Is suggestible, that is, easily influenced by others or circumstances. 8. Considers relationships to be more intimate than they actually are."

Axis III: Medical conditions that are directly related to the diagnoses on Axis I are to be listed here. None were present.

Axis IV: Psychosocial and environmental stressors: From a list provided in the Manual the diagnostician is asked to describe those stressors that contribute to an understanding of the diagnoses on Axis I. Those that apply to Mr. Forest are occupational problems—stress on the job, job loss, litigation (which is specifically listed as a stressor).

Axis V: Global Assessment Scale of Functioning: On a scale from 1, profound, to 100, absent, the diagnostician is asked to rate the severity of the patient's symptoms. During the last few years at work I rated Mr. Forest's symptoms in the 51–60 moderate range. Currently, I rate them in the 71–80 minimal ranges.

The treatment prescribed for the Major Depressive Disorder diagnosis made by his psychotherapist and others was appropriate. His therapist later described this condition as resolved. I did not make this diagnosis because I did not feel that Mr. Forest's depression was severe enough to warrant that diagnosis. Some of the impression of severity was due to his histrionic tendencies to exaggerate.

Treatment

No psychiatric treatment related to the termination of his job is indicated at this time.

The treatment that Mr. Forest received over a span of several years in the past was appropriate and achieved a good result.

Although not directly related to the issues of this lawsuit, I feel that the continued use of anti-depressant medication on a long-term basis is questionable.

Prognosis

The prognosis for this intact, intelligent man, is excellent.

Calvin A. Colarusso, M.D.
Clinical Professor of Psychiatry
University of California at San Diego

DIAGNOSTIC SUMMARY FOR THE DEFENSE

This attorney did not want a full report. A diagnostic summary conveys the most essential facts in the case and the diagnostician's diagnoses and impressions, thus providing the lawyer with the information he needs in the form that he prefers. The diagnostic summary also serves as a useful document for the diagnostician when preparing for deposition or trial.

Opinions are based on:

A Diagnostic Interview of 1 hour 50 minutes with the plaintiff, Miss Shift. *Working for the defense, I was not allowed to see the plaintiff more than once.*
Review of Records:
Cross Complaint
Joan Shift's Responses to Cross-Defendant Joseph B.'s Form Interrogatories (set one)
First Amended Cross-Complaint
Joan Shift's Responses to Special Interrogatories
Records of medical doctor:
Records of medical doctor:
Records of medical doctor:
Deposition Joan Shift
Psychological Testing—Dr. L.:

Diagnostic Interview, Miss Shift

Identifying Information:

Joan Shift, in early midlife. Not working. Bought her home four years ago.

Developmental History:

Parents divorced when she was a young child. Sees parents regularly.

Several siblings.

Early development—fine. Fibromyalgia in early teens. Actual diagnosis in her 20s.

Did well in elementary school

Puberty age 13. High school graduate.

No drugs, alcohol, or problems with police.

Ages 20–30: Married and divorced after several years. Good guy. Just not right. PTSD Dx made in this decade due to constant sexual harassment by a supervisor. AA degree in science.

Ages 30–40: Second marriage. Divorced after a few years. Second instance of harassment by a male supervisor. "Exact same scenario." Given several thousand dollars to close case. Not sure who gave diagnosis of PTSD.

Ages 40–present: Bought house. Problems with tree began soon after moved in.

Mental Status Examination:

Cooperative, talkative. Affect bright, not depressed. Thinking—logical, goal directed. Oriented.

Issues of Law Suit:

Large tree in back yard. Issues with neighbors over fence and cutting branches on tree. Took neighbors to small claims court. New trial after neighbors appeal. Awarded $2,000.

Afraid go outside. Neighbors yell obscenities.

Symptoms:

Withdrawal, isolation, anxiety, extreme fatigue, anger, increased pain, night terrors.

Therapy:

Began August 2012. Was once/week, now once/month. Described as paranoid. Connecting dots that weren't there. Dxs: PTSD, paranoid personality.

Psychological Testing
Dr. F.

Mental Status: appears euthymic with appropriate affect during the interview. Says is hypervigilant, not paranoid.

Full Scale IQ—105

MMPI-2: "She appears to exaggerate the extent of her physical complaints and disability, while also denying minor personal faults and limitations to which most people will readily admit."

"Cognitively, Ms. Shift demonstrates evidence of paranoid ideation. . . . Because of her general suspiciousness and alienation from others, she is likely to have significant interpersonal difficulties."

Diagnosis
DSM- V

A diagnosis of PTSD is not indicated now, or in the past. There was no life threatening danger during the sexual harassments or from the neighbors.

DX: Adjustment Disorder 309.0
Paranoid Personality Disorder 301.0
Discord with Neighbor, Lodger or Landlord, V60.89

Treatment

Specifically to deal with the situation with her neighbors, individual psychotherapy, once per week for six months. Cost $250 per 45-minute session.

Long-standing personality issues and emotional consequences of fibromyalgia are clearly in need of continuing therapy and pain management but are not related to the dispute with the neighbors.

Prognosis

For resolution of the Adjustment Disorder related to the dispute with the neighbors—good.

THREE

Components of a Thorough Adult Forensic Evaluation

The Case of Robert Rose

> In scientific terms, the law expects *incremental*—not absolute—validity. The question is whether mental health professionals' opinions will *assist* legal decision not whether the opinions meet a particular standard of scientific rigor.
>
> —Melton et al., 2007, p. 4

PSYCHOLOGICAL TESTING REPORTS

There are significant differences between conducting a clinical evaluation and a forensic evaluation. As opposed to clinical evaluations, forensic evaluations must be conducted in a short period of time (particularly when working for the defense), are not for the subjects own benefit, are often focused on highly charged emotional events, and commonly involve matters about which there is motivation to distort information. Consequently, forensic interviews are often confrontational and address traumatic memories faster than would be common in clinical assessment and intervention (Melton et al., 2007, p. 102).

Doing a complete, thorough adult forensic evaluation or IME (independent medical examination as it is called by some) serves two basic purposes. First, as with any psychiatric diagnostic process, it is the best way to arrive at the most comprehensive understanding of the individual's mental and emotional state, diagnoses, treatment recommendations, and prognosis. Second, and critically important to a forensic expert, a thorough evaluation permits you to provide the lawyer who retained you with a detailed understanding of his client and allows you to successfully resist the efforts of the opposing attorney to denounce or dismiss your opinions at deposition or trial. Further, a thorough evaluation ensures that your opinions will be at least the equal of the opposing psychiatric expert and more than likely superior and more credible.

As previously stated, the best data sources that underlie your opinions are a review of all relevant records, diagnostic interviews, and psychological testing. *You can be certain that the opposing lawyer will ask you for the bases of your opinions. Indeed, this may occur multiple times, particularly during depositions.*

All of the information gathered during the diagnostic evaluation will usually be formalized in a report. Report writing will be referred to throughout this chapter. Case examples of reports were already presented in chapter 2.

REVIEW OF RECORDS

The complaint, interrogatories, police and medical records (others as well), depositions, and opposing expert reports are obviously not a part of the diagnostic process in nonforensic settings; but they are an integral part of every forensic psychiatric evaluation. They provide you with detailed information about the event(s) that lead to the Filling of the lawsuit and the assertions and opinions of the opposing parties. Other information such as medical records, family history, and education and work histories are a familiar and necessary component of any psychiatric evaluation.

When the number of records to be reviewed is large, a not infrequent occurrence, many hours will be spent reviewing and summarizing the information contained therein. Each expert will develop his own method of summarizing large bodies of data. I personally chose to receive all records on paper. I would rather have the law firm take the time to prepare the records for me to review than my having to download them from my computer or take them to Kinko's to be copied. Paper records allow me to review the records wherever I choose as opposed to being chained for hours to a computer screen. The only notations I ever make on the records themselves are the date that they were reviewed and the number or minutes or hours doing so. I take notes in long hand as I go along, summarizing the major points and noting the pages involved (in case I want to return to the original material at a later date). This allows me to refresh my memory and summarize the pertinent facts in the case easily and quickly as the lawsuit progresses. Keep all records provided to you until the case is resolved, then return them to the law firm or shred them if so instructed.

DIAGNOSTIC INTERVIEWS—LEGAL CONSIDERATIONS

It is essential for you to understand, and explain to the examinee, that you and he or she are not entering into a doctor-patient relationship. You are doing the evaluation as an expert witness and your primary relationship is with the retaining law firm (Macbeth et al., 1994).

When serving as a plaintiff expert you will have the freedom to see the plaintiff more than once if you chose. I prefer to see the individual at least twice because most persons are apprehensive about legal examinations and are uncertain of what to expect. Thus, you will often get a different perspective—and often more detailed information—during a second interview.

When serving as an expert for the defense your flexibility is much more circumscribed. Almost always you are allowed to see the plaintiff only once. Very often the time allotted is limited, sometimes by the judge, to two or three hours. Occasionally the court will not allow you to ask questions about certain subjects. Plaintiff lawyers will often insist on being present during the diagnostic interview. I *always* make it clear that this is completely unacceptable because the presence of a third party in the room skews the diagnostic process, particularly when that individual has a vested interest in the outcome of the evaluation. If the plaintiff lawyer insists, ask the lawyer who retained you to present the issue to the court for a final determination.

Taping interviews: I personally do not tape record my diagnostic interviews. Doing so requires hours of additional time to review the tapes and provides the opposing side with more data to criticize and attack. It is not unusual when working for the defense to have the plaintiff bring a recorder and tape the interview. This is perfectly acceptable as long as the plaintiff—and not you—operates the recording device. Recently, a colleague was accused by a plaintiff lawyer of purposely turning off the recorder (totally untrue) in order to deprive the lawyer of information about the interview process and content. The proper place for the opposing lawyer to question you about any aspect of your evaluation and opinions is at deposition or trial.

PSYCHOLOGICAL TESTING

A complete evaluation includes psychological testing. I make a request for psychological testing *during my initial contacts* with the retaining lawyer. That way the testing evaluation, which often takes weeks or a month or two to complete (including a report), can be occurring simultaneously with your record review and diagnostic interviews. A psychologist who has had experience with the court system, writes reports that are easy to read, is able to focus on the issues involved in the law suit, and is not afraid to give a deposition or testify in court is worth his weight in gold. Make every effort to find such a person in your community or nearby.

If is often necessary to educate relatively inexperienced lawyers about the value of psychological testing. When explaining, I usually compare the importance of lab tests or radiographic diagnostic measures to an internist or a surgeon. Experienced lawyers are sometimes wary of psychological testing reports because the opposing attorney will sometimes focus on a sentence or two that seems to contradict the psychologist's or my conclusions. Less data means less damaging material. However, since both sides use psychological testing, it is usually easy to compare the relative value versus the possibility of benefit for the opposing side.

As a psychiatrist, I was not trained to administer and interpret raw data, hence the need for a psychologist of my choosing to administer the tests and prepare a report, which I use as part of the data available to me as I consider my opinions. Some lawyers will argue that getting psychological testing amounts to designating a second psychiatric expert. The court often decides this issue. In my experience the court has usually allowed me to use the testing as an adjunct to my clinical interviews, much as a physician diagnosing a medical problem would use lab tests and radiographic data, and not consider the psychologist administering the testing as a second designated expert.

I often ask one of the three experienced forensic psychologists that I utilize to do the testing. In their report they always make it clear that they are not conducting a complete evaluation. For example, this opening comment by a psychologist who worked on a case with me: "In this instance, the undersigned is working with Calvin Colarusso, M.D., in an adjunctive role. This is, Dr. Colarusso is the principle evaluator in this case. I will be performing a psychological evaluation in order to assist him in reaching diagnostic and causative conclusions, but I will not be forming such opinions myself" (from a psychological testing report).

Two psychological testing reports are provided at the end of this chapter.

ADULT DIAGNOSTIC INTERVIEWS—THE CONTENT

Since anyone interested in becoming a forensic psychiatric expert has done many clinical evaluations of adults, I will not focus on the components of a standard evaluation. But I will comment on the forensic usefulness of the information gathered.

Identifying Information

Name, age, occupation, spouse, names of children are important details because they provide a basic framework on which to build an understanding of the individual. Date of birth, for instance, allows you to determine exactly how old the person was when the event(s) leading to the lawsuit began.

The History of the Law Suit

The history of the lawsuit is the forensic equivalent of the present illness in clinical evaluations. You should already know many details about these issues and/or experiences from the complaint and other records that were provided to you for review prior to the diagnostic interview. But it is absolutely essential that you hear the story from the plaintiff. Otherwise you are basing your understanding on the opinion of the lawyer who wrote the complaint and will be attacked for basing your conclusions on information formulated by the referring or defending lawyer and not on information you obtained directly from the plaintiff or defendant.

Take down as many direct quotes as you can, particularly about the individual's emotional responses to the events involved in the lawsuit. Here are two examples: "When I saw the other car coming right at me and I couldn't get out of the way, I thought I was going to die" or "When my boss kept trying to touch me I wanted to scream but I needed my job."

Symptoms

I ask the individual to list, not describe, first any physical, and then any psychological symptoms that he feels developed as a direct result of the issues in the lawsuit. Then, as with any clinical evaluation, I ask for a description of each symptom, when it began, when it was most severe, and if it still exists, what is the severity at the time of the evaluation. Legally the presence or absence of symptoms and their severity is important because in civil actions any emotional damages that are awarded by the judge or jury are translated into money. How much are the individual's symptoms and diagnoses resulting from the lawsuit worth.

As a psychiatric expert it is very important to recognize that you are not qualified to give expert opinions on physical symptoms or diagnoses. There are board certified specialists in whatever medical areas that are involved to do that. If you do, prepare to be severely attacked at deposition or on cross-examination at trial for rendering opinions in areas where you do not have the formalized training to do so. However, physical symptoms are often a component of recognized psychiatric diagnoses and therefore can be addressed in that context.

DSM-V Diagnoses

The following advice, if followed, will render you relatively bulletproof at deposition or on cross-examination. When making a diagnosis be sure that you have considered each and every criteria listed in DSM-V for that diagnosis and have recorded the evidence for each of the requirement in your notes.

For example, if you determined that a diagnosis of Post-traumatic Stress Disorder was indicated, ask the individual about each of the symptoms in each of the sections and record the responses in long hand. Then when you are questioned about the basis for your diagnosis you can respond with conviction.

When organizing your diagnostic thoughts be sure to have a clear understanding of what any other mental health experts involved in the case (as treater or expert on the other side) have concluded. Occasionally, you will find that treaters or opposing experts have not detailed the DSM-V bases for their opinions and are thus vulnerable to criticism from you or the retaining lawyer. You will also find that there is often disagreement between opposing expert and treaters in regard to diagnosis and treatment (Large, Nielssen, and Elliott, 2010).

Developmental History

The developmental history traces an individual's life from birth to the chronological present, comparing this person's experience against a large body of knowledge on normal and pathological processes. Although I'm dealing with the history of an adult in this chapter, remember that a complete developmental history traces the individual's life from pregnancy to the chronological present, regardless of age.

When dealing with adults it is important to cover the adult years as well as the childhood developmental stages. If you are familiar with adult developmental theory the following outline of adult developmental phases and tasks will be rudimentary. If you are unfamiliar with these concepts the following outline will serve as a guide to help you organize your questions about both childhood and adulthood.

Childhood Developmental Phases

Pregnancy, Labor, and Delivery
The First Year of Life (the Oral Phase)
Ages 1–3 (the Anal Phase)
Ages 3–6 (the Oedipal Phase)
Ages 6–11 (Latency)
Ages 11–20 (Adolescence)

Young Adulthood (Ages 20–40)

Middle Adulthood (Ages 40–60)
Late Adulthood (Ages 60–80)
Late, Late Adulthood (Ages 80 and beyond)

For more information about child and adult developmental theory and processes I refer you to two books on the subject: *Adult Development* (Colarusso and Nemiroff, 1981) and chapter 2 (pp. 11–28) and chapter 9 (pp. 121–132) in *Child and Adult Development* (Colarusso, 1992). These chapters contained detailed examples of areas to be covered and questions that may be asked.

Now why is this information important to you as an expert witness? Because plaintiff lawyers want to focus causation of all emotional difficulties on the experiences and issues that led to the law suit and defense lawyers want to blame the symptoms on everything *but* the issues that lead to the law suit. Remembering that thoroughness and integrity are your greatest strengths as an expert witness, take a complete development history of both childhood and adulthood and describe any and all preexisting issues that help explain the individual's symptoms and diagnoses.

If you were hired by the plaintiff attorney, if he is worth his salt at all, he will want to hear about, and be prepared to deal with, preexisting factors from his expert, not from the defense expert. If the retaining lawyer is a defense attorney, he will be impressed with your thoroughness and providing him with information that can be extremely useful to his defense.

In some cases, the developmental history will be relatively "clean"—meaning that there are little or no preexisting emotional difficulties that relate to the issues and symptoms resulting from the experiences related to the lawsuit. In other cases there may be considerable evidence of preexisting psychopathology that significantly contributed to the symptoms and diagnoses claimed by the plaintiff. I repeat, regardless of which side hired you, do a thorough evaluation and honestly state your opinions about preexisting factors.

The developmental framework is also extremely important for determining how the major issues/traumas leading to the lawsuit will affect the individual's future. The life care planner will translate future physical and psychological care into a dollar figure, in severe cases totaling millions of dollars. *Predicting the need for future psychological care is an integral part of your role as a psychiatric expert.* For example, chronic child sexual abuse has lifelong consequences, affecting future development as much or to a greater degree than current functioning (Colarusso, 2010). A case that I was involved in recently concerned a young boy who was hit by a vehicle while crossing a street. As a result a limb was amputated and he required a permanent colostomy, supra-pubic catheter, and a non-functioning penis.

A knowledge of adolescent development allowed me to predict the emotional consequences of his being unable to function sexually or the ability in adulthood to consider a range of career choices and the greatly diminished chances of marriage and parenthood.

Mental Status Examination

A complete mental status examination is a required component of any clinical psychiatric evaluation, covering appearance and behavior, speech, affect or feeling tone, thinking and orientation, and memory. The role of the mental status examination in forensic evaluations is no different. There should be evidence in your notes taken during the diagnostic interview(s) that clearly indicate that you have conducted, and recorded, your impressions and the person's response to questions for each section of the mental status exam.

An experienced lawyer will note the absence of an organized mental status examination and thus, undermine your expertise and credibility. On the other hand, if you have recorded a full mental status examination and the expert on the other side has not, you become the more credible expert.

In nonforensic settings we do not think of ourselves as competing against or comparing ourselves with other mental health professionals but the legal system is adversarial in nature—plaintiff against defendant, plaintiff lawyers against defense lawyers; and like it or not, mental health plaintiff expert against defense mental health expert. This fact is distasteful to most mental health professionals and explains, in part, why so few of us are willing to have anything to do with the legal system. However, evaluation and involvement in the system provides an extremely valuable, and necessary function for plaintiff and defendant and society in general. In 1973, the American Psychiatric Association published the first edition of the *Principles of Medical Ethics with Annotations Especially Applicable to Psychiatry*. There have been numerous revisions since then but all contain a section stating that a psychiatrist should recognize a responsibility to participate in activities contributing to an improved community. In particular, psychiatrists are encouraged to serve society by advising and consulting with the executive, legislative, and judiciary branches of government.

I believe the solution to this distressing aspect of the law is to do an honest, thorough job and describe areas of agreement and disagreement between and among experts in a respectful, professional manner.

Review of Records

Although not always possible because of their unavailability due to legal wrangling over what should be made available to you, always try to review the complaint, interrogatories, and physical and mental health records before conducting your diagnostic interviews. This allows you to ask the person being evaluated for details about events that are mentioned in the records, particularly about their opinions and feelings about treating physicians and mental health practitioners and experiences that you need to explore in order to get the most complete knowledge of the individual's mental and emotional state.

Considering Diagnostic Possibilities

Toward the end of the diagnostic interview(s), with DSM-V in front of you so that you can assess the presence or absence of all criteria required to make a diagnosis, consider various diagnostic possibilities and memorialize the various diagnoses considered in your notes so that you will be able to discuss why you ruled a particular diagnosis in or out at deposition or trial. Final determination of diagnosis will await the results of psychological testing and the arrival of all necessary records. At that point you are ready to formalize your opinions in whatever form the retaining attorney requests (diagnostic summary or formal report).

As DSM-V clearly states the diagnostic criteria and text contained therein were primarily designed for clinical assessment, case formulation, and treatment planning and not for use in the courts. There is an imperfect fit between the ultimate concerns of the law and the information contained in a clinical diagnosis. However, DSM-V can facilitate legal decision maker's understanding of mental disorders and serve as a check for ungrounded speculation about diagnosis and the functioning of a particular individual (DSM-V Desk Reference, 2013, p. 13).

Gathering Information from Other Sources

It is not unusual during diagnostic evaluations to discover sources of information that were either unknown to the referring attorney or were not considered to be important by him, or more likely, by his paralegal. Most of your dealings with law firms will be with assistants or paralegals who take care of the management of information for a case such as procuring and sending records, arranging times for interviews, and scheduling phone calls or meetings with attorneys.

At the end of a diagnostic interview I frequently need to call an assistant or paralegal and ask for additional data such as school or work records, medical records, or records from mental health providers who were unknown to the law firm. A frequent question at deposition is were you provided with all of the records that you requested. We'll discuss depositions in chapter 5, but for the moment it is sufficient to state that the lawyer taking your deposition will ask for a list of all the records that you have reviewed. Although he won't say so, he is comparing your list with those records reviewed by his expert.

Treatment Recommendations

Recommendations for psychotherapy should be expressed in detail. The estimated cost of the therapy, per session, should be described. For example: "Individual psychotherapy, once per week for eighteen months. An experienced psychiatrist or psychologist in San Diego would charge $250 per 45-minute session." If medication is indicated I make a recommendation for antidepressant or antianxiety medication but do not mention a specific drug, leaving that decision to the treating therapist. An approximate monthly cost of the medication is described.

If other forms of psychological intervention are indicated, such as group or couples therapy, therapy for cognitive impairments, or vocational rehabilitation, are listed also.

Prognosis

Since the Global Assessment Scale of Functioning from DSM-IV is no longer utilized, I describe prognosis as poor, fair, good or excellent. I always include the phrase "with treatment as recommended," in my prognosis. "The prognosis, if the recommendations described above are followed, is good."

Discussion

The case is summarized in the discussion section of the report and the rationale behind diagnosis and treatment recommendations is described. In many instances, such as chronic child abuse or significant injury, discussing the consequences on future developmental tasks and stages throughout adulthood is indicated. Examples of such recommendations will be found in case examples throughout this book.

THE CASE OF ROBERT ROSE: EVALUATION AND REPORT

The initial phone call and discussion with the retaining attorney were described in chapter 1.

Mr. Rose called a few days after the initial phone call from his attorney. I had asked his attorney to tell him that I would be calling. I explained who I was and what would occur during the evaluation. He easily agreed to a date for the first diagnostic interview. I also called the psychologist whom I had chosen to do the psychological testing and he agreed to do the psychological evaluation. I gave him the attorney's name and phone number so he could make his independent financial arrangements. The initial diagnostic interview lasted two hours and thirty-five minutes. During that time I gathered information on all of the areas described in this and the previous chapter. That included identifying information, the history of the accident and subsequent treatment, physical and psychological symptoms, mental status examination, reviews of records, and consideration of various diagnostic possibilities.

My report, which provides a detailed consideration of the information gathered during the diagnostic evaluation, follows. The full report of the psychologist, which is summarized in my report, also follows. I always attach the complete report of the psychologist with my report, providing convincing evidence of the thoroughness of my evaluation.

REPORT OF THE FORENSIC EVALUATION OF ROBERT ROSE

Introduction

This is a report of a psychiatric evaluation of Robert Rose of [address]; by Calvin A. Colarusso, M.D., Board Certified Adult and Child Psychiatrist; at the request of Attorney [name and address].

The conclusions contained herein are based on a two hour and thirty-five minute diagnostic interview with Mr. Rose and psychological testing performed at my request by [psychologist's name]. In addition the following records were reviewed:

Traffic collision report
County fire rescue
The treating medical center
The treating rehabilitation hospital
Radiology
Treating physician
Treating neurologist

The Diagnostic Interview

Mr. Rose was seen in my office. No one else was present. He was informed that unlike the usual doctor-patient relationship, this evaluation was being performed as part of his lawsuit and there was no doctor-patient confidentiality. My records would be available to the attorneys for the defense as well as his attorney.

Identifying Information:

Robert Rose, born February 2, 1953, was the general manager of a real estate office.

Rebecca Rose, his wife, was born on March 14, 1955. She was employed, full time, as an elementary school teacher.

The couple has been married for 21 years. They have a son who was in college.

The Accident:

On January 3, 2008, Mr. Rose was standing at the valet stand outside of a restaurant waiting for his car. When the valet, in a car directly in front of Mr. Rose, mistakenly floored the car in reverse, instead of putting the gearshift into forward, he slammed Mr. Rose against the brick wall of the restaurant. Mr. Rose ended up on the ground with the bumper in his crotch. His right leg was up in the air and a tire was against his left shoulder. A nurse and a man standing by encouraged him to hang on. Mr. Rose could wiggle his right foot so he had the thought that he wasn't paralyzed. He lay on the floor for a long time and yelled, "Get the car off of me."

While he was pinned against the wall Mr. Rose thought "I'm going to die on my mother's birthday." He began to cry as he described his thoughts. Both of his parents were dead. "Mom and Dad, I'm not coming to see you yet!" Mr. Rose sobbed as he described thoughts of dying and the "excruciating pain." "I wished I would lose consciousness." The pain in his penis was severe. "I was embedded in the wall. It was worse than having your balls hit."

After approximately 15 minutes the car was pulled off of Mr. Rose. He was given oxygen and pain medication and put on a gurney. *In the ambulance* on the way to the hospital Mr. Rose wondered if he was going to make it. The paramedics told him to hang on. He was in "horrible pain, beyond anything you can imagine" and wondered if he would live.

Hospitalization and Return Home:

At the hospital emergency measures such as a check for internal bleeding, insertion of a catheter, and various radiological procedures were performed. Then Mr. Rose was transported by helicopter to a major trauma treatment center. In the helicopter he asked the physician if he would see his family again. At the trauma center evaluation continued until the middle of the night. Mr. Rose had a fractured pelvis and lumbar vertebra. The pain continued to be extreme. "I thought I'd be out of work for a long time but I'd live. But how would my body work?" Surgery was not performed. At the end of a several day hospital stay Mr. Rose was told that it would take him up to two years to recover. At that time he would be "somewhat back to normal."

Mr. Rose was transferred to a rehabilitation center where he remained for two weeks. He was still in great pain and asked to be put in a coma but the staff wanted him awake and forced him to move. "I could feel my bones crushed in me." Mr. Rose spent much of his time in physical therapy. Despite morphine and other drugs he was still in "unbelievable pain." Mr. Rose worried if he would be able to perform sexually and if his right leg would work. His wife told him that his penis and testicles were black and blue.

The trip to the airport and the flight home were very difficult since Mr. Rose couldn't walk or go to the bathroom. He was at home for nearly five months before he was able to return to work on a limited basis. While recovering at home Mr. Rose saw several physicians and went to physical therapy. Because the pain continued to be severe the physicians prescribed various narcotic pain medications. At the time of this evaluation the pain was "tolerable."

Mr. Rose had no penile sensations and did not get erections.

Symptoms:

Physical Symptoms:

Mr. Rose can walk but not run or jog due to the injuries. His right leg, below the knee, is numb.

His back in the right lumbar area is sore during the morning and becomes more painful as the day goes on. By the end of the day Mr. Rose has no feeling in his right leg.

Mr. Rose can feel the bones in his pelvis when he sits on the toilet. They are fractured and have not healed yet.

He is not able to get an erection. Viagra doesn't help. Mr. Rose had his first orgasm during the week before the interview, achieving an erection through a self-administered needle injection of his penis. Mr. Rose doesn't expect to be able to get spontaneous erections in the future but hasn't asked the urologist for a prognosis because he is fearful of the answer he might receive. A penile implant is the next step. Mr. Rose had no difficulty with sexual functioning prior to the accident.

Mr. Rose has not had any serious illnesses in his life.

Psychological Symptoms:

"I'm on edge."

"I think about it all the time. I try not to."

"I worry about getting hit again."

"Now I know how people give up and die. I'm so fortunate I'm alive."

"Internally I'm disabled, not to mention my sexuality."

"My wife has been patient. On our anniversary, in a suite, I couldn't get an erection."

"I'm jumpy. If people come up to me I jump."

"I love my job. I never missed except for this. I set the tone as general manager. I don't want to have my problems interfere."

Mr. Rose cried as he told how warmly the office staff greeted him when he returned to work.

"I can't sit through an entire football game."

"I want it to be next summer so I'll be better."

"All I do is work and come home. I don't have a life beyond that. I want to golf with my guy friends. I don't want people to feel sorry for me."

"I'm frustrated, tired, and disappointed."

"Before the accident I was friendly, had best friends, and was active and jovial. I'm a very humble guy with morals and integrity."

Mr. Rose did not have any emotional problems or treatment prior to the accident.

Developmental History:

The developmental history traces an individual's life from birth to the chronological present and allows the diagnostician to compare this person's experience against a large body of knowledge of normal and pathological development, thus tracing any connection between present symptomatology and past problems.

Mr. Rose was raised in an intact family with one sibling. His parents were married for more than 45 years when his father died. The parents had a very good marriage and the atmosphere in the home was "great."

Ages 0–6: Pregnancy, labor, and delivery were normal. Mother was at home as the full time caretaker. Early developmental milestones such as walking and talking occurred on schedule.

Ages 6–12: Mr. Rose was an excellent student in elementary school. He was well liked, had lots of friends, and was interested in sports. The family went camping and on vacations to the shore.

Adolescence, ages 12–20: Puberty occurred at age 11/12. Mr. Rose began dating at 16 and developed a heterosexual orientation. In junior and senior high school he achieved a 3.8 grade point average and was on the track team. He experimented with pot and alcohol but never had problems with the police. After high school Mr. Rose got an AA degree before beginning work.

Ages 20–30 (1975–1985): Mr. Rose married at age 23. His first child was born three years later. He worked as a salesman for his current employer during this decade.

Age 30–present: Mr. Rose received several promotions and eventually became office and regional manager. During these years he advanced in the work place, had a happy marriage, enjoyed raising his child, and had a full social life. The accident occurred when Mr. Rose was 55 years of age.

Mental Status Examination:

The mental status examination is the standard method by which a mental health professional evaluates an individual's mental and emotional state assessing appearance and behavior, speech, affect or feeling tone, thinking and orientation, and memory.

Mr. Rose presented as a somewhat overweight middle-aged man. He walked with a limp. Mr. Rose had a good vocabulary and spoke clearly. He was emotionally labile, crying as he described various aspects of his injuries and symptoms. Although he denied being depressed, his affect was obviously depressed. Thinking was logical and goal directed (normal). There was no evidence of a thinking disorder, delusions, or hallucinations. He was oriented as to time, person, and place and interpreted proverbs abstractly (normal finding).

Psychological Testing

A full battery of psychological tests was administered by Dr. B. at my request. Dr. B. saw Mr. Rose on three separate occasions. His complete report accompanies this document. A summary of the findings will be reported here.

On the Structured Clinical Interview test "Mr. Rose reported the following symptoms associated with major depression: consistent dysphoria or depressed mood, periods of diminished interest or pleasure in many activities, sleep difficulty (requiring prescription medication), intermittent periods of agitation, feelings of guilt and diminished self-worth, focus and concentration difficulties, fears and recurrent thoughts about dying (not suicidal in nature). Mr. Rose also described the following symptoms and features of Post-traumatic Stress Disorder: exposure to a horrific and terrifying event which was life threatening and resulted in extreme bodily injury, recurrent and intrusive distressing recollections of the accident, recurrent distressing dreams and nightmares associated with the accident, intense psychological distress and psychological reactivity to internal or external cues associated with the accident, persistent avoidance of stimuli associated with the traumatic accident, persistent symptoms of increased arousal, and a significantly negatively altered view of the expected course and quality of his life."

"Based on Mr. R.'s sustained and appropriate level of engagement and participation in the various voluntary components, these testing results should be considered a valid and useful assessment of his current level of cognitive and psychological functioning."

On the Wechsler Adult Intelligence test Mr. Rose achieved a full-scale IQ in the average range. "Among the various subtests that assess different aspects of learning, memory, and problem solving, Mr. Rose evidenced some notable errors and inconsistencies in his ability and overall performance. Such inconsistencies are often indicative of mild to moderate intermittent cognitive disruption associated with underlying psychological difficulties secondary to features of depression, anxiety, or sustained psychological trauma.

On the Minnesota Multiphasic Personality Inventory-2 elevated clinical scales indicated severe concerns, difficulty, and symptoms regarding many aspects of physical functioning, sleep disruption, gastrointestinal problems, and chronic pain. "Mr. Rose also endorsed items reflecting major concerns and difficulty with his sexual functioning and performance. . . . Additional scores suggest tension, worry, and some degree of guardedness, distrust, resentment, or perceived hostility from others."

On the Rotter Incomplete Sentences Blank test, a relatively highly structured self-report projective measure, "Mr. Rose's responses vacillated between attempts to remain positive and hopeful while painfully acknowledging his current difficulties, limitations, and worries about his future functioning and well-being. . . . Mr. Rose expresses major concerns and worries about his current and future prospects for a satisfying and happy life. . . . He is in constant pain and acknowledges that his greatest fear 'is being in pain and disabled for life.'"

"Themes and projections from the Thematic Apperception Test were notable for a distinct alternation between normative, optimistic, hopeful, and mastery-oriented responses juxtaposed with associations reflecting dysphoria, despair, loss, and death." Mr. Rose often feels overwhelmed by "the profound physical and emotional challenges facing him."

"Structural data and indices from the Rorschach Inkblot Test are consistent with multiple indications of pronounced depressive emotional and cognitive features and extremely limited and failing coping capacities and resources. . . . He is likely to be in a relatively constant and intense degree of psychological distress and overload. . . . Mr. Rose sees himself as quite physically damaged. He has pronounced concerns over his body integrity and physical functioning, with a marked tendency to view himself as vulnerable, compromised, and broken."

Dr. B. suggested diagnoses of Major Depressive Disorder, Single Episode, Post-traumatic Stress Disorder, Chronic and Pain Disorder Associated with a General Medical Condition. He rated Mr. Rose's symptoms in the moderate to serious impairment range.

Review of Records

The records from the rescue service and the treating and rehabilitation hospitals describe the accident and Mr. Rose's injuries and treatment prior to returning to his home. Upon discharge from the rehabilitation hospital diagnoses of pelvic and sacral fracture, small pelvic hematoma, mild elevated liver function tests, and newly diagnosed diabetes were noted.

The records of the treating physician and neurologist describe regular office visits monitoring Mr. Rose's rehabilitation efforts once he returned home.

Diagnosis

The Diagnostic and Statistical Manual of Mental Disorders of the American Psychiatric Association, 4th Edition, is the only widely recognized diagnostic nomenclature in the field. (At the time of the evaluation.) Based on the required criteria for each diagnosis listed in the manual the diagnostician is asked to divide his or her diagnostic impressions into five subdivisions called Axes. Using this nomenclature I arrived at the following diagnostic conclusions regarding Mr. Rose.

Axis I: Major diagnoses are to be listed here.

Post-traumatic Stress Disorder, Chronic (309.81). Mr. Rose meets all of the criteria for this diagnosis. He experienced "an event or events that involved actual or threatened death or serious injury . . . and experienced intense fear, helplessness, or horror." The traumatic event was reexperienced through intrusive thoughts, dreams of the acciden, and intense psychological and physiological distress and reactivity. Persistent avoidance of stimuli associated with the trauma and numbing of general responsiveness not present before the trauma were experienced by unsuccessful efforts to avoid thoughts, feelings, and conversations associated with the trauma, markedly diminished participation in significant activities, feelings of detachment or estrangement from others, restricted range of affect, and a sense of a foreshortened future. Persistent symptoms of increased arousal not present before the trauma were indicated by sleeping difficulties, irritability, difficulty concentrating, hyper-vigilance, and exaggerated startle response. The Post-traumatic Stress Disorder is chronic because it has lasted more than three months. It causes "clinically significant distress or impairment in social, occupational, or other important areas of functioning."

Major Depressive Disorder, Single Episode (296.22). Although Mr. Rose denied being depressed, depressive affect was noted on clinical interview and there was marked evidence of depression on psychological testing. In addition to the depressed mood markedly diminished pleasure in activities, difficulty sleeping, loss of energy, feelings of worthlessness, diminished ability to concentrate, and recurrent thoughts of death were present.

Male Erectile Disorder Due to Pelvic Trauma (607.84). Clinically significant sexual dysfunction has resulted in marked distress and interpersonal difficulty due to severe physical injury resulting from the accident.

Pain Disorder Associated with a General Medical condition (625.9, pelvic). A general medical condition has a major role in the onset and severity of the pain. Psychological factors are not judged to have a major role in the onset, severity, exacerbation, or maintenance of the pain.

Axis II: Character disorders, long standing patterns of maladaptive behavior, are to be listed here. None were present.

Axis III: General Medical Conditions: All of the diagnoses listed on Axis I are directly attributable to and the result of the injuries suffered during the accident.

Axis IV: Psychosocial and Environmental Factors: From a list in the manual the diagnostician is asked to describe those factors that amplify an understanding of the diagnoses on Axis I.

Problems with primary support group—significant interference in marital relationship due to injuries and in particular, inability to function sexually.

Problems related to the social environment—inability to participate in sports and other activities with friends.

Occupational problems—absence from work and limited work schedule due to injuries.

Litigation is specifically listed as a stressor.

Axis V: Global Assessment of Functioning Scale. On a scale from 1, profound, to 100, absent, the diagnostician is asked to rate the severity of the individual's symptoms. I listed Mr. Rose's symptoms in the 41–50 serious ranges.

Treatment

Mr. Rose is in need of an immediate course of psychotherapy, two to three times per week for two to three years to help him cope with the ongoing physical and psychological consequences of the accident. An experienced psychiatrist or psychologist in San Diego would charge $225 per 45-minute session. Antidepressant medication may be indicated during the course of the treatment at a cost of $100–$200 per month.

At some point, to be decided by clinical evaluation at the time during the decade following the completion of the first course of psychotherapy, an additional course of once to twice per week psychotherapy for one to two years is indicated to help Mr. Rose continue to deal with sexual issues, relationship problems, pain and physical injury consequences, and the relationship between physical and psychological consequences of the accident and the aging process. The need for medication would be evaluated at that time.

Prognosis

Due to the permanent nature of physical injuries and the several emotional consequences the prognosis is guarded to fair.

Discussion

As a result of a cruel and devastating act of fate Mr. Rose went from being a happy, active individual one moment to being a significantly injured person in great pain and in a life threatening situation the next. The consequences of the severe injuries he suffered have been devastating physically and psychologically. Major psychiatric diagnoses have come into being as a direct result of the restaurant accident. They will require intensive long-term intervention. The inability to function sexually without penile injections is devastating to self-esteem and masculine identity and has complicated the marital relationship. Restrictions in the ability to work and limited social and recreational interactions are contributing to the significant depression that is present.

Fortunately, Mr. Rose was a high functioning, emotional intact individual before the accident. With ongoing medical and psychiatric help, likely for the rest of his life, he will persevere but never be able to return to the rich, rewarding life that was present before the accident.

Calvin A. Colarusso, M.D.
Clinical Professor of Psychiatry
University of California at San Diego

Psychodiagnostic Evaluation of Mr. Rose

Dr. B.
Address and Phone

Name: Robert Rose
Date of Birth: [date]
Referral Source: Calvin Colarusso, M.D., [date]. Dates Examined: [three]
Report Date: [date]

Tests Administered:

Structured Clinical Interview
Wechsler Adult Intelligence Scale-Revised: Seven Subtest Format (WAIS-R)
Rotter Incomplete Sentences Blank
Thematic Apperception Test
Minnesota Multiphasic Personality Inventory-2 (MMPI-2)
Rorschach Inkblot Test

Background Information:

All of the information in this evaluation was reported directly by Mr. Rose. No additional records were reviewed in the preparation of this report. Robert Rose (in his 50s), Caucasian, married father. He resides with his wife. Mr. Rose is a college graduate and has been employed in business for many years.

Mr. Rose was the victim of a very serious accident on [date]. He was waiting to have his automobile returned by a valet attendant. The attendant apparently mistakenly depressed the accelerator and pinned and crushed Mr. Rose between the automobile and a wall. Mr. Rose sustained very serious and potentially life threatening injuries. He was crushed and trapped between the auto and wall, requiring extrication and emergency medical services from first responders. Mr. Rose was transported by ambulance to a local hospital for evaluation and treatment. Upon assessing the seriousness of his injuries, he was then air lifted to a regional trauma center. Mr. Rose spent five days in that hospital and was transferred to a rehabilitation hospital for an additional ten days. Unable to walk and wheelchair bound, he returned home to continue extensive treatment and rehabilitation efforts.

The extent of the sustained injuries included multiple fractures to both sides of his pelvis, a fractured lumbar,and extensive nerve damage with severed nerves in his right leg. Mr. Rose suffers from chronic pain in his lower back, and his pelvic region remains fractured. His right hip, leg, and foot also have chronic issues including pain, tingling, and numbing. Mr. Rose takes a number of powerful painkillers to assist with the intense chronic pain associated with these injuries. As a result of the injuries sustained in the accident, Mr. Rose developed complete erectile dysfunction. After unsuccessful trials of pill-form erectile dysfunction medication, it was determined that it would be necessary to directly inject medication into the base of Mr. Rose's penis in order for him to achieve and maintain an erection. Even with this highly uncomfortable method, Mr. Rose experiences limited stimulation and pleasure due to sustained nerve damage.

Prior to the accident and resultant injuries Mr. Rose described himself as a very positive, happy, outgoing person. He very much enjoyed being around others and was recognized as a top manager who successfully trained and mentored colleagues at work. He cherished family, socializing and friends, performing well at work, traveling, attending various events, and regularly playing golf. Since the traumatic accident and resultant injuries and limitations, nearly every aspect of Mr. Rose's psychosocial functioning has been severely and dramatically negatively impacted. He attempts to remain hopeful and optimistic, but explains that "now I feel on edge, especially around cars. . . . I have nightmares of others getting run over. . . . I feel lucky to be alive, but I'm emotionally treading water and often overwhelmed." Mr. Rose describes his family as loving, available, and very supportive. Unfortunately, the sustained injuries and resulting erectile dysfunction have significantly decreased the frequency, performance, and pleasure of sexual intimacy with his wife. The necessity of administering penile injections prior to intimacy has resulted in a significant decrease in Mr. Rose's libido and interest in intercourse. Until very recently, Mr. Rose had been unable to achieve an orgasm, and the pleasurable sensations of sexual behavior have been greatly diminished by the impact of chronic pain and nerve damage. Mr. Rose is unable to engage in most physical activities, including the regular golf outings he so previously enjoyed. He now tends to spend much less time with friends, and realizes he has become "much more pulled back" from many friends and social activities. He continues to enjoy his work, but his work schedule and duties have needed to be greatly modified and reduced to accommodate his limitations and chronic pain. He experiences increased pain and fatigue as his workday proceeds. He is very worried and disappointed about not being able to function and perform occupationally as he did prior to the accident. Mr. Rose denies any history of psychiatric difficulties, treatment, or evaluation prior to the accident.

In the Structured Clinical Interview:

Mr. Rose reported the following symptoms associated with Major Depression: consistent dysphoria or depressed mood, periods of diminished interest or pleasure in many activities, sleep difficulties (requiring prescription medication), intermittent periods of agitation, feelings of guilt and diminished self-worth, focus and concentration difficulties, and fears and recurrent thoughts about dying (not suicidal in nature). Mr. Rose also described the following symptoms and features of Post-traumatic Stress Disorder: exposure to a horrific and terrifying event which was life threatening and resulted in extreme bodily injury, recurrent and intrusive distressing recollections of the accident, recurrent distressing dreams and nightmares associated with the accident, intense psychological distress and physiological reactivity to internal or external cues associated with the accident, persistent avoidance of stimuli associated with the traumatic accident, persistent symptoms of increased arousal, and a significantly negatively altered view of the expected course and quality of his life.

Test Results:

Mr. Rose appeared his stated age, was nicely groomed, and presented as pleasant and cooperative. He walked with some noticeable pain and difficulty, especially after sustained periods of sitting. It was physically uncomfortable for Mr. Rose to remain in a stationary position, so he frequently required short breaks to allow for stretching and repositioning. Mr. Rose had taken his typical regimen of medication for chronic pain and nerve difficulties, but did not report or evidence any obvious sedation or undue impact related to the evaluation procedures. On a number of occasions, Mr. Rose became obviously distressed or tearful when directly acknowledging or discussing the traumatic accident and resultant physical and emotional impact. Mr. Rose appeared oriented, engaged, and adequately motivated throughout the assessment process. Based on Mr. Rose's sustained and appropriate level of engagement and participation in the various evaluation components, these testing results should be considered a valid and useful assessment of his current level of cognitive and psychological functioning.

On the WAIS-R Seven Subtest Form, Mr. Rose achieved a Full Scale IQ score of 99 ± 5. This places him in approximately the 50th percentile and the Average range of cognitive functioning as compared to the standardization group. He demonstrated no statistically significant differences between IQ scores associated with Verbal Comprehension and acquired knowledge (VIQ = 103) as compared to nonverbally mediated problem-solving skills and Perceptual Organizational abilities (PIQ = 93). Among the various subtests that assess different aspects of learning, memory, and problem solving, Mr. Rose evidenced some notable errors and inconsistencies in his abilities and overall performance. Such inconsistencies are often indicative of mild to moderate intermittent cognitive disruption associated with underlying psychological difficulties secondary to features of depression, anxiety, or sustained psychological trauma. It is very possible that the observed scores and results represent a mild to moderate underestimation of Mr. Rose's premorbid functioning and cognitive capacities. It is also quite likely that the existence of chronic physical pain and discomfort interferes with Mr. Rose effectively and efficiently engaging and demonstrating his intellectual abilities at their highest level.

Findings from the MMPI-2 are consistent with a reliable and consistent test taking approach. Individuals with similar validity profiles have responded consistently and with an appropriate balance of self-disclosure and willingness to acknowledge existing symptoms and difficulties. Clinical scale elevations indicate severe concerns, difficulties, and symptoms involving specific somatic complaints. These complaints range across a wide area of suffering including acute pain, neurological symptoms, back and neck pain, fatigue, numbness, sleep disruptions, gastrointestinal problems, and chronic pain. Mr. Rose also endorsed items reflecting major concerns and difficulties with his sexual functioning and performance. These results are obviously consistent with his extensive physical and neurological injuries which have left him extremely physically limited, in constant pain, and unable to achieve or maintain an erection without first administering an injection at the base of his penis. Mr. Rose clearly views himself as quite physically damaged and limited.

Additional scores suggest tension, worry, and some degree of guardedness, distrust, and resentment, as well as perceived hostility from others. Such individuals may find it difficult to trust the intentions of others, or find it necessary to remain hypervigilant and "on guard" relative to perceived potential personal dangers. Data are also consistent with some unusual ideation and thought processes that may result in periods of mild reality distortion. Many of these unusual perceptions and peculiar experiences are also a likely response to the strange new sensory events and difficulties Mr. Rose encounters as a result of neurological injuries and pronounced chronic pain. Such intermittently strained and distorted thought processes, as well as heightened alertness to potential dangers and attacks are frequently the result of marked hypervigilance and the mild-moderate dissociative features that may result from experienced psychological trauma.

On the Rotter Incomplete Sentences Blank (RISB), a relatively highly structured self-report projective measure, Mr. Rose's responses vacillate between attempts to remain positive and hopeful while painfully acknowledging his current difficulties and limitations and worries about his future functioning and well-being. He derives great pleasure and support from his wife and family. Mr. Rose also feels very fortunate and grateful to be alive following such a horrific accident. He is hopeful and motivated regarding the possibility of recuperating and attempting to resume his premorbid lifestyle and level of functioning.

Despite his outwardly positive outlook, Mr. Rose expressed major concerns and worries about his current and future prospects for a satisfying and happy life. He feels extremely physically limited and unable to participate in many enjoyable and important activities. He is in constant pain and acknowledges that his greatest fear "is being in pain and disabled for life." He also attempts to protect his wife and others by not revealing the true depths and intensity of his feelings and fears. He is extremely frustrated that his injuries, pain, and physical limitations preclude him from participating in previously enjoyed activities and sports. He is a man who generally exhibits a great "zest and zeal" for life, but is very anxious, fearful, and unsure of what the future actually holds for him.

Themes and projections from the Thematic Apperception Test (TAT) were notable for a distinct alternation between normative, optimistic, hopeful, and mastery-oriented responses juxtaposed with associations reflecting dysphoria, despair, loss, and death. A number of responses were rather defensively brief, simplified, and concrete in an apparent attempt to avoid or minimize negative and painful emotional stimulation. Even with such a protective psychological approach, many stories revealed underlying feelings of sadness, hopelessness, and great pessimism about current circumstances and the future. Mr. Rose wishes to remain strong, positive, and able to successfully confront the profound physical and emotional challenges facing him. Frequently, however, these great challenges feel overwhelming, disorganizing, and potentially insurmountable. Projected material also included perceptions of significant and catastrophic illness or injury resulting in marked loss of physical functioning or death.

Structural data and indices from the Rorschach Inkblot test are consistent with multiple indications of pronounced depressive, emotional, and cognitive features and extremely limited and failing coping capacities and resources. Mr. Rose evidences markedly impaired and limited psychological resources that frequently give way to periods of being overwhelmed and experiences of acute cognitive and emotional disruption. He is likely to be in a relatively constant and intense degree of psychological distress and overload. Mr. Rose is defensively attempting to avoid and minimize painful, negative, and destabilizing thoughts and feelings. His current processing style is quite constricted with clear efforts to limit emotional stimulation and engagement. These defensive efforts, however, are currently woefully ineffective leaving Mr. Rose to encounter frequent episodes of major emotional and cognitive disruption. In those instances when emotions do color ideation and processing, such experience is often dysphoric, painful, negative, pessimistic, and significantly distorted. The level of overall cognitive and perceptual distortion is consistent with intermittent lapses in formal reality testing operations. This presentation of avoidant/simplified processing, emotional constriction, overwhelmed and impaired coping capacities, and significant perceptual distortion is often seen in respondents who have experienced significant psychological trauma.

Rorschach data also reveal quite painful, negative, and pessimistic self-perceptions. Mr. Rose sees himself as quite physically damaged. He has pronounced concerns over his body integrity and physical functioning, with a marked tendency to view himself as vulnerable, compromised, and broken. There was very little focus or interest involving normative interpersonal contact and gratifying relationships. Instead, most responses gravitated toward images and associations involving negative, damaged, crushed, bleeding components of the human anatomy. Many of these damaged anatomical regions were clearly references to the injuries and ongoing physical consequences resulting from being crushed in the accident.

Diagnoses

Axis I:

1. Major Depressive Disorder, Single Episode (296.22)
2. Post-traumatic Stress Disorder, chronic (309.81)
3. Pain Disorder Associated with a General Medical Condition

Axis II: No Diagnosis on Axis II (V71.09)

Axis III: Chronic pain and physical injuries and limitations including multiple pelvic fractures and significant nerve damage

Axis IV: Problems related to social environment, problems related to occupational functioning, problems related to primary support group (intimacy)

Axis V: GAF (current) = 50–60; moderate to serious impairment

Recommendations

Deferred to Calvin Colarusso, M.D., who is performing a comprehensive Independent Medical Evaluation of Mr. Rose.

TWO EXAMPLES OF NEUROPSYCHOLOGICAL REPORTS

The following two examples of psychological testing reports, written by the examining psychologist, are presented in their entirety. The reports were edited to protect confidentiality.

Confidential Neuropsychological Evaluation

This is an example of comprehensive neuropsychological evaluation, conducted by an experienced forensic neuropsychologist, intended to primarily assess mental functioning after an assault to brain substance, in this case following a head injury. It utilizes different tests than those chosen for administration when psychological issues are the primary concern.

Identifying Data

Name: Alice Williams
Date of Birth: A woman in her late 30s
Date of Evaluation: Two testing sessions occurred, 14 months after the accident that lead to the evaluation.
Referred by: Name of the attorney
Examined by: The psychologist's name

Ms. Williams is a married, Caucasian female in her late 40s. She is a college graduate. She is currently unemployed and lives with her husband. She is a world-class athlete. English is the only language she speaks, and she is right-hand dominant. She explains that although she was born left-handed, she was made to use her right hand when she began school. She now does everything with her right hand, although she will occasionally eat with her left.

Reason for Referral

Ms. Williams suffered a head injury in a bicycling accident. She is referred for neuropsychological evaluation in order to determine her current level of cognitive and personality functioning. In this instance, the undersigned is working with [name] in an adjunctive role. That is, [name] is the principle evaluator in this case. I will be performing a neuropsychological evaluation in order to assist him in reaching diagnostic and causative conclusions, but I will not be forming such opinions myself.

Informed Consent

The purpose of this evaluation and limitations of confidentiality were explained to Ms. Williams. In particular, Ms. Williams was told that the examiner would perform a neuropsychological evaluation in order to assess her current level of cognitive and personality functioning. She was told that the results of this evaluation would be provided to both Dr. [name] and to her attorney, who may in turn share these results with opposing counsel. The plaintiff was also told that if she reported incidents of child or elder abuse or if she indicated she was a danger to herself or others, that these concerns would be reported as mandated by law. Ms. Williams indicated that she understood the purpose of the evaluation and the limitations of confidentiality, agreed to participate in the evaluation, and read and signed a statement of informed consent to that effect.

Means of Assessment

Clinical interview with Ms. Williams and her husband
Adverse Childhood Experiences Scale (ACES)
Neurobehavioral Symptom Inventory (NSI)
Ruff Neurobehavioral Inventory (RNBI)
Mental Status Examination
Validity Indicator Profile (VIP)
Test of Premorbid Functioning (TOPF)
Wechsler Adult Intelligence Scale, 4th Edition (WAIS-IV)
Meyers Neuropsychological Battery (MNB)
Forced Choice Test
Finger Identification Test
Token Test
Animal Naming
One Minute Estimation
Controlled Oral Word Association Test
Sentence Repetition
Boston Naming Test
Judgment of Line Orientation

Rey Auditory Verbal Learning Test
Rey Complex Figure Test and Recognition Trial
Dichotic Listening
Trail Making Test
Category Test
Finger Tapping Test
Visual Confrontation Subtest from the Dean-Woodcock Sensory-Motor Battery
Grooved Pegboard (GP)
Grip Strength Test (GST)
Integrated Visual & Auditory Continuous Performance Test, Advanced Edition (IVA-AE)
Barkley Deficits in Executive Functioning Scale (BDEFS)
Minnesota Multiphasic Personality Inventory, 2nd Edition, Restructured Form (MMPI-2RF)
Beck Depression Inventory, 2nd Edition (BDI-II)
Barkley Functional Impairment Scale (BFIS)

The Neuropsychological Impairment Scale (NIS) and the Barkley Deficits in Executive Functioning Scale (BDEFS) were also completed by Mr. Williams.

I also reviewed medical records regarding Ms. Williams that were provided by Ms. Williams.

Presenting Problem

According to hospital records, Ms. Williams was brought to the ER following a fall from her bicycle. As she was cycling a dog ran in front of her. She swerved to miss the dog and crashed. The odometer on her bicycle indicated she was going 22 miles per hour when she crashed. She was reported to have had a loss of consciousness (LOC) at the time of injury of 5 minutes, but was awake with repetitive speech when paramedics arrived. At the time she was brought to the hospital her Glasgow Coma Scale (GCS) was 15/15. Reported injuries included a laceration over her left eye and dental trauma. A toxicology screening was negative. A CT scan of the head revealed no acute intracranial findings and no evidence of a fracture. Soft tissue swelling was noted in the supra/preorbital region along with chronic sinusitis involving the right sphenoid sinus. A CT scan of the spine was also essentially unremarkable. Her jaw was broken and she chipped a tooth. She was discharged from the hospital after an overnight stay with a prescription for Vicodin, 500 mg as needed for severe pain.

Two days later Ms. Williams was seen at her HMO. At that time Ms. Williams described having amnesia for the accident, stating that she recalls seeing the dog and then remembers being in an ambulance. She had her jaw wired by her dentist earlier this same day. Ms. Williams told her physician that she felt well. She was diagnosed with a closed head injury and continued to be treated for her facial injuries.

Four days later the plaintiff reported having symptoms of headache, dizziness, and memory loss. Left arm weakness was also noted. She was found to have intact cranial nerves during an evaluation at her HMO. It was recommended that she return to sports one week after her symptoms resolved.

A follow-up head CT scan was performed. No significant brain abnormality or intracranial hemorrhage was found during this procedure.

Nine days after the accident Ms. Williams had an orthopedic consult because of pain complaints in her left biceps, right wrist and thumb, and left inner thigh. She was diagnosed with a right ulnar collateral ligament sprain and a contusion of her left bicep. She was counseled to refrain from sports for three to four weeks. An MRI of her left upper arm was notable for mid-left humeral disphyseal sclerotic lesion that appeared to be benign, but which was opined to be the source of pain.

Nine months after the accident Ms. Williams underwent a neuropsychological evaluation at her HMO. The test results were considered valid. At that point she complained of symptoms that included headaches, dizziness, occasional fatigue, difficulty focusing attention and concentrating, memory problems, difficulty following conversations in groups, difficulty remembering people's names, and occasional word-finding problems. She noted that when sitting at the computer for a length of time, all these symptoms seem to worsen. She also reported that when exercising, she would give up or slow down more readily than in the past. Her premorbid level of intelligence was estimated to be in the average to high average range.

She also scored in the average range on a measure of confrontation naming (missing three items on the Boston Naming Test). Both verbal and category fluency were also average. Overall performance on measures of both verbal and visual memory was also average, as was her performance on measures of executive functioning. No significant emotional or psychiatric difficulties were noted on personality testing with the exception of mild depression. The psychologist concluded that Ms. Williams might have experienced some declines in functioning form previous levels in the verbal domain, adding that she experienced rapid forgetting between the encoding and retrieval stages of her verbal memory performance. The psychologist concluded: "While we cannot say definitely that this plaintiff had experienced declines from previous levels, there are indications that would support such a hypothesis."

During the current interview, Ms. Williams states that she was training for a race by bicycling early in the morning with her husband. She says the driver of a small truck opened the door and a large dog jumped from the vehicle into her path. She says that she struck the dog, went over the handlebars, and landed on her head. Her helmet remained intact as she fell on the right side of her face. Mr. Williams notes that his wife's face was protected to some degree by her sunglasses. Her husband indicates that it took paramedics approximately twenty minutes to arrive. She was taken to [name of hospital].

Asked about her ongoing problems, Ms. Williams indicates she has difficulty reading ("I have to repeat paragraphs. I have a lack of focus. I can't read for as long or as fast for comprehension. I used to be a voracious reader."). She also reports having difficulties paying attention ("I'll miss my exit on the freeway."). She complains of having "floaters" in both eyes since the accident, and complains of having blurred vision when fatigued or if her heart rate is high from exercise. She also complains of short-term memory loss ("I have trouble learning new things. I forget what I'm doing. I misplace things."). Mr. Williams notes that his wife seemed to improve slowly from her injury until a few months ago when she "plateaued. She's not back to where she was."

Ms. Williams is administered the NSI, a self-report instrument that allows her to report the presence and severity of postconcussion. Her raw score of 29 places her at the 99th percentile, suggesting the presence of post concussive symptoms. She reports impairment with regard to her cognitive symptoms only not in regard to affective or somatosensory problems. She reports that she experiences the following symptoms as severe or very severe.

Sensitivity to light
Poor concentration, can't pay attention; easily distracted
Forgetfulness, can't remember things
Slowed thinking, difficulty getting organized, can't finish things
Fatigue, loss of energy, getting tired easily.

The plaintiff reports that bright lights bother her, particularly when irritated or tired, causing her to have headaches. She also reports that with regards to sleeping, "I don't sleep as well or as long." Loud noises also used to cause headaches after her injury; now she says it must be a prolonged exposure to a loud noise to have this effect. A tingling sensation in the fingertips or both hands, but mostly on the right "comes and goes." She says she is not as sharp as she used to be mentally, that it is harder to stay on task, and harder to do more than one thing at a time. She sometimes cannot remember how she got somewhere and continues to occasionally miss her freeway exit because of a lack of focus. She adds that she is not as strong as she used to be: "I'm sometimes weak and achy if I haven't slept." Psychologically, she complains of greater impatience and a lack of energy and motivation: "I don't do as much training as I did before." She notes that her race times have dropped since her injury as she takes an additional hour to complete a half-ironman event.

Ms. Williams is also administered the RNBI. The RNBI is designed to measure the current status of individuals whose lives have been altered by a catastrophic event such as a major illness or injury. It is a self-report measure of the cognitive, emotional, physical, and psychosocial functioning of individuals both before and after the illness or injury. Ms. Williams responds to this instrument in a consistent manner, indicating that she had no difficulty reading and understand the test items. She does not endorse a significant number of items that are rarely endorsed by members of the standardization sample for this instrument. There is also no evidence that she exaggerates or minimizes her self-reported symptoms either prior to or after her injury indicating that Ms. Williams responded to the RNBBI in an open and self-disclosing manner.

Ms. Williams denies having any significant problems in any areas of functioning prior to her injury. She reports having a significant discrepancy between her pre- and post-morbid functioning in the cognitive domain. She denies having any significant difference in her emotional or physical functioning or in her overall quality of life when considering her life before and after the injury. Her most significant cognitive complaints lie in the areas of attention and concentration, learning and memory, and speech and language functioning, in which she demonstrates a significant elevation postinjury. She reports a moderate elevation in symptoms of executive dysfunction. All of these differences are statistically significant with regards to her pre- and post-morbid functioning. She also reports a statistically significant difference in symptoms related to posttraumatic stress from before the accident, although her current reported symptoms remain in the average range. She endorses none of the critical items on this measure.

Neuropsychological Impairment Scale—Mr. Williams

The NIS is an observer-report measure of neuropsychological symptoms for adults. It includes four validity scales, global measures of impairment, and subscales regarding specific aspects of cognitive functioning. Mr. Williams responds to this measure regarding his wife's current neuropsychological functioning in a consistent manner. He may have also responded in a slightly defensive manner suggesting a protective attitude toward his wife. His responses do not suggest that emotional factors contribute to her neuropsychological difficulties, and indeed he observes her as demonstrating a restricted range of emotional expression. The obtained global measure of impairment (GMI) based on his responses to the NSI is significantly higher than would be expected from Ms. William's predicted GMI, which is based upon her actual performance on currently administered neuropsychological tests (Digit Span and Digit Symbol). This pattern of test scores suggests that Mr. Williams may overestimate the severity of his wife's cognitive impairment.

Mr. Williams reports that his wife has significant cognitive impairment. Problems with reasoning, problem-solving, psychomotor slowness, cognitive rigidity, and difficulty coping with fast-paced environments are to be expected given his ratings. In addition, difficulties with concentration and vision are reported.

I also reviewed medical records regarding Ms. Williams that were provided by her lawyer.

Nine months after the accident Ms. Williams underwent a neuropsychological evaluation. The test results were considered valid. At that point, she complained of symptoms that included headaches, dizziness, occasional fatigue, difficulty focusing attention and concentrating, memory problems, difficulty following conversations in groups, difficulty remembering people's names, and occasional word-finding problems. She noted that when sitting at the computer for a length of time, all these symptoms seem to worsen. She also reported that when exercising, she would give up or slow down more readily than in the past. Her premorbid level of intelligence was estimated to be in the average to high average range. During that evaluation, she achieved the following test scores on the WAIS-IV:

WAIS-IV	*Standard Scores*	*Percentile*	*Level of Performance*
Full Scale IQ	126	96%	Superior
Verbal Comprehension	107	68%	Average
Perceptual Reasoning	119	90%	Superior
Working Memory	131	98%	Superior
Processing Speed	132	98%	Superior

She also scored in the average range on a measure of confrontation naming (missing three items on the Boston Naming Test). Both verbal and category fluency were also average. Overall performance on measures of both verbal and visual memory was also average, as was her performance on measures of executive functioning. No significant emotional or psychiatric difficulties were noted on personality testing with the exception of mild depression. The psychologist concludes that Ms. Williams may have experienced some declines in functioning from previous levels in the verbal domain, adding that she experienced rapid forgetting between the encoding and retrieval stages of her verbal memory performance. The psychologist wrote: "while we cannot say definitely that this plaintiff has experienced declines from previous levels, there are indications that would support such a hypothesis."

During the current interview, Ms. Williams stated that as she was bicycling she saw the driver of a small truck open his door and a large dog jumped from the vehicle into her path. She says that she struck the dog, went over the handlebars, and landed on her head. Her helmet remained intact as she fell on the left side of her face. Mr. Williams notes that his wife's face was protected to some degree by her sunglasses. Her husband indicates that it took paramedics approximately 20 minutes to arrive.

Asked about her ongoing problems, Ms. Williams indicates she has difficulty reading ("I have to repeat paragraphs. I have a lack of focus. I can't read for as long or as fast for comprehension. I used to be a voracious reader."). She also reports having difficulties paying attention ("I'll miss my exit on the freeway."). She complains of having "floaters" in both eyes since the accident, and complains of having blurred vision when fatigued or if her heart rate is high from exercise. She also complains of short-term memory loss ("I have trouble learning new things. I forget what I'm doing. I misplace things."). Mr. Williams notes that his wife seemed to improve slowly from her injury and then she "plateaued. She's not back to where she was."

Ms. Williams is administered the NIS, a self-report instrument that allows her to report the presence and severity of post-concussive symptoms. Her raw score of 29 places her at the 99th percentile, suggesting the presence of post-concussive symptoms. She reports impairment with regards to her cognitive symptoms only, not in regard to affective or somatosensory problems. She reports that she experiences the following symptoms as severe or very severe:

Sensitivity to light
Poor concentration; can't pay attention; easily distracted
Forgetfulness, can't remember things
Slowed thinking, difficulty getting organized, can't finish things
Fatigue, loss of energy, getting tired easily

The plaintiff reports that bright lights bother her, particularly when irritated or tired, causing her to have headaches. She also reports that with regard to sleeping, "I don't sleep as well or as long." Loud noises also used to cause headaches after her injury; now she says it must be a prolonged exposure to a loud noise to have this effect. A tingling sensation in the fingertips of both hands, but mostly on the right, "comes and goes." She says she is not as sharp as she used to be mentally, that it is harder to stay on task, and harder to do more than one thing at a time. She sometimes cannot remember how she got somewhere, and continues to occasionally miss her freeway exit because of a lack of focus. She adds that she is not as strong as she used to be: "I'm sometimes weak and achy if I haven't slept." Psychologically, she complains of greater impatience and a lack of energy and motivation: "I don't do as much training as I did before." She notes that her race times have dropped since her injury as she takes an additional hour to complete a half-Ironman event.

Ms. Williams was also administered the RNBI. The RNBI is designed to measure the current status of individuals whose lives have been altered by a catastrophic event such as a major illness or injury. It is a self-report measure of the cognitive, emotional, physical, and psychosocial functioning of individuals both before and after the illness or injury. Ms. Williams responds to this instrument in a consistent manner, indicating that she had no difficulty reading and understanding the test items. She does not endorse a significant number of items that are rarely endorsed by members of the standardization sample for this instrument. There is also no evidence that she exaggerates or minimizes her self-reported symptoms either prior to or after her injury, indicating that Ms. Williams responded to the RNBI in an open and self-disclosing manner. She scores in the following manner on the RNBI Composite Scales:

WNL = Within Normal Limits

RNBI Composite	*Premorbid*		*Postmorbid*	
Domain	*T-score*	*Range*	*T-score*	*Range*
Cognitive	42	WNL	87	Significantly Elevated
Emotional	40	WNL	47	WNL
Physical	40	WNL	43	WNL
Quality of Life	40	WNL	50	WNL

Ms. Williams denies having any significant problems in any area of functioning prior to her injury. She reports having a significant discrepancy between her pre- and post-morbid functioning in the cognitive domain. She denies having any significant difference in her emotional or physical functioning or in her overall quality of life when considering her life before and after the injury. Her most significant cognitive complaints lie in the areas of attention and concentration, learning and memory, and speech and language functioning, in which she demonstrates a significant elevation postinjury. She reports a moderate elevation in symptoms of executive dysfunction. All of these differences are statistically significant with regard to her pre- and post-morbid functioning. She also reports a statistically significant difference in symptoms related to posttraumatic stress from before the accident, although her current reported symptoms remain in the average range. She endorses none of the critical items on this measure.

At the present time, Ms. Williams reports that she gets up at 4:00 a.m. and goes to bed at 8:00 p.m. She exercises daily. She shops, fixes meals, and does laundry for her and her husband and enjoys reading, scrapbooking, and jewelry making. She denies having any problems with activities of daily living. She uses a computer and drives without any difficulties or restrictions.

Neuropsychological Impairment Scale—Mr. Williams

The NIS is an observer-report measure of neuropsychological symptoms for adults. It includes four validity scales, global measures of impairment, and subscales regarding specific aspects of cognitive functioning. Mr. Williams responds to this measure regarding his wife's current neuropsychological functioning in a consistent manner. He may have also responded in a slightly defensive manner suggesting a protective attitude toward his wife. His responses do not suggest that emotional factors contribute to her neuropsychological difficulties, and indeed he observes her as demonstrating a restricted range of emotional expression. The obtained global measure of impairment (GMI) based on his responses to the NIS is significantly higher than would be expected from Ms. William's predicted GMI, which is based upon her actual performance on currently administered neuropsychological tests (Digit Span and Digit Symbol).

Mr. Williams reports that his wife has significant cognitive impairment. Problems with reasoning, problem-solving, psychomotor slowness, cognitive rigidity, and difficulty coping with fast-paced environments are to be expected given his ratings. In addition, difficulties with concentration and vision are reported.

Background Information

Ms. Williams was born and raised in an intact family. Her parents were well-educated professionals. She has two siblings who are functional well. She denies any history of significant childhood trauma or loss.

Adverse Childhood Experiences Scale: Score of "0" indicating an absence of childhood abuse, neglect, molest, or exposure to family violence or instability.

The plaintiff is unaware of any complications suffered by her mother during her pregnancy, labor, and delivery. She denies any history of developmental, social, emotional, or behavioral difficulties while growing up.

Ms. Williams denies any history of learning disabilities or special education. Indeed, she was in advanced placement classes in high school. She reports that she graduated from college with a GPA close to 4.0. She states that she excelled at math and science.

The plaintiff has been married for 24 years. She has two children who are doing well. She is a homemaker who has a happy marriage and enjoys raising her children.

Medical History

Ms. Williams reports being in good physical health. She denies any other history of significant illness, surgery, or injury. There are no known allergies. She denies any history of substance abuse and does not smoke cigarettes. The family medical history is unremarkable. At the time of assessment, she is prescribed no medications for any physical concerns.

Psychiatry

Ms. Williams denies any history of psychiatric symptoms or treatment. She denies any history of trauma exposure as an adult. The family psychiatric history is unremarkable. She denies having any current psychiatric symptoms. Current stresses include only her cognitive difficulties. At the time of assessment, the plaintiff is not taking any prescribed psychotropic medications.

Mental Status Examination

Ms. Williams arrives on time for her appointments. She was driven by her husband to her initial appointment, but drove herself to the second one. She is a well-groomed woman who is casually and appropriately dressed. She describes herself as 5'4" and as weighing 135 pounds. She reports having a scar on her eyebrow from the bicycle accident and a surgical scar on her abdomen. She denies having any significant wounds, tattoos, or piercings, and none are visible. Posture and gait are unremarkable. Although initially reserved, she is cooperative and becomes friendlier with the examiner over time, making good eye contact. Behavior and level of activity are appropriate. There is no evidence of any tics or tremor.

During the administration of the various testing procedures, Ms. Williams demonstrates a high tolerance for frustration and good persistence on tasks she finds difficult. She attempts to solve problems in a systematic and reflective manner, working at a rapid pace. She demonstrates occasional impulsivity in the assessment situation, particularly after she became frustrated by a previous task. Twice she becomes tearful during the evaluation session: on the vocabulary subtest from the WAIS-IV, she says, "I know these words but I can't explain them. It's so frustrating!" Following the immediate recall trial of the RCFT, she also starts crying and says, "I should remember more!" She seems to make excellent effort to do her best. She demonstrates no difficulties focusing, shifting, or sustaining attention in the assessment situation.

The plaintiff's speech is fluent and of normal rate and volume. She speaks in a monotone voice. There is no evidence of any paraphasias or errors in articulation. She initiates conversation spontaneously and appropriately, and has no evident difficulty understanding questions and directions. Associations are logical and goal-directed.

When asked to describe her usual mood during the past month, Ms. Williams replies, "I don't know." While she denies having recent symptoms of depression, she admits having some anxiety "about what's going on with me." She appears depressed with flat or constricted affect during interview.

Thought content is negative for hallucinations, delusions, paranoid ideation, obsessions, compulsions, phobias, suicidal, or homicidal ideation. She denies any history of suicidal thoughts or behaviors. She also denies any history of intentional self-mutilation.

Level of Effort and Validity of Performance

During interview, Ms. Williams reports her symptoms and history in a manner that is consistent with that contained in her medical records. There is no indication that she attempts to minimize or exaggerate her reported symptoms during interview. On the measures of effort she is given with regards to the neuropsychological tests, as well as those imbedded in the tests themselves, she performs within expected limits on all of them, suggesting that she puts forth adequate effort on these tasks. She responds to the MMPI-2RF in a consistent and valid manner. What follows is considered as an accurate description of her current level of cognitive and emotional functioning.

Test Results

The following test results reflect comparisons using norms based upon a neurologically intact control group. The scores are corrected for age, gender, ethnicity, level of education, and handedness, and a specific level of performance is given. Level of performance is described using a range from Superior to Severely Impaired, as follows:

Clinical Interpretation	*T-Scores*	*Percentiles*
Superior	61 or above	85–100
High Average	58–60	76–84
Average	43–57	25–75
Low Average	40–42	16–24
Mild Impairment	35–39	7–15
Mild to Moderate Impairment	30–34	2–6
Moderate Impairment	25–29	1 or lower
Moderate to Severe Impairment	20–24	1 or lower
Severe Impairment	0–19	1 or lower

Test performance will be reported using either T-scores that have a mean of 50 and a standard deviation of 10 or standard scores that have a mean of 100 and a standard deviation of 15. Consistent with recommendations by Heaton, Miller, Taylor, and Grant (2004), performance is considered to be impaired or deficient when scores fall at least one standard deviation below the mean. Norms for the WAIS-IV and TOPF are provided by the scoring program for these instruments published by Pearson. All tests included in the MNB rely on the demographically corrected normative data contained in the scoring program for this instrument. All other tests are scored and interpreted based on information contained in their respective test manuals.

Ms. William's overall neuropsychological test results are summarized as follows:

Neuropsychological Domain	*T-Scores*	*Percentile*	*Level of Performance*
Premorbid Functioning	53	63%	Average
Overall Test Battery Mean	52	58%	Average
Full Scale IQ Score	65 (IQ = 123)	94%	Superior
Attention/Working Memory	52	58%	Average
Processing Speed	60	84%	Superior
Verbal Reasoning	53	62%	Average
Visual Reasoning	56	73%	Average to High Average
Verbal Memory	55	69%	Average
Visual Memory	47	38%	Average
Sensory-Motor, Dominant hand	51	54%	Average
Sensory-Motor, Non-dominant hand	52	58%	Average

Several procedures for assessing the plaintiff's premorbid level of intellectual functioning are performed during this evaluation. Relying solely on demographic factors, Ms. Williams's premorbid intellectual functioning is estimated to be in the high average range (79th percentile). The TOPF provides an estimate of an individual's premorbid intellectual functioning using a combination of demographic characteristics of the individual along with their performance on a measure of their ability to read irregularly spelled words. The plaintiff's predicted IQ score based on the TOPF lies in the average range (58th percentile). The MNB also allows for the determination of the lowest expected estimated Overall Test Battery Mean (OTBM), which is the average of the sixteen tests that make up the test battery, based on demographic factors. Ms. Williams's estimated OTBM as determined by this method lies in the average range at the 58th percentile. In other words, it would be expected, based on these estimates of premorbid functioning, that the plaintiff should demonstrate at least average to high average intelligence and average neuropsychological functioning in most areas. This is consistent with her premorbid educational history.

In terms of global measures of cognitive functioning, the OTBM is considered a valid measure of Ms. Williams's overall neurological functioning because there is no significant variation in her test scores. She achieves an OTBM in the average range (58th percentile). There is no significant difference between her predicted and actual OTBM scores, suggesting no loss of ability in her overall neuropsychological functioning. There is little evidence of lateralization in her test scores, with tests sensitive to functioning in the left hemisphere lying in the average to high average range (73rd percentile) and tests sensitive to functioning in the right hemisphere lying in the average range (61st percentile). There is also no significant discrepancy between her average dominant right hand sensory-motor functioning (38th percentile) and her average non-dominant, left hand sensory-motor functioning (31st percentile).

The plaintiff is given an individually administered test of intellectual functioning the WAIS-IV. Using standard norms, she scores in the superior range of intellectual ability (94th percentile). There is a 95 percent chance that her true IQ score as measured by this instrument lies between 118 and 127. The 15-point difference between Ms. Williams's predicted IQ of 103 and her actual Full Scale IQ scores is significant and unusual as only approximately 2 percent of the standardization sample demonstrates a discrepancy of this magnitude. She scores significantly above expectation on her full scale IQ, Perceptual Reasoning, Working Memory, and Processing Speed Indices, but demonstrates no loss of ability on the Verbal Comprehension Index. Her performance on the various WAIS-IV subtests ranges from average to superior.

Ms. Williams is administered measures of sensory-perceptual functioning. On a measure of finger recognition (finger agnosia), she scores in the average range with her dominant, right hand (69th percentile) as well as with her non-dominant, left hand (66th percentile). She commits one error with her right hand. On a measure of double simultaneous visual stimulation, the plaintiff scores within normal limits in her left visual field, but demonstrates mild impairment with her right visual field. In particular, she demonstrates a partial loss of vision in her lower right visual field. She also demonstrates evidence of decreased range in her right peripheral vision.

Simple attention is related to the ability to focus and sustain concentration. Ms. Williams demonstrates the following scores on measures of functioning in this area:

Simple Attention	*T-Scores*	*Percentile*	*Level of Performance*
Span of Attention			
Digits Forward	57	75%	Average to high average
Sentence Repetition	67	96%	Superior
AVLT Trial 1	51	54%	Average
Focused Attention/ Processing Speed			
WAIS-IV Symbol Search	60	84%	High average to superior
WAIS-IV Coding	67	96%	Superior
TMT-A	53	62%	Average
Sustained Attention	56	73%	Average to high average

Attention span is a limited capacity system, as most adults Ms. Williams's age can retain seven to eight "chunks" of information in awareness at one time. Ms. Williams is able to correctly recall seven numbers in the correct sequence after a single presentation, placing her in the average range on a measure of *span* of auditory attention. This is consistent with her superior performance on a measure of her ability to repeat sentences of increasing length. On a more complex measure of this ability that involves the immediate recall of a list of unrelated words, she scores in the average range. *Focused* (or selective) attention refers to the ability to maintain a cognitive set in the presence of background noise or distraction. Processing speed, or mental quickness (the ability to fluently and automatically perform cognitive tasks), is often a factor in one's ability to focus attention. Ms. Williams scores in the high average to superior range on these tasks overall. She scores in the high average to superior range on a measure of speed of visual processing and in the superior range on a measure of rate-of-test taking that also involves working memory and motor speed. She scores in the average range on another measure of focused attention that involves connecting randomly arranged numbers in order as quickly as she can. She scores in the average to high average range in her ability to *sustain attention* across tasks on the MNB.

On a measure of auditory processing, Ms. Williams's scores in the average range on a measure of dichotic listening with her dominant, right ear (66th percentile), and with her non-dominant, left ear (69th percentile).

The plaintiff is administered several measures of language functioning. She achieves the following scores:

Language Tests	*T-Scores*	*Percentile*	*Level of Performance*
MNB Verbal Reasoning	53	62%	Average
Token Test	57	76%	High Average
WISC-IV Vocabulary	53	67%	Average
Boston Naming Test	53	62%	Average
Sentence Repetition	67	96%	Superior
Animal Naming	60	84%	Superior

On measures of general language functioning, Ms. Williams scores in the average range on the MNB Verbal Reasoning Domain. She also scores in the average range on the Verbal Comprehension Index from the WAIS-IV (68th percentile). On a measure of *receptive language* ability involving the auditory comprehension of subtle linguistic cues, she scores in the average to above range as she commits no errors on this task. She is also administered several measures of *expressive language* ability. Her expressive vocabulary lies in the average range. On a measure of confrontation naming that involves mentally retrieving the names of a variety of objects presented visually as line drawings, Ms. Williams also scores in the average range. She scores in the superior range on a measure of repetition in which she is asked to repeat sentences of increasing length. Category fluency lies in the high average to superior range.

On measures of visual-spatial processing, Ms. Williams achieves the following scores:

Visual-Spatial Processing Tests	*T-Scores*	*Percentile*	*Level of Performance*
MNB Visual Reasoning	56	73%	Average
JOL	49	46%	Average
WISC-IV Block Design	60	84%	Superior

Visual-Spatial Processing Tests	*T-Scores*	*Percentile*	*Level of Performance*
RCFT Copy Trial	44	27%	Average

She scores in the average to high average range on the MNB Visual Reasoning Domain. She scores in the superior range on the Perceptual Reasoning Index from the WAIS-IV (96th percentile). She scores in the average range on a rather pure measure of spatial perception while scoring in the superior range on a more complex measure of spatial relations. On a measure of visual-motor integration where she is asked to copy a complex, abstract figure, she scores in the average range, but completes this task rather quickly (84th percentile).

Ms. Williams achieves the following scores on measures of memory functioning:

Memory Functioning Tests	*T-Scores*	*Percentile*	*Level of Performance*
Verbal Memory Composite	55	69%	Average
Immediate Memory	59	82%	High Average
Delayed Memory	55	69%	Average
Recognition	50	50%	Average
Visual Memory Composite	47	38%	Average
Immediate Memory	44	27%	Average
Delayed Memory	46	34%	Average
Recognition	51	54%	Average

Short-term memory is the ability to hold information in immediate awareness and then use it within a few seconds. On a measure of immediate verbal memory in which she is asked to recall a list of unrelated words she has learned over several trials following a distracter task, she scores in the high average range. On a measure of visual immediate memory in which she is asked to recall a complex, abstract figure she had copied three minutes earlier, she scores in the average range.

In contrast to short-term memory, long-term memory is the ability to store and fluently retrieve new or previously acquired information. Ms. Williams scores in the average range in her overall *verbal memory* ability. When asked to recall a list of unrelated words she had previously learned following a half-hour delay, she scores in the average range as she is able to recall all but three out of fifteen words. Her performance remains in the average range when presented with this information in a recognition format, as she is able to accurately identify all but one of the words on the list. Retrieval fluency lays in the low average to average range (27th percentile). She demonstrates average functioning in her ability to learn and retain information in the verbal modality (58th percentile).

The plaintiff scores in the average range in her overall *visual memory* ability. However, her score on this domain is significantly lower than would be expected given her scores in all other areas of neuropsychological functioning, indicating that this is an area of personal weakness for her. When asked to recall a complex, abstract drawing she had copied following a half-hour delay, she scores in the average range. Her performance remains in the average range when presented with this information in a recognition format.

Complex attention and executive functions consist of those capacities that enable a person to engage successfully in independent, purposive, self-serving behaviors. These include the capacity for self-control and self-direction, and the ability to initiate, inhibit, plan, and organize goal-directed activities. Ms. Williams scores in the low average range overall on measures of executive functioning from the MNB as follows:

Executive Functioning Tests	*T-Scores*	*Percentile*	*Level of Performance*
Executive Functioning Composite	55	69%	Average
Divided Attention/Mental Flexibility			
WAIS-IV Digits Backward	63	91%	Superior
WAIS-IV Arithmetic	60	84%	Superior
TMT-B	63	90%	Superior
Dichotic Listening	60	84%	Superior
Verbal Reasoning			
WAIS-IV Similarities	53	62%	Average
WAIS-IV Information	57	76%	High Average
Visual Reasoning			
Visual Puzzles	67	96%	Superior
Matrix Reasoning	70	98%	Superior
Category Test	51	54%	Average
Verbal Fluency (COWAT)	48	42%	Average

Divided attention refers to the ability to respond to more than one task or event at the same time. It involves both working memory (the ability to mentally manipulate information) and mental tracking. On a relatively easy measure of working memory that requires her merely to reverse the order of numbers presented auditorially, she is able to recall six digits (most adults her age can recall five or six). She scores in the superior range when asked to mentally perform mathematical calculations. She also scores in the superior range on a visual measure of this ability that involves connecting numbers and letters in alternating order. On a measure of *mental flexibility*, she scores in the superior range on a measure of dichotic listening in which she is asked to attend to two words being spoken simultaneously, one in each ear.

On measures of problem solving and reasoning, Ms. Williams scores in the average range on a measure of verbal, abstract thinking. She also scores in the average range on a measure of her acquired fund of information. She scores in the superior range on measures of non-verbal, fluid reasoning. She scores in the average range on a measure of verbal fluency. Finally, on a measure of complex non-verbal problem solving, Ms. Williams also scores in the average range.

The IVA-AE is a measure of sustained-attention and response control in both the auditory and visual modalities. The task involves clicking the mouse when she sees a "3" on the computer screen or hears a "5" through her headphones, but to refrain from responding when the stimulus is a visual "5" or an auditory "3." Ms. Williams responds to this instrument in a valid manner, indicating that she put forth adequate effort and did not respond randomly. She achieves the following scores on this instrument:

IVA-AE Global Scale Scores	*T-Scores*	*Percentile*	*Level of Performance*
Full Scale Response Control	65	94%	Superior
Auditory Response Control	63	91%	Superior
Visual Response Control	65	94%	Superior
Full Scale Attention Scale	58	81%	High Average
Auditory Attention	56	73%	Average
Visual Attention	60	84%	Superior
Combined Sustained Attention	58	81%	High Average

Ms. Williams scores in the high average range overall on measures of sustained attention while demonstrating no significant discrepancy between her performances in the auditory or visual modalities. She scores in the superior range on measures of behavioral inhibition. There is again no discrepancy between her visual and auditory response control. This performance pattern suggests that the plaintiff has excellent ability to inhibit and shift her mental set. She is likely to have the ability to be accurate in detailed tasks and to remember and follow rules well. She is capable of sustaining attention without being unduly distracted. No problems with fine motor regulation are noted, and she is unlikely to exhibit problems with inappropriate off-task behavior in her home or work environment. Consistent with other test results, she has strong working memory skills. Of note, she demonstrates mild impairment in her visual processing speed during the test. Most notably, her simple reaction time in both the auditory and visual modalities is extremely impaired.

The BDEFS is a self-report measure of executive functions. This is conceptualized in the test manual as the ability to engage in self-regulation or self-control over time in order to achieve goals (self-interests). Because of the limited ability of neuropsychological tests to accurately assess this aspect of functioning, self-report measures are often considered as more accurate. Ms. Williams achieves the following scores on this measure:

BDEFS-LF Domain	*Percentile*	*Level of Performance*
Summary Score	51–75%	Average
Self-Management to Time	1–25%	Average
Self Organization/ Problem-Solving	97%	Moderate Impairment
Self-Restraint	1–25%	Average
Self-Motivation	87%	Borderline
Self-Regulation of Emotions	94%	Mild Impairment
ADHD-EF Index	51–75%	Unlikely

The plaintiff reports having no significant impairment in her overall executive functioning. However, she reports having moderate impairment in her ability to be organized and to problem-solve. In particular, she reports having difficulties saying what she wants to say, finding herself at a loss for words, putting her thoughts down in writing as well or quickly as before, being distracted, and having difficulty with focusing and sustaining attention and with reading comprehension. She reports having mild problems with emotional self-regulation, noting that she has difficulty calming herself down once she is upset. She also notes that she does not seem to have the willpower or determination that she used to have. Mr. Williams's rating of his wife on the same scale indicates that he also perceives her as having no impairment in her overall executive functioning. However, he perceives his wife as having problems of moderate severity in her ability to be organized and to problem-solve. He does not perceive her as having difficulties in any other area of executive functioning.

On measures of motor functioning, Ms. Williams demonstrates a right-handed preference in response to questioning. She achieves the following scores on measures of motor functioning:

Motor Tests	*T-Scores*	*Percentile*	*Level of Performance*
Dominant (right) hand			
Finger Tapping	48	42%	Average
Grooved Pegboard	55	69%	Average
Grip Strength	50	50%	Average
Non-dominant hand			
Finger Tapping	51	54%	Average
Grooved Pegboard	47	39%	Average
Grip Strength	55	70%	Average

On a measure of fine motor speed, she scores in the average range with both her dominant, right hand and her left. On a measure of manual dexterity, the plaintiff again scores in the average range with both her right and left hands. Finally, on a measure of grip strength, Ms. Williams scores in the average range with both hands.

Personality Functioning

The MMPI-2RF is a self-report measure of psychopathology and personality functioning in adults. Ms. Williams responds in a very consistent and valid manner to this instrument. There is no evidence of symptom exaggeration. If anything, she may have minimized her self-reported problems and symptoms because she presents herself as being very well adjusted.

Ms. Williams denies having any significant emotional, social, or behavioral difficulties. There is no evidence of any type of disordered thinking. She reports having below average levels of anxiety and worry. However, she also reports a diffuse pattern of cognitive difficulties including problems with concentration and memory, along with a low tolerance for frustration. She also reports having low energy. Consistent with her self-report during interview, she reports having a conflict-free past and present family environment. She has good behavioral self-control and is very unlikely to act out painful emotions in a self-defeating manner. Cognitively, she perceives herself as being decisive and effective. She perceives others as well intentioned and trustworthy and denies having any social anxiety.

The BDI-II is a self-report measure of the symptoms of depression in adults and older adolescents. Ms. Williams's raw score of 11 places her in the minimal range of depression at the 84th percentile. She denies having any significant *affective* or *physiological symptoms* of depression. The only significant *cognitive symptom* she reports is that of having difficulty concentrating. On a question related to suicidal ideation, Ms. Williams denies having any thoughts of self-harm.

Psychological Functioning

The BFIS is a self-report measure of an individual's perception of the degree of psychosocial impairment they are currently experiencing in relation to their medical, psychological, and/or neuropsychological condition(s). It can be used with adults ranging in age from 18 to 89 who reside in the United States, and allows for comparison of that individual's impairment relative to the representative standardization sample of 1,242 adults. Higher scores indicate higher levels of impairment. Ms. Williams achieves the following scores on the BFIS:

BFIS Domain	*Percentile*	*Level of Functioning*
Mean Impairment Score	51–75%	Average
Home—family	51–75%	Average
Home—chores	51–75%	Average
Work	96%	Moderate Impairment
Social—strangers	51–75%	Average
Social—friends	76–84%	Marginal
Community activities	1–50%	Average
Education	97%	Moderate Impairment
Marriage/cohabiting/dating	1–50%	Average
Money management	1–50%	Average
Driving	91%	Borderline
Sexual relations	1–50%	Average
Daily responsibilities	51–75%	Average
Self-care routines	1–50%	Average
Health maintenance	1–50%	Average

BFIS Domain	Percentile	Level of Functioning
Childrearing	N/A	

Overall, Ms. Williams reports that her head injury does not have a significant impact on her psychosocial functioning at the present time ever. With regards to her friends, she says, "I've been forgetting their birthdays. I've never done that before." When driving, she says, "I miss my exit, forget where I'm going or how to get there." Overall she says, "I forget to do things. I'm not as organized, not as focused. I have to write everything down. I can't train at the same level I used to."

Diagnostic Impressions Supported by Neuropsychological Assessment

Axis I: No diagnosis (V71.01)

Axis II: No diagnosis (V71.01)

Axis III: History of head injury

Axis IV: None

Axis V: Current GAF—48 (Symptoms of significant severity that interfere with psychosocial functioning)

Summary of Findings

Ms. Williams is a 49-year-old woman of likely above average premorbid intelligence. She suffered a mild head injury 15 months ago when she fell from her bicycle. She continues to experience cognitive symptoms related to this injury, but denies having any social or emotional symptoms. Her continued symptoms include those of sensitivity to light, poor concentration, forgetfulness, slowed thinking, difficulty getting organized, fatigue, and a loss of energy. These symptoms are suggestive of a post-concussive syndrome. However, neuropsychological test results, which are valid, suggest no overall loss of intellectual or cognitive ability. Indeed, she is functioning in the average range or better in all areas of neuropsychological functioning. She is likely to have little to no problem in her daily life outside of problems related to fatigue which may impair her ability to concentrate and therefore remember things. Her current test results are quite similar to those obtained in a previous evaluation.

The current assessment did reveal two areas of difficulty. First, the plaintiff appears to have a mild right visual field loss. This is not likely to cause her any practical difficulties as she is likely to compensate for this loss without realizing she is doing so. On the other hand, she may miss something that is at or comes toward her feet on the right hand side, causing her to collide with that object and/or fall.

Secondly, Ms. Williams demonstrates severe impairment in her reaction times in both the visual and auditory modalities. Again, this may have little practical impact on her functioning with one exception. When she is judging skating events, she notes that she is behind in scoring the individual skating moves, and it could well be that her slowed reaction time is causing this difficulty. She says that this was never a problem prior to her injury.

Overall, it is unclear why the plaintiff continues to experience symptoms of post concussive syndrome. It may be related to her high levels of exercise, but that is speculation.

Final diagnostic conclusions and other opinions and recommendations will be left to the referring psychiatrist who has the benefit of additional historical and clinical information.

I appreciate the opportunity to evaluate Ms. Williams. Please contact me should you have any further questions.

Name
Signature
License number

This is a second example of a neuropsychological evaluation, conducted by a different neuropsychologist, following a severe, self-inflicted anoxic experience.

Psychologist's Name
CLINICAL NEUROPSYCHOLOGY

Address
License Number
BOARD CERTIFIED IN CLINICAL NEUROPSYCHOLOGY
AMERICAN BOARD OF PROFESSIONAL PSYCHOLOGY, INC. (ABPP)
AMERICAN BOARD OF CLINICAL NEUROPSYCHOLOGY, INC. (ABCN)
FELLOW, NATIONAL ACADEMY OF NEUROPSYCHOLOGY
CERTIFIED REHABILITATION COUNSELOR (CRC)

Date

Attorney's name
Attorney's address

Clinical Neuropsychological Evaluation of an Adolescent Boy

Re: Patient's name	Date of Evaluation: Date	(6.5 hours)
SSN	Review of Records: Date	(1.5 hours)
Date of Birth: Age 16	Date of Dictation: Date	(5.5 hours)
Date of Injury: One year before testing		

Purpose of Evaluation:

[Patient's name] is a 16-year-old, right-handed, single, male, 10th-grade student. David has a history of being born methamphetamine positive, and subsequently being placed in foster care. His adoptive parents initially cared for him as an infant and subsequently adopted him.

David was reported to have performed well in school until 11 years of age. At 11 years of age, without any preparation or his parents' permission, he was informed that he was adopted. He subsequently seemed to develop depressive symptoms. Then, two years later when he was 13, an older male on a camping trip kissed him, precipitating confusion about his sexuality. Approximately 5 months after this the same older male and an 18-year-old male raped him. The same adult male raped him again the following year.

Last year David reviewed a diary he had stopped using approximately two months earlier, which precipitated painful feelings and confusion regarding the sexual assaults. In response, he attempted suicide by ingesting a large amount of drugs. He was discovered by his father, who performed CPR. David was subsequently hospitalized at a major medical center. He was in a therapeutic coma for three days and diagnosed with Major Depressive Disorder, Severe, PTSD, Rule out conduct disorder, Rule out borderline personality disorder. The physician at the time indicated there were no signs of an anoxic episode.

David was subsequently transferred to a psychiatric center where he remained until a few months before this neuropsychological evaluation. He was referred for the current evaluation to further explore cognitive, behavioral, and affective changes noted since the suicide attempt.

The current clinical neuropsychological evaluation is requested to better understand David's current neurobehavioral status, the nature of any neurobehavioral impairments he has approximately eight months post-injury, the most probable causes of his presenting neurobehavioral complaints, the practical implications for his presenting problems with respect to his current activities of daily living, and the most appropriate treatment/rehabilitation interventions.

David was examined with the following psychological and neuropsychological examination procedures.

Procedures Administered:

Wechsler Abbreviated Scale of Intelligence, 2nd Edition (WASI-II)
Wechsler Memory Scale, 3rd Edition (WMS-III)
Wisconsin Card-Sorting Test, Computer Version 4 for Windows, Research Edition (WCST-CV: 4 for Windows-Research Edition)
Boston Naming Test
Controlled Oral Word Association Test (COWAT)
Trail Making Test
Stroop Neuropsychological Screening Test
Consonant Trigrams Test
d2 Test of Attention
BDAE Complex Material Test
Reitan-Indiana Aphasia Screening Test
Peabody Individual Achievement Test–Revised (PIAT-R)
Lateral Dominance Examination
Personality Assessment Inventory–Adolescent (PAI-A)
Detailed Assessment of Posttraumatic Stress (DAPS)
Trauma Symptom Checklist for Children (TSCC)
Child Neuropsychological History
Pre- and Post-Testing Clinical Interview

Review of Records:

Records from psychiatric treatment center were submitted for review.

The recent Discharge Summary by [name], M.D., provided a history that David was exposed to in utero alcohol and methamphetamine, and was born methamphetamine positive. He was placed in foster care after birth, was placed in his current parents' home at the age of 4 months, and was adopted at the age of 24 months. His biological parents were allowed to visit until he was 24 months of age. He was reported to have performed well in school through 11 years of age. At that time he was told by a respite worker that he was adopted (without his parents' prior preparation or consent).

David was described as being quite devastated by the news that he was adopted, and he seemed to develop a depressed mood. Then he was sexually molested between the ages of 13 and 15 by two older males while camping with his troop. His depression subsequently worsened and he had engaged in cutting behaviors since the sixth grade. Symptoms of depression included poor concentration, initial and secondary insomnia, nightmares, excessive shame, and guilt. One perpetrator had been arrested, while the other had not.

David was reported to have attempted suicide approximately 26 days before admission, after reading his old diary and reliving the sexual assault. He claimed that the suicide attempt was an impulsive act, although he had had chronic suicidal thoughts since at least the sixth grade.

Laboratory and x-ray findings were identified. Hospital course was remarkable for improved depressive symptoms with medication. Results of the Kaufman Test for Educational Achievement included the following:

Math	> 12.8 grade level
Reading	> 12.8 grade level
Spelling	> 12.8 grade level
Reading Comprehension	> 12.9 grade level
Math Comprehension	> 12.8 grade level

David was reported to have struggled with poor boundaries upon admission. He also struggled with anxiety and depression, as well as self-harm, which gradually improved. He had flashbacks and nightmares, which also resolved. However, he had problems throughout his hospital course with lying and manipulation, as well as purposeful targeting of peers. He had significant difficulty in his relationship with others and refused to take responsibility for his actions. He was frequently entitled and engaged in defiance as well as disregard of rules and authority in order to increase his own excitement level, as he was frequently bored. He also seemed to lack remorse for the actions that were hurtful to other peers.

In therapy, David addressed his negative choices. His family was described as being very motivated and engaged in treatment. David was eventually able to talk about his emotional distress. Safety concerns in the home also were addressed, and appropriate boundaries between David and his siblings were discussed.

At discharge, mood was euthymic and stable. Affect was relaxed. Thought processes were linear. However, insight and judgment were poor.

The Behavioral Health Discharge Summary provided a history that David was admitted on after being recently discharged from a major medical center following treatment after a near fatal suicide attempt.

History of the present illness indicated that David was developing normally and enjoying a happy normal adolescence when he went on the camping trip where an older male kissed him. This precipitated confusion regarding his sexuality and, approximately 5 months later, the same individual and an older male who was 18 years of age raped David.

David was reported to be somewhat vague about the details of the rape, but indicated they did "pretty much everything." He described experiencing a dissociative state at the time, and not telling anyone about the incident. Then, months later, the same older male raped him again two nights in a row. Again, David did not tell anyone. However, his father found out what had happened when he discovered an e-mail from the perpetrator to David describing the events. The perpetrator was subsequently arrested.

David was reported to have been keeping a diary, but had stopped using it approximately two months prior to the suicide attempt. He indicated that, just before the suicide attempt, he was reading the diary, which brought back painful feelings and confusion, caused distress, embarrassment, confusion, shame, and guilt.

Additional history indicated David had experienced a history of suicidal ideation approximately one year prior to admission. In addition, he had a history of climbing on the roof as a means to escape his overwhelming feelings. He also had a history of drinking on one occasion to the point of needing to go to the emergency room. He had experienced multiple school suspensions due to negative interactions with teachers and peers. He also had a history of acting out violently and had been expelled from the school. He was on independent study and attending school one period per day.

David also had a history of noncompliance with medication, as well as a history of lying and stealing, including taking jewelry from his mother and giving it to friends. He displayed poor boundaries and an inability to maintain relationships, with the tendency to become overly consumed in a relationship and then sabotaging it. His parents expressed concern regarding poor insight, poor judgment, and lack of communication.

Hospital course suggested he was very superficial and engaged in a flight into health. He denied any problems whatsoever. When told he was going to residential treatment, David withdrew and became isolative and appeared more depressed.

David was described as being fairly tightlipped during interviews. However, when informed he would be going to a residential treatment center, he was reported to be looking forward to it as an appropriate place to recover and heal from his traumas.

On discharge, David was described as being alert and oriented. He was described as being at high risk for suicidal acting out, with little in the way of open communication or working on issues in treatment. Cognition was reported to be intact and unchanged from admission. Insight and judgment were poor.

The diagnostic impression included Major depression, severe, with a near fatal suicide attempt; Posttraumatic Stress Disorder; Rule out Conduct Disorder; Rule out Borderline Personality Disorder; GAF-35 on admission; 40 at discharge. Stressors were reported to be severe, with sexual assault. The prognosis was reported to be fair.

David indicated he could not remember the suicide attempt, but was overwhelmed with emotional distress after having reread his diary. A CT scan of the head revealed no damage, and he was reported to have not suffered any neurologic sequelae. He lived with his mother, father, and siblings.

On examination, David was alert and oriented and made fairly good eye and emotional contact. Mood was a little bit depressed and affect was blunted. Expressive speech was within normal limits. Thoughts were goal-directed and logical. Cognition was intact. David had poor memory for the events leading up to and subsequent to his suicide attempt, but otherwise had good memory function. He was to be admitted to the Adolescent Unit and was to receive group, family, and individual therapies, with continued medications

Memory for the Events:

David was asked to recount his memory of the events surrounding the suicide attempt. The purpose of this exercise was to ascertain any retrograde and/or anterograde amnesia, as well as to obtain an impression of his perception of, and response to, the significant events. David described the events leading to the suicide attempt as follows:

"That morning, I went to work . . . nothing happened . . . I came home and I went upstairs . . . then, I went downstairs . . . I found my journal and began to read about some of my problems . . . I couldn't see a reason to be alive anymore."

When asked if the above description was based solely on his own recollection of events, or if some of the information was what he had been told by others, he was unable to effectively differentiate which elements were distinctly from his own memory.

Current Symptoms and Complaints:

David generally denied any significant neurobehavioral symptoms and changes in functioning since the suicide attempt. His description of current symptoms is detailed below.

Physical: David denied any significant physical symptoms.

Cognitive: With respect to cognitive symptoms, David denied any problems. However, his parents describe memory problems, primarily incidental memory difficulties, as well as difficulty with sustained attention and concentration.

Emotional and Behavioral: When David was questioned regarding his current emotional state, he reported that he is emotionally "doing great now." He reported that if he has "an issue, I bring it up." However, when asked specifically regarding vegetative depressive symptoms, he acknowledged a pervasive feeling of sadness, crying spells on two occasions since his psychiatric hospitalization, diminished interest in activities (e.g., drawing and reading, and possible hypersomnia. He denied any significant fatigue).

When his parents were asked, they indicated that David appears to display poor sleeping habits and a greater propensity for risk-taking than he did prior to the suicide attempt. Additional symptoms they have noticed since then included swearing a lot and being unmotivated.

History:

Personal and Social: David reported that he was born in California in 1997. His biological parents were apparently heavily involved in the use of illicit substances and David was born with methamphetamine and alcohol in his system. He was adopted as an infant. His adoptive father and adoptive mother, in their fifties, were in good health.

David has never been married, but does have a girlfriend. He describes this relationship as being a supportive one. He does not have any children.

His criminal legal history is unremarkable.

Education: David reported that he is currently a 10th-grade student in an independent study program. He described himself as being an above-average student. His best subjects are English, art and language arts, in which he earns As. He indicated that he struggles with mathematics, but he still gets good grades, typically As. He denied any history of special education interventions, failing any grades, repeating any grades, or of being diagnosed with a learning disability or attention-related disorder.

Vocational: David does not have an employment history.

Medical: David and his parents indicated that his biological mother's pregnancy with him was remarkable for her use of alcohol and methamphetamines. He was delivered approximately two weeks early, weighing 5 lbs. 4 oz. He was jaundiced, displayed difficulty breathing and appeared inactive at birth, with elevated tone, a large head, and underdeveloped lungs. Developmental history was remarkable for diminished gross motor skills especially affecting the lower extremities, although he also had trouble sucking. However, he otherwise developed language skills and self-help skills within expected time frames.

His parents described him as being a happy and very active infant, and very outgoing. His childhood medical history, beyond the typical childhood illnesses and injuries, was unremarkable.

Past psychiatric history was unremarkable until the molestation and subsequent suicide attempt. The outpatient services David is currently receiving include psychiatric medication and talk therapy provided by a psychiatrist and licensed psychologist, respectively.

Biological family medical and psychiatric history is unknown, with the exception of the noted substance abuse. David denied any history of alcohol or substance abuse, with the exception of experimental usage on a few occasions. He denied any current consumption of alcohol. He also denied drinking caffeinated beverages, but reported using tobacco products. He was unaware of any exposures to neurotoxins.

Family medical history of stroke, seizure, or other neurological disease is unknown.

Mental Status Examination:

David arrived promptly for the evaluation, accompanied by his parents. He was casually dressed, well groomed, and appeared to be his stated age. He was alert and cooperative. Eye contact during the evaluation was good. Motor function was within normal limits; no apparent abnormalities or gait disturbances were observed. David displayed no vision or hearing deficits that would interfere with the current evaluation.

David was articulate; speech volume and rate were moderate, and prosody was normal. The amount of spontaneous speech was within the range of what is typical of these testing circumstances. No word-finding problems were apparent. In addition, no auditory comprehension difficulties were observed. Moreover, no obvious disturbances in immediate, recent, or remote memory were noted on interview. His intellectual ability was estimated to be within the *average* to *high average* range.

No gross disturbances in executive functioning were identified. Mood was euthymic and affect was appropriate to content, although his countenance appeared sad. David reported a history of suicidal ideation, diminished currently in comparison to relatively frequent thoughts before the suicide attempt, but he denied any current intent or plan. He also denied any homicidal ideation.

Thought processes were coherent, relevant, goal-directed, and logical. Hallucinations and delusional thought patterns were absent. Judgment, reasoning, and insight appeared fair.

Clinical Neuropsychological Testing Results

The WASI and WMS-III were scored with reference to the Psychological Corporation norms (1999). The Boston Naming Test, Trail Making Test, Controlled Oral Word Association Test, and Auditory Consonant Trigrams measures were scored with reference to the Mitrushina, Boone, Razani, and D'Elia norms (2005). The Stroop and d2 Test of Attention were scored with reference to their respective manuals. The Wisconsin Card-Sorting Test was scored according to the norms by Heaton, Talley, Chelune, Kay, and Curtiss (1993). The remaining tests were scored with reference to their respective manuals.

Procedural Considerations: The interview and mental status examination were performed in our outpatient office. David reported that he sleeps well, and he did not display any obvious fatigue during the evaluation. He was taking his usual medications (i.e., Zoloft for depressive symptoms and Vistaril for sleep, as well as a 10-day course of antibiotics apparently to treat acne). He is right-hand dominant. He had no obvious difficulties seeing test materials or hearing test instructions. His general activity level was task-appropriate.

Behavioral observations during testing, review of patterns of test results, and results of specific tests that are sensitive to emotional and motivational factors indicated that David put forth consistent effort during this evaluation. Thus, the current evaluation results are judged to be a valid reflection of David's current abilities.

Test performance descriptions provided below take into account David's age, education, intellectual attainment, and gender, as appropriate. The results are described below.

Intellectual Functions: David was administered the four subtests of the Wechsler Abbreviated Scale of Intelligence-Second Edition (WASI-II), from which Verbal Comprehension and Perceptual Reasoning index scores were derived. The Full-Scale IQ is the aggregate of the Verbal Comprehension and Perceptual Reasoning index scores and is usually considered to be the most representative measure of g, or global intellectual functioning. David's general cognitive ability is within the *high average* range of intellectual functioning, as measured by the WASI-II. His overall thinking and reasoning abilities exceed those of approximately 81 percent of children his age (FSIQ = 113). Subtest results were as described below.

	Verbal Comprehension Subtests Percentile (Psych. Corp. Norms)	
Vocabulary	96	
Similarities	73	
Perceptual Reasoning Subtests		
Block Design		42
Matrix Reasoning		76

The combination of Verbal Comprehension subtest performances results in a Verbal Comprehension Index in the *superior* range (VCI = 119), exceeding that of approximately 90 percent of David's peers. The combination of Perceptual Reasoning subtests results in a Perceptual Reasoning Index that is in the *average* range (PRI = 104), exceeding that of approximately 61 percent of his peers.

There is a statistical significant difference between verbal and nonverbal abilities as measured by the VCI and PRI. In general, David demonstrated better-developed abilities in the areas of (1) vocabulary and verbal abstract reasoning than in the areas of (2) spatial reasoning/motor coordination and nonverbal abstract reasoning. However, this disparity is primarily attributable to his *very superior* range performance on the Vocabulary subtest. Otherwise, spatial reasoning was a relative weakness, although solidly within the *average* range. Nonverbal abstract reasoning was within the *high average* range and verbal abstract reasoning was near the top end of the *average* range.

Academic Achievement: The PIAT-R Reading Recognition, Reading Comprehension, and Spelling Subtests were administered and scored according to the instructions found in the test manual. The advantage of the PIAT-R over other tests of academic skills is its separate assessments of oral reading and reading comprehension, as well as the fact that reading comprehension and spelling are assessed by using a multiple-choice format that does not require speech.

David performed within an expected range on all three PIAT-R subtests. Reading Recognition and Reading Comprehension subtest performances were within the *average* range and *high average* range, at the 70th percentile and 87th percentile, respectively. The Spelling subtest performance also was within the *high average* range, at the 79th percentile.

Language: David spoke with moderate volume, adequate melody, and normal intonation. In addition, he answered questions with logical responses, thus demonstrating no difficulty tracking conversation during the interview. In addition, he required few repetitions of instructions during introduction to various tasks and did not display any word-finding difficulties. On formal testing, David's verbally mediated intellectual skills within the *superior* range, at the 90th percentile (Verbal Comprehension Index).

Verbal fluency was assessed with the Controlled Oral Word Association Test. David was able to carry out this procedure with performances consistent with measured verbal IQ. He performed within the *high average* range on both fluency tasks, at the 85th percentile for letter fluency and at the 84th percentile for category fluency. Similarly, on the Boston Naming Test, he was able to name correctly 57 out of 60 items, a performance that fell within the *high average* range, at the 84th percentile. On the Reitan-Indiana Aphasia Screening Test, he made one error of articulation, a performance within an expected range. Moreover, on the Complex Ideational Material subtest of the Boston Diagnostic Aphasia Examination (BDAE), a relatively simple measure of receptive language, David made no errors, a performance within an expected range.

The results described above provide evidence of expressive language function consistently within an expected range. David displayed *high average* range performances on expressive language tasks requiring confrontational naming, initiation, retrieval, and semantic categorizing, and the development of phonemic strategies. Moreover, his performance on a simple task requiring receptive language skills was within an expected range.

Attention, Concentration, and Memory Functions: During the full day of the examination (6.5 hours), David was alert, oriented to date, person, place, and situation, and easily directed without incident. He displayed some difficulty with estimating the passage of time, believing it was 10 a.m. when the actual time was close to noon. His attention to the interview was adequate, with no obvious conversational tracking problems. In addition, there were no significant behavioral indications of fatigue that might have significantly affecting performance. Several formal tests of attention were administered.

The d2 Test of Attention is a timed test of selective attention. It represents a standardized refinement of the so-called Cancellation Test. The test measures processing speed, rule compliance, and quality of performance and response to the discrimination of similar visual stimuli, thereby allowing for an estimation of individual attention and concentration performance.

David's total number of completions over 14 trials on the d2 fell within the *average* range, just above the 38th percentile. His total error rate was improved in comparison, with a performance that fell within the 75th–90th percentile band (*high average range*). His overall completion performance, taking into account errors, returned to the *average* range, at approximately the 46th percentile. His concentration performance was within the top half of the *average* range, within the 50–75th percentile band. Moreover, his fluctuation rate performance was at the top end of the *average* range, at the 75th percentile. The overall performance is indicative of adequate processing speed and attention to detail on a visual-motor task. The formatted scores are as follows.

d2Test of Attention	Standard Score	Percentile Rank
Total	97	38.2
Errors	107–112	75–90
Total-Errors	99	46.0
Concentration Performance	100–110	50–75
Fluctuation Rate	106/107	75

Selective attention was assessed using the Stroop Neuropsychological Screening Test. Selective attention refers to the ability to focus attention on one or more relevant aspects of a stimulus or situation while ignoring irrelevant aspects. One method of examining this function is through the use of the Stroop procedure, in which David was asked to selectively attend to the color of ink used to print words, as opposed to the actual words themselves. Since reading is such a dominant response to letters grouped in this fashion, mental effort is required to suppress the tendency to read the words. This results in slowing of processing, as well as errors, especially in individuals with reduced selective attention ability. David successfully completed 111 items within the allotted time frame, a performance that fell within the *average* range, at the 69th percentile.

On a measure of visual scanning (Trail Making Test A), David performed within the *average* range, at the 36th percentile. This is a pencil-and-paper task that requires an individual to connect consecutively numbered items as quickly as possible. Trail Making Test B is a somewhat more complex task, requiring the individual to alternately connect consecutive numbers and letters. Thus, this task requires more complex memory and planning, cognitive flexibility, mental maintenance of parallel sets, as well as the visual-motor coordination required on Trail Making Test A. David's performance on Trail Making Test B was diminished in comparison with the Trail Making Test A, within the *borderline* range, at the 9th percentile.

In summary, attention and concentration measures, using a variety of selective attention procedures listed above, demonstrated an expected level of function in all cases but one. On a highly speed-dependent visual scanning task, David's performance ranged from the *average* to the *high average* range, while his performance on a second highly speed-dependent visual scanning task was within the bottom half of the *average* range. Selective attention requiring suppression of an automatic response also was within the *average* range. On the other hand, on another task requiring mental maintenance of parallel sets, his performance was within the *borderline* range.

Memory Functions: Memory functions are organized into six sections: (1) Working Memory; (2) Ability to learn and retain new material; (3) Auditory Learning; (4) Modality-specific memory; (5) Retention of information; and (6) Retrieval of information. Each section is intended to provide interpretative hypotheses about various aspects involved in the ability to process and retrieve newly learned information.

Of course, when reviewing the succeeding results, it is always important to consider other factors that may have contributed to test performance, such as difficulties with vision, hearing, motor functioning, and speech/language performance. However, given the background information provided in the current evaluation, none of these specific factors were identified in the background screens as potential confounding variables.

The Wechsler Memory Scale-III is a memory assessment battery that consists of 11 primary subtests and 6 optional subtests. During the current evaluation, the primary subtests were administered. Primary Index scores are provided below.

Primary Indexes:	Age-Corrected Percentile (Psychological Corporation Norms)
Auditory Immediate	94 (*superior range*)
Visual Immediate	84 (*high average range*)
Immediate Memory	95 (*superior range*)
Auditory Delayed	82 (*high average range*)
Visual Delayed	73 (*average range*)
Auditory Recognition Delayed	50 (*average range*)
General Memory	77 (*high average range*)
Working Memory	77 (*high average range*)

Working Memory on the WMS-III: The Working Memory Index of the WMS-III is a measure of an individual's ability to hold information temporarily in memory for the purpose of using that information to perform a specific task. Working memory (i.e., a higher level attentional ability) is an important prerequisite of many cognitive abilities. As a consequence, inadequate working memory skills will likely affect an individual's ability to perform other mental operations efficiently.

Overall, David's working memory capacity falls within the *high average* range and exceeds that of 77 percent of individuals in his age norm group (Working Memory Index = 111). This level of performance suggests that David's ability to temporarily retain information facilitates his performance of mental operations. On the other hand, his ability to hold and process auditory information is a relative strength in comparison to his ability to hold and process visual-spatial information.

Ability to Learn and Remember New Material: Learning refers to a person's ability to encode and store novel information, while memory refers to the persistence of learned material that can be retrieved after a brief (immediate) or long (delayed) interval. The WMS-III is intended to provide information regarding learning and memory under a specific set of conditions, but is not intended to provide direct information regarding academic achievement or to reflect the more general academic usage of the term ability to learn.

David's ability to recall new information after a brief interval is in the *superior* classification range. In situations requiring the learning of new information, David will likely recall more information than will most of his peers. His Immediate Memory Index score indicates that his performance exceeds that of 95 percent of individuals in his age group (Immediate Memory Index = 124). His performances on the Auditory Immediate Index and Visual Immediate Index are comparable, suggesting approximately equal capabilities in both modalities. However, he exhibited variability in his performance on the subtests of the Visual Immediate Index, suggesting diverse memory abilities within the visual modality. Specifically, David displayed *superior* range ability to remember faces and an average range ability to remember relatively complex social scenes.

David also demonstrated a well-developed ability to retrieve recently learned information after a 25- to 35-minute delay. Based on these results, he will likely remember more information than will his peers in situations requiring the learning and long-term storage of new information. His General Memory Index score is within the *high average* classification range and exceeds 77 percent of individuals within his age group (General Memory Index = 111). An analysis of the delayed modality-specific indexes reveals that David's performances on the Auditory Delayed Index and the Visual Delayed Index are comparable, suggesting approximately equal delayed memory capabilities in both modalities.

Auditory Learning: On the WMS-III, the rate at which an individual learns new information is determined by the difference between the amount of information learned after a single presentation of the material and the amount of information learned after multiple learning trials. The Single-Trial Learning and Learning Slope process composites provide information regarding the extent to which repetition of information improves auditory memory functioning. Compared to the performance of individuals of similar age, David's acquisition of auditory information after a single presentation is in the *high average* range, exceeding 87 percent of individuals within his age group. Similarly, his ability to acquire auditory information over multiple trials is within the *average* range (52nd percentile), suggesting a rate of learning comparable to that of others his age.

Modality-Specific Memory: A comparison of memory performance when information is presented visually and orally can reveal modality-specific strengths and weaknesses. Visual memory refers to information presented to the individual visually, whereas auditory memory refers to the oral presentation of information. However, the terms visual memory and auditory memory should not be used to refer exclusively to how the information is encoded and retrieved from memory. Most likely, individuals use visual and verbal strategies to encode and recall information regardless of the modality of presentation.

David's performance on auditory and visual memory measures is relatively consistent. However, he shows a relative strength with respect to auditory working memory. Therefore, emphasizing the oral presentation of information, or supplementing a visual presentation with oral instruction, may help him to improve overall learning and retrieval.

Retention of Information: The difference between an individual's immediate and delayed memory capabilities is an indication of the amount of previously learned information retained after an interval of time. Substantially lower delayed memory performance relative to immediate memory capabilities suggests a rapid rate of forgetting, or retrieval difficulties. David's delayed memory performance relative to his immediate memory capabilities does not suggest retention difficulties for either auditory or visual information.

Retrieval of Information: The difference between an individual's Auditory Recognition Delayed Index and Auditory Delayed Index scores can indicate the extent that cues or choices help the individual in retrieving auditory information. A discrepancy between these index scores, with recognition greater than recall, may suggest auditory retrieval difficulties. Retrieval problems suggest that, although the individual has learned the information, he has a reduced capacity to access that information without external prompts or structure.

David's performance on the Auditory Recognition Delayed Index (Index Score = 100) and the Auditory Delayed Index (Index Score = 114) shows a somewhat unusual pattern of better recall performance than recognition performance. This pattern may indicate that the presentation of choices or cues might have interfered with, rather than enhanced, memory performance.

In summary, the memory testing results were generally within the *high average* range or better, with the exception of auditory recognition. When compared to his general intellectual ability, within the *high average* range (FSIQ = 113), the overall performances were within an expected range.

Working Memory on the Consonant Trigrams Test: The Consonant Trigrams Test consists of oral presentation of three consonants that the individual must remember. The initial five trials require that the individual repeat the three consonants immediately. On the 15 subsequent trials, the three consonants are presented and followed by presentation of a number from which the individual must immediately start counting backwards. At a given interval following initiation of counting backwards, 3 seconds, 9 seconds, or 18 seconds (five trials for each time condition), the individual must repeat the three consonants. A perfect performance of recalling all three consonants on five trials (15 total possible) is expected without a distraction delay. As the distraction delay grows longer, decreased performance is expected. David was able to recall 15/15 without a distraction delay, 14/15 at a 3-second delay, 15/15 at the 9-second delay, and 12/15 at an 18-second delay. His performance on the 9-second delay was within the *superior* range, at approximately the 95th percentile. Moreover, his performance on the 18-second delay condition was within the *average* range at approximately the 50th percentile.

As a whole, the auditory and visual memory test results suggest an individual who possesses an expected level of abilities with respect to encoding, storing, and retrieving verbal and visual information. Auditory and visual memory function on the WMS-III was generally within the *high average* range, or better, and performance did not diminish when a distractor variable was introduced on the Consonant Trigrams Test. On the other hand, his relative performance on the WMS-III auditory recognition task was a relative weakness. This relatively diminished performance was felt to be attributable to a functional psychiatric component affecting attentional mechanisms, rather than to an organic etiology.

Reasoning and Abstract Thinking: David's concept formation abilities were assessed using the Wisconsin Card-Sorting Test: Computer Version 4 for Windows, Research Edition. On this test, Cody obtained an error score of 7, equivalent to a T-score of 69 (97th percentile, *very superior* range). The Wisconsin Card-Sorting Test: Computer Version 4 for Windows, Research Edition, is a card-sorting task requiring him to sort card stimuli along one of three dimensions: according to color of stimulus depicted, form of stimulus, and number of stimuli on the card. After he has begun to sort to the correct stimuli, the sorting criteria are changed without warning. This is done repeatedly, requiring him to flexibly adapt on the basis of visual and auditory feedback. The test is thought to provide an objective measure of perseveration.

David completed all six possible categories, using only 73 of the 128 possible sorts. Of his overall responses, 66 were correct sorts and, as mentioned earlier, there were a total of 7 errors, which is within the *very superior* range. He completed six categories, producing a score that fell above the 16th percentile band, within the *average* range. In addition, he required only 10 trials before completing the first category, a performance that fell above the 16th percentile, within the *average* range.

David's conceptual level of responses was within the *very superior* range, at the 96th percentile. Of his overall responses, only two were perseverative. When this latter score, which is quite sensitive, is compared to detailed normative values, it reveals that David performed within the *very superior* range (T-score = >80, >99th percentile). The overall results suggest a more than adequate ability to develop a strategy and shift/maintain mental set on tasks, generally consistent with intellectual ability described earlier.

Executive Functions: David was socially appropriate throughout our contacts with him. He had no difficulty initiating or directing behavior to the task at hand, and no significant distractibility was observed. He approached tasks in an orderly fashion, and there were no obvious instances of impulsive errors.

On formal testing, he performed within the *average* range on a task requiring inhibition of automatic responses (Stroop). In addition, he performed within the *average* range on a simple task of sequencing (Trails A).

Moreover, he was adequately able to develop good strategies on less structured tests (e.g., WCST and Matrix Reasoning). Furthermore, he displayed no difficulty shifting or maintaining mental set on the WCST. Thus, he performed consistently within an expected range on tasks requiring various executive functions, with one exception. On Trail Making Test B, David performed within the *borderline* range, suggesting mild difficulty maintaining parallel sets.

Emotional and Personality Status

Personality Assessment Inventory–Adolescent (PAI-A): The Personality Assessment Inventory–Adolescent (PAI-A), a 264-item self-report, provides a number of validity indices that are designed to provide an assessment of factors that could distort the results of testing. Such factors could include failure to complete test items properly, carelessness, reading difficulties, confusion, exaggeration, malingering, or defensiveness. For this protocol, the number of uncompleted items is within acceptable limits.

Also evaluated is the extent to which David attended appropriately and responded consistently to the content of test items. David's responses suggested that he attended appropriately to item content and responded in a consistent fashion to similar items.

The degree to which response styles may have affected or distorted the report of symptomatology on the inventory also is assessed. The scores for these indicators fall in the normal range, suggesting that David answered in a reasonably forthright manner and that there do not appear to be factors that might distort the profile, which would make it appear either more negative or more positive than the clinical picture would warrant.

The PAI-A clinical profile is marked by a significant elevation on the ARD scale, indicating that the content tapped by this scale may reflect a particular area of difficulty for David. He indicates that he is experiencing specific fears or anxiety surrounding some situations. The pattern of responses reveals that he is likely to display significant phobic symptoms and behaviors. These behaviors are likely to interfere in some significant way in his life, and it is probable that he monitors his environment in a vigilant fashion to avoid contact with the feared object or situation. He is more likely to have multiple phobias or a more distressing phobia, such as agoraphobia, than to suffer from a simple phobia.

David describes himself as being more wary and sensitive in interpersonal relationships than the average adolescent. Others are likely to see him as tough-minded, skeptical, and somewhat hostile. He also describes himself as being rather moody, and others may view him as being overly sensitive. He may be dissatisfied with his more important relationships, and uncertain about major life goals to a greater degree than is typical of others his age.

David reports that drug use may be the source of some problems in his life. These problems may include strained interpersonal and family relationships, school and/or legal problems, and use of drugs to manage stress.

David's self-concept appears to involve a generally positive self-evaluation. He is generally a confident, resilient, and optimistic person, although his self-esteem may be reactive to changes in his current circumstances. During times of stress, he may inwardly be troubled by more self-doubt and misgivings about his adequacy than are readily apparent to others. Reactive changes in self-esteem may be accompanied by uncertainty about goals, values, and important life decisions.

His interpersonal style seems best characterized as friendly and extraverted. He will usually present a cheerful and positive picture in the presence of others. He is able to communicate his interest in others in an open and straightforward manner. He usually prefers activities that bring him into contact with others, rather than solitary pursuits, and he is probably quick to offer help to those in need of it. He sees himself as a person with many friends and as one who is comfortable in most social situations.

With respect to perceived stressors and the availability of social supports with which to deal with these stressors, David's responses indicate that both his recent level of stress and his perceived level of social support are about average in comparison to normal adolescents. The reasonably low-stress environment and the availability of a social support system are both favorable prognostic signs for future adjustment.

David's interest in, and motivation for, treatment is somewhat below average in comparison to adolescents who are not being seen in a therapeutic setting. Furthermore, his level of treatment motivation is substantially lower than is typical of individuals being seen in treatment settings. His responses suggest that he is satisfied with himself as he is, that he is not experiencing marked distress, and that he sees little need for change, despite his recognition that a number of areas of his life are not going well at this time.

If treatment were to be considered, particular areas of attention or concern in the early stages of treatment could include his defensiveness and reluctance to discuss personal problems, as well as a reluctance to participate or cooperate in treatment.

Trauma Symptom Checklist for Children (TSCC): The TSCC consists of 54 items and provides a measure of posttraumatic stress and related psychological symptomatology in children ages 8–16 years who have experienced traumatic events, such as physical or sexual abuse, major loss, or natural disasters, or who have been a witness to violence. The TSCC includes two validity scales (Under response and hyper response), six clinical scales (Anxiety, Depression, Anger, Posttraumatic Stress, Dissociation, and Sexual Concerns), and eight critical items. Profile Forms allow for conversion of raw scores to age- and sex-appropriate T-scores. The TSCC-A, which was administered during the current evaluation, is an alternate 44-item version of the measure, which makes no reference to sexual issues.

On the TSCC, David produced responses to all 44 items. In addition, his scale score on the under response scale was within normal limits. However, his T-score on the hyper response scale exceeded the validity cutoff score. Therefore, the TSCC was considered invalid.

Detailed Assessment of Posttraumatic Stress (DAPS): The Detailed Assessment of Posttraumatic Stress (DAPS) is a 104-item test that provides detailed information about an individual's symptomatic responses to a specific traumatic event. The DAPS contains two validity scales, three trauma specification scales, and eight clinical scales. The eight clinical scales evaluate the extent to which individuals experience each of the three clusters of symptoms common to PTSD, the overall severity of the PTSD symptoms, and the impact these symptoms may be having on overall psychosocial functioning.

David endorsed several items that were rarely endorsed by traumatized individuals in the standardization sample. Possible explanations include an attempt to present himself as especially symptomatic, random responding, or the existence of an unusual number of atypical symptoms. In addition, the possibility of psychosis or mania should be ruled out. In either case, elevations on the Negative Bias scale of this magnitude suggest the possibility of an invalid administration. Thus, the interpretive hypotheses described later should be interpreted with this precaution.

David provided a description of the traumatic event as follows:

"Over the course of two years, I was led into a relationship with an adult leader that I met through a camping experience. . . . I was molested on three occasions and sodomized on another. I was emotionally and mentally abused, as well as sexually and physically."

David's responses indicate that he experienced more distress, as well as dissociation, during or soon after the incident than the average trauma victim. His responses resulted in scale elevations indicative of a significant level of reexperiencing of the event, avoidance, and hyper arousal. He is likely regularly bothered by intrusive recollections of the events and may feel unable to control these reexperiencing symptoms. He experiences significant withdrawal, apathy, and emotional numbing, as well as a tendency to avoid people, places, or situations that remind him of the accident. He may be reluctant to discuss his symptoms with therapists or others. He is likely experiencing a combination of tension and irritability, and a tendency to be "jumpy" or "on edge." He also may complain of various somatic concerns that reflect the effects of sustained hyperarousal. His overall Posttraumatic Stress score reflects clinically significant, severe, symptomatology.

Diagnostic Impression—DSM-IV-TR:

AXIS I:	294.9 Cognitive Disorder NOS, Mild in Nature;
	309.81 Posttraumatic Stress Disorder, Chronic, Severe in Nature;
	296.32 Depressive Disorder, Chronic, Moderate in Nature
AXIS II:	799.9 No Diagnosis on Axis II
Axis III:	Anoxic Brain Injury, DOI: 9/27/12; With Mild Cognitive Deficits; Defer to Medical Records

Discussion: David was born methamphetamine positive and displayed neurological soft signs in infancy. Nevertheless, he reportedly performed well in elementary school until developing depressive symptoms after being informed by a nonfamily member that he was adopted. Then, two years later, an adult and juvenile raped him on multiple occasions during camping trips.

After his father became aware of the sexual molestation, the adult perpetrator was arrested. Then, some months later, after becoming distressed while reading a diary that recounted the sexual assaults, David became suicidal and attempted to kill himself. After he was treated emergently with a three-day therapeutic coma, he underwent residential treatment.

At discharge from the residential treatment center David's problems with anxiety, depression, and self-harm (cutting) were reported to have gradually improved. Flashbacks and nightmares also had resolved. However, he had problems throughout his hospital course with lying and manipulation, as well as purposeful targeting of peers, significant difficulty in his relationship with others, and refused to take responsibility for his actions. He was reported to be frequently entitled and engaged in defiance as well as disregard of rules and authority in order to increase his own excitement level, as he was frequently bored. He also seemed to lack remorse for the actions that were hurtful to other peers.

During the current evaluation, David generally denied any significant neurobehavioral symptoms and changes in functioning since the traumatic events. He denied any significant physical or cognitive symptoms, and reported that he was emotionally "doing great." On the other hand, his parents reported incidental memory difficulties, as well as difficulty with sustained attention and concentration. Moreover, they indicated that he had developed poor sleeping habits and a greater propensity for risk-taking than he did prior to suicide attempt. They also described increased levels of swearing and a tendency to be unmotivated. For his part, on direct questioning, David admitted to a pervasive feeling of sadness, crying spells on two occasions since his psychiatric hospitalization, diminished interest in activities (e.g., drawing and reading, and possible hypersomnia).

With respect to cognitive function, the current evaluation results provide evidence of intellectual functioning within the *high average* range, with a Full-scale IQ of 113 (81st percentile). Furthermore, David possesses *high average* range academic skills. In addition, multiple measures of expressive language function revealed performances within the *high average* range. Similarly, his performance on a simple task requiring receptive language skills was within an expected range.

Immediate and delayed auditory and visual memory performances generally ranged from the *high average* range to the *superior* range. In addition, performances on most measures of executive functions were within the *average* to *very superior* range. Furthermore, multiple measures of attention and concentration tended to be within the *average* to *high average* range, with one exception. On Trail Making Test Part B, David performed within the *borderline* range, suggesting mild difficulty with maintenance of parallel sets.

Thus, in summary, the entirety of the cognitive testing suggested an individual with *high average* range innate intellectual ability, as well as relatively intact functions in all domains. On the other hand, a relative weakness was identified with respect to cognitive processing speed.

All of the tasks on which David performed within the bottom half of the *average* range or worse contained a speed-dependent variable (e.g., Block Design, Trail Making, and the d2). Of course, even his performances on tasks involving cognitive processing speed were generally within the bottom half of the *average* range and, thus, not representative of "impaired" function. However, this level of diminished processing speed could represent a residual of an anoxic injury, as it is known that individuals who experience acute oxygen deprivation can display a variety of cognitive deficits (Fitzgerald et al., 2007). Furthermore, his parents described personality and behavioral changes since September 2012, symptoms which are not uncommon following anoxic injuries, as the hippocampus, basal ganglia, and cerebral cortex are particularly vulnerable to anoxia (Caine and Watson, 2000).

In addition to the diminished cognitive processing speed described above, administration of a personality instrument and multiple self-report forms revealed symptoms consistent with a chronic Posttraumatic Stress Disorder associated with the sexual molestations. Furthermore, despite his protestations that he is emotionally feeling "great," on direct questioning, he admits to vegetative depressive symptoms. Moreover, the tendency is to believe that David is repressing depressive symptoms and avoiding addressing important issues, as he apparently has for the last few years, because the feelings are simply too overwhelming to confront.

Given the entirety of the available data in this case, including reviewed medical records, clinical interview, and evaluation results, the likelihood is that David sustained a very mild traumatic brain injury as a result of the suicide attempt. *The Journal of Head Trauma Rehabilitation,* volume 8 (3), page 86, 1993, provides an excellent definition of mild traumatic brain injury, developed by the Mild Traumatic Brain Injury Committee of the Head Injury Interdisciplinary Special Interest Group of the American Congress on Rehabilitation Medicine. The definition reads as follows:

> The patient with a mild traumatic brain injury is a person who has had a traumatically induced physiological disruption of brain function, as manifested by at least one of the following:
>
> 1. Any period of loss of consciousness;
> 2. Any loss of memory for events immediately before or after the events;
> 3. Any alteration in mental state at the time of the events (e.g., feeling dazed, disoriented, or confused); and
> 4. Focal neurological deficits, which may or may not be transient; but where the severity of the injury does not exceed the following:
>
>   a. Loss of consciousness of approximately thirty minutes or less;
>   b. After thirty minutes, an initial Glasgow coma scale (GCS) of 13–15; and
>   c. Posttraumatic amnesia (PTA) not greater than 24 hours.

The rationale for the very mild traumatic brain injury diagnosis in this case is as follows. David was involved in an event that restricted blood flow and oxygenation, resulting in an anoxic episode and loss of consciousness that subsequently required CPR and a therapeutic coma before he was revived.

In summary, David was born amphetamine positive, showed neurological soft signs, performed well in school until he was 11 years old, developed depressive symptoms after learning he was adopted, and developed symptoms of Posttraumatic Stress Disorder and severe depressive symptoms months after being sexually molested. The current evaluation documents high average range innate intellectual ability and generally intact cognitive function. However, he also displays relatively diminished levels of cognitive processing speed accompanied by severe psychiatric symptoms.

With respect to prognosis, David obviously possesses above-average levels of innate cognitive ability, which suggests likelihood of greater success in adapting to the relatively minor cognitive deficits. Moreover, the possibility certainly exists that these cognitive deficits will diminish over the next several months. On the other hand, prognosis regarding his psychiatric symptomatology is much more tenuous. In fact, his elevated intellectual ability facilitates his well-defended repression of symptoms to some extent. However, these symptoms also "leak" on a regular basis (e.g., through self-mutilation and other behavioral manifestations).

Psychotropic medication appears to have been somewhat effective to this point at least in mitigating the depressive symptoms. Ongoing psychiatric medication management is necessary. In addition, David should be provided and ongoing psychotherapeutic environment where he can be encouraged to address the ramifications of the molestations when he feels emotionally strong enough to do so.

Thank you for referring David for a comprehensive neuropsychological evaluation. I hope this report has answered the pertinent questions. If I can respond to any additional information, please do not hesitate to contact me.

Declaration

I declare under penalty of perjury that the information contained in this report and its attachments, if any, is true and correct to the best of my knowledge and belief, except as to information that I have received from others. As to that information, I declare under penalty of perjury that the information accurately describes the information provided to me and, except as noted in this report, that I believe it to be true. I have not violated Labor Code Section 139.3, and the contents of this report and bill are true and correct to the best of my knowledge.

Respectfully submitted,

Psychologist's Name
Address
License number

The child psychiatric forensic evaluation is presented in chapter 4. A case example follows the theoretical discussion.

FOUR

Components of a Thorough Child Psychiatric Evaluation

The Case of William Rain

There are many similarities between the forensic evaluation of an adult and a child or teenager, but there are also important differences. Just as psychiatrists and psychologists need proper credentials in order to succeed as forensic experts in regard to adults, so do mental health professionals who choose to serve as experts in cases involving children. For psychiatrists, the requirements are clear—two years of full-time accredited residency training in child psychiatry in addition to the two or three years of full-time residency training in adult psychiatry, and board certification in child psychiatry. There is no exact equivalent for psychologists but those who wish to serve as experts in child cases should have additional training in child development and psychopathology and experience in evaluating and treating children and adolescents.

Anyone who does not have at least the minimum requirements mentioned above and who chooses to serve as an expert witness in law suits that are focused on children, will certainly have his credentials challenged and his opinions undermined.

COMPONENTS OF THE EVALUATION

As with adults, a thorough child psychiatric evaluation consists of a review of records, diagnostic interviews with parents and the child or teenager and, depending on the age of the child, psychological testing.

Review of Records

All of the records relevant in adult evaluations are also important in child forensic evaluations. The complaint, accident reports, medical records, interrogatories, and depositions should be reviewed. With children and adolescents school records are often very helpful as are those from the pediatrician because they provide independent information about the child's physical, mental, and intellectual development over time allowing the diagnostician to place the current symptoms and issues into a developmental context. All requests for records are made to the retaining law firm who perform the sometimes, difficult job of obtaining the records requested by you.

Diagnostic Interviews

In clinical, non-forensic, evaluations I always interview the parents and have at least two diagnostic interviews with the child or adolescent. With young children the parents are seen first since the child cannot give an adult perspective on the child's problems. Then after preparing the parents on how to introduce the subject of coming to see me to their child, I interview the child.

When dealing with adolescents in any setting an understanding of adolescent development theory is particularly useful. The adolescent is in the process of psychologically separating from his or her parents and wants to be treated and thought of as an individual. Because of the upsurge of sexual feelings generated by puberty, adolescents are unable to enter easily or quickly into a close, open relationship with adults, particularly adults who within a session or two focus on painful and embarrassing subject matter. However, they have the intellectual capacity to understand the nature of the legal system and will usually cooperate, although reluctantly.

Because of these reasons the procedure that I use in clinical evaluations with adolescents is different than my approach with children. When the parent makes the initial phone call, after explaining the evaluation process and getting their agreement to proceed, I ask the parents to tell their son or daughter that they have talked to me about the problems at hand and that I asked to see him or her. Then, I make a phone call to the adolescent, introduce myself, and arrange the first appointment with the adolescent. This tells the adolescent that I respect them as an individual and want to involve them in the process from the beginning. After one or two sessions with the adolescent I see the parents, explaining to the adolescent that whatever they choose to tell me is confidential but if they wish to know, I will share with them any information I obtained during parental interviews. When the evaluation is finished, I meet with the adolescent first, explain my findings and what I will be telling their parents when a hold a second summary conference with the parents. The purpose of this seemingly convoluted exercise is an additional attempt to gain the confidence and respect of the adolescent in order to form a therapeutic alliance that allows therapy to begin and hopefully succeed.

In forensic evaluations the interaction with the adolescent and his or her parents is different. The goal is to quickly obtain the information required to serve as an expert witness. The focus is not on building a long term alliance since the adolescent will not be coming into therapy with me. I consider it a conflict of interest to treat adults or children whom I have seen in the role of an expert witness and always refer them, when asked by the parents or retaining lawyer, to experienced colleagues.

Further, the need to tell the adolescent that there is not confidentiality in a forensic evaluation process, that lawyers from both sides, and possibly their parents, will have access to my file and all of the information in it, makes gaining the confidence of the adolescent much more difficult. This can be particularly difficult when serving as a defense expert when almost always you are only allowed to see the adolescent once and the subject matter is often highly personal and embarrassing, for example, in sexual abuse cases. Because the adolescent is often in duress and has some understanding of the legal process, a sensitive, kind approach will usually allow you to get the information that you need in order to perform your diagnostic function.

Diagnostic Interviews with Children

During diagnostic sessions with children, up to the age of eleven or twelve, the presence of toys, doll houses, puppets, and drawing material usually become the immediate focus of attention and make the young child comfortable in a strange setting. Toys often because the vehicle for the expression of issues related to the lawsuit. These objects are an integral part of psychotherapy with young children because they often express themselves most easily through play rather than words. They serve the same function in diagnostic interviews.

For example, one nine-year-old girl whom I evaluated forensically had watched her mother fall fifteen feet through a second floor railing and saw her bleeding and unconscious on the floor below. She was hesitant to talk about the experience in the first diagnostic interview. During the second diagnostic session she was busily playing with a two-tiered doll house and, without prompting, began to shove the dolls off of the second story so that they would land on their heads. Clearly, she was telling me about the traumatic experience of watching her mother fall and, utilizing the repetition compulsion, was attempting to master the experience through the use of play. I observed but did not comment since I would not be seeing her again. If this were a psychotherapeutic situation, the play would have been explored and eventually interpreted.

Standard child psychiatric techniques, such as asking for three wishes and drawings, can provide useful information. Older children are occasionally able to discuss the events that led to the lawsuit and the symptoms that resulted from it. They can also provide some developmental history.

Adolescent Diagnostic Interviews

Adolescents consider toys to be infantile and will almost always sit and talk. Treating the adolescent like an adult by informing them at the beginning of the interview who you are and why you are seeing them usually creates a positive tone for the interaction. So does asking if the adolescent has any questions for you. Beginning by asking general questions about interests, hobbies, school, and friends also helps to create a nonthreatening relationship. But sooner or later, in one session or two, the subject matter of the lawsuit must be addressed. Obviously, if you are seeing a plaintiff and were retained by the plaintiff lawyer, cooperation is more likely to occur than if you were retained by the opposing side. Lawyers will sometimes coach adolescents in interviews with opposing experts to refuse to discuss certain subjects.

Diagnostic Interviews with Parents

I make every effort to make parents comfortable by meeting them in a pleasant, but non-pretentious office, and offering water, coffee, or tea. I schedule appointments with parents from the side that retained me directly with them in order to establish a rapport prior to the face-to-face meeting. Appointments with parents from the opposing side are made through the retaining attorney or his or her office staff. You will be contacted by the retaining attorney's office asking for several dates when you will be available to conduct the interview.

I make a particular effort to be friendly and sensitive to parents from the opposing side because we have not had any prior contact and they often approach their meeting with me with the assumption that I will be unfriendly, or even hostile. Their preconceived notions often lead to failure to keep the scheduled appointment, in some instances more than once. That's the reason for the cancellation policy stated in the fee agreement with the retaining attorney. When such a parent fails to show, I call the retaining attorney who then contacts opposing counsel in order to reschedule the diagnostic interview.

Skeptical parents may ask questions about credentials or procedures (MacBeth et al., 1994) which, of course, are answered openly and nondefensively. If psychological testing is planned, the reasons for the procedure and an outline of what the child will expect to encounter during the testing is explained. Since many psychologists ask parents to provide clinical information and complete test protocols about their child, their part in the testing process is explained.

The next stop is to explain the subject matter to be covered and to begin to ask questions. As with the evaluation of an adult, information is obtained about identifying information, the events leading to the law suit, the child's or adolescent's symptoms, a complete developmental history, and a review of records. The diagnostic interview or interviews with parents usually take me approximately three hours to complete.

Identifying Information

The identifying information provides the basic realities of the child's life and a skeletal framework on which to build an understanding of his or her problems. Symptoms and development will be influenced by the presence or absence of parents and siblings, socioeconomic status, and other life circumstances. All of these factors have relevance in the courtroom since they can be used by both sides either to minimize or maximize damage.

History of the Events Leading to the Law Suit

This would be the equivalent of the chief complaint and history of the present illness in a clinical evaluation. Before obtaining this information from the parents you should have reviewed the complaint and other records that have informed you about the matter at hand. As with adult evaluations, obtaining the information directly from parents refutes any claim that you have based your opinions and conclusions primarily on secondary sources. Although my handwriting is not the best, I prefer to take notes in long hand, thus indicating with certainty that I obtained the information directly from the party involved. Because they are talking about physical or psychological damage to their child, sensitivity to their pain is particularly important.

Symptoms

Young children cannot give an organized comprehensive description of the symptoms that developed from the trauma that lead to the lawsuit. Parents have the capacity to do so. As, always, it is important to continually watch for understatement or exaggeration of symptoms or outright malingering.

As in adult evaluations I ask the parents to first list any physical or psychological symptoms that they feel occurred as a direct result of the trauma that led to the lawsuit. Then I ask for a detailed description of each, when the symptoms were most severe, what external influences made the symptoms better or worse, and how the symptoms diminished or increased in intensity from inception to the chronological present. Then, when I interview the child or adolescent, I am in a position to ask sensitive questions, if compatible with the child's mental and emotional state, and gain a comprehensive knowledge of the symptom picture. In addition, there is often additional information on symptoms from physician and therapist records and psychological testing.

Developmental History

As explained in chapter 3 on adult evaluations, a developmental history provides detailed information about an individual's life course and allows the diagnostician to place current symptoms into a lifelong context and prepares you and the retaining attorney for attempts to maximize or minimize symptoms related to the causative events in the lawsuit. For a detailed description of developmental themes to be explored and questions to be asked about them, I refer you to *Child and Adult Development* (Colarusso, 1992, pp. 17–20).

Review of Records

Records serve the same function as they do in an adult evaluation. They provide additional information that cannot be provided by parent or child and often give an independent, objective picture of the child. School records are particularly useful in this regard because of the amount of time that children spend in school being observed, and sometimes evaluated psychologically, by teachers and psychological professionals. Pediatric records also provide a longitudinal, developmentally oriented view of the child, adding to an in depth understanding of the child and his or her symptoms and problems.

Psychological Testing

Psychological testing with very young children is not recommended by most psychologists. It can be useful in latency-aged children when there are questions about the diagnosis. However, most of the child cases that come into the civil litigation system involve some form of personal injury or sexual abuse. In such cases the primary psychological issue is whether or not the physical or psychological trauma resulted in the development of an Adjustment Disorder or Posttraumatic Stress Disorder. In my experience, psychological testing adds little to the knowledge needed to arrive at a diagnosis and confronts the child with an additional stressful situation. Psychological testing can be quite helpful in providing a more complete picture of adolescent psychopathology than can be obtained from clinical interviews alone.

Diagnosis

As with adults, diagnostic impressions and conclusions must be expressed in terms of the criteria in DSM-V. DSM-V clearly recognizes the developmental differences between a child and an adult and gives specific instructions about utilizing the Manual with children. I will use the example of Posttraumatic Stress Disorder to illustrate: "The following criteria apply to adults, adolescents, and children older than 6 years. For children 6 years and younger, see corresponding criteria below." Under section B the following note is found: "Note: In children, trauma-specific reenactment may occur in play" (DSM-V Desk Reference, p. 143, 144). The Manual then has an entire section on "Posttraumatic Stress Disorder for Children 6 Years and Younger."

Treatment

As with recommendations for adults, the length, frequency, and cost of psychotherapy should be described. With children and adolescents, the effect of trauma on subsequent developmental tasks and phases often leads to recommendations for additional courses on psychotherapy (and possibly medication) later in childhood or adolescence or in adulthood. For example, when the psychological trauma is severe, or when the effects of the trauma (such as facial scarring from dog bites or other physical injury) remain obvious for months or years. Recommendations for therapy for parents may be indicated because of their enormous influence on the child's development. Recommendations to the school about how to respond to the child's symptoms is also often indicated.

Prognosis

As with adult patients, since DSM-V eliminated Axes, I classify the prognosis in terms of poor, fair, good, or excellent.

AN EXAMPLE OF A CHILD PSYCHIATRIC FORENSIC EVALUATION AND REPORT

This is a case example of serious dog bites.

Calvin A Colarusso, M.D.
1020 Prospect St., Suite 145
La Jolla, California 92037

Date

Introduction

This is a report is a child psychiatric evaluation of William Rain of [address]; by Calvin A. Colarusso, M.D., Board Certified Adult and Child Psychiatrist practicing at the above address; at the request of [attorney's name and address].

The evaluation consisted of a diagnostic interview with Edwenna Rain, William's mother, of one hour and thirty-five minutes duration, in my office on [date] and two diagnostic interviews with William on [dates] in my office, each lasting fifty minutes.

In addition the following records were reviewed:

The complaint
Children's Hospital
Children's Services
Elementary School Records.
Abel Evans, M.D., Independent Medical Examination
Updated Children's Hospital records
Deposition of William Rain
Deposition of Mrs. Rain

Both William and his mother were told that I was serving as an expert witness in their lawsuit and that the usual doctor/patient relationship and confidentiality was not present. My records would be available to the attorneys for the plaintiff and defense.

Diagnostic Interview with Mrs. Rain

Identifying Information:

Mother was born in 1972 and worked as a secretary on a local college campus.

Her former husband, Robert, was 40 years of age. He was a government employee who had not remarried. He lived in another part of the country.

The parents divorced when William was age seven.

William Rain, born October 7, 1997, was a 13-year-old student at the local high school in his area. He had just begun the eighth grade.

William had a brother, Joe, age 10, who lived with William and his mother. The children visit father every summer. They had just returned from spending several weeks with father and his parents.

The Dog Bites:

Mother received a phone call at work. An officer told her that William had been attacked by dogs and was taken to Children's Hospital. Mrs. Rain knew immediately that it must have been two dogs that she had seen in the neighborhood.

When mother arrived at the hospital William was in the emergency room. A paramedic said the owner of the dogs was on the phone. He said, "My kid left the gate open and the dogs got out." He apologized. Mrs. Rain noted that his "kid" was 21 years old. They exchanged information about the owner's insurance. Mother had called a family friend on the way to the hospital. He got there first.

William was in "a zombie state." His eyes were glazed and he was not talking. Mother began to cry. The rabies shots that William received were very painful. Anesthesia and medicine were shot into his wounds as they were repaired. William screamed during the rabies shots. Mother held him and coached him through the procedures. All five shots were given at the same time. "He never said a word. He never talked."

William was released that evening. On the way home he was subdued and concerned about leaving his backpack at the hospital.

"I was so happy this morning." William was looking forward to getting to school and while on his way had told the dog owner that his new truck was nice.

Later that evening at home he screamed about his bottom. There was a bite on the inner side of one of the cheeks of his buttocks that the doctors had missed. Mother cried with her son.

The dogs were put down by the Humane Society.

Symptoms:

I asked mother to describe any physical and psychological consequences of the dog bites.

Physically, the bites healed but William is still disturbed by the scars on his body. He still complains of pain in his right upper arm and abdomen.

Emotionally, William is angry. He has fears and has had dreams and nightmares. He tries to protect his mother, brother, and friends from anything bad happening to them.

"He looks at himself in the mirror and cries. Will these marks ever go away? Why did they do this to me?"

William's right nipple was bitten. Yesterday he said, "I'll never have a good chest."

"He sits in the middle of the bathroom floor in a daze. He's thinking about it. He gets really angry." The intensity of his emotional response has not diminished since the bites occurred.

William is angry. "You don't understand it's my body. I have braces [on his teeth] and I'm small and now the dogs did this to me." Later

William apologizes to his mother for his outbursts that occur about once per week to the present. William was very even-tempered prior to the dog bites.

William attended therapy sessions (at a local clinic) after he was bitten. Mother lost her insurance and could not afford to continue the sessions.

William is very fearful of dogs, even small ones. He has stopped going outside on his own and doesn't want to go to his best friend's house. His friend has a puppy. When mother and he are walking in the neighborhood if William hears a dog barking he will run. He avoids the area where the owner of the dogs lived. "We don't even drive that way." William had no fear of dogs before he was bitten. The family had a Yorkie that they gave away because of his fears.

William is very protective of his mother and brother. Mother likes to walk in the morning. William is anxious the entire time mother is out of the house. He insists that she take her cell phone and calls her during the walk to make sure that she is OK. This symptom has diminished slightly recently.

In addition, William doesn't like to be left alone at home.

When friends come to the house to play with William he wants to stay inside. They often want to play outside. William worries that he will lose his friends because of this.

Shortly after he was bitten William had a nightmare that dogs came into the house and were chasing him.

None of these symptoms were present before William was bitten.

Developmental History:

The developmental history traces an individual's life from birth to the chronological present and allows the diagnostician to compare this person's experience against a large body of knowledge of normal and pathological development.

Ages 0–6: Mother had no problems during the pregnancy. William was born vaginally. He weighed 5 pounds and was 19 inches in length. William was bottle fed and weaned at approximately one year of age. Mother returned to work shortly after William's birth. During the day, from shortly after birth until age two, he was cared for by a woman in her home. Then William attended day care. There were no major separations from either parent during the early years of life. William did not wet the bed or soil his pants and has not had any major illnesses or operations.

Ages 6–12: The parents separated when William was seven years of age. William was upset by the separation. He tries to be the man of the house, checking doors and becoming protective of his younger brother. William misses the things that boys do with their fathers. At his thirteenth birthday party, when asked where his father was, he refused to tell his friends that his parents were divorced.

William made good grades in elementary school, had friends, and was well behaved.

Ages 12–present: William is very small for his age. His lack of size bothers him. Mother is considering the use of growth hormones. William has always been smaller than his peers. However, there are signs that puberty is not far away. He has a few hairs under his arms and in the pubic area.

First Diagnostic Interview with William

William Rain was a 13-year-old who had just begun the eighth grade at his local high school. He presented as a somewhat shy, early adolescent. William was cooperative throughout both interviews. After gathering identifying information about William and his family we discussed his activities and then discussed the dog bites.

Hobbies and Interests:

William likes to spend time with friends and play video games. He wrestled for his junior high school team, competing in the lightweight class. William reported having lots of friends. They "hang out" and go to the mall. When he and his brother visited his father they swam and went on a trip. William talks to his father frequently but doesn't see his dad very often during the school year.

When I asked William what was his favorite sport he told me about playing on the flag football team at school. Unfortunately, he wasn't able to play for a while after being bitten.

When asked for three wishes, a standard child psychiatric evaluation technique, William replied that he would like to have a nice family when he grew up. He also wished that his mother and father were together and that the accident (meaning the dog bites) didn't happen.

The Dog Bites:

Since William introduced the subject I asked him to tell me what happened. On the day of the attack he was walking alone to school. There were no people around. The dogs ran at him. He tried to be calm because he knew it was not good to act scared. "Bad boys" he said to the menacing dogs. Soon after when a car drove by William tried to jump on the hood. As he did one of the dogs bit his right arm. As he fell both dogs began to bite him. A second woman pulled up as the first woman tried to protect him. She fell on the sidewalk.

The women told William to run with them. The dogs had them pinned against a wall. Both women tried to protect William with their bodies. One of the dogs bit him repeatedly on his backside. When he fell the dogs continued biting. The owner of the dogs showed up and told the dogs to walk home. He offered to buy William a new pair of pants. One of the woman's young children watched the whole thing from the car. Then an ambulance came and took William to the hospital.

I asked William to tell me what he was thinking and feeling while he was being attacked.

"I thought I was going to die."

"I saw a chunk of my shirt in the dog's mouth. I thought it was my skin."

"I cried and screamed. I wanted my Mommy."

"They just kept biting at me."

"I lost all my strength. In the hospital I learned my right arm was torn open."

William remembered being in the ambulance for a long time. They checked his heart rate and wrapped his wounds. "I thought they were going to do surgery on me. They tried to calm me down." William did not realize that he was being transported to Children's Hospital.

At the hospital William was met by his mother's friend. Later mother arrived. Both were crying. The doctors sewed up his wounds. They couldn't give him much anesthesia because he was so small. "I had to tolerate the pain. I got rabies shots. They put six needles in my bottom at the same time." William was allowed to go home after six or seven hours.

Second Diagnostic Interview with William

After obtaining permission from his mother I looked at the scars on William's right and left arms, shoulder, chest, and abdomen. Many were large enough to be quite obvious. William was a bit embarrassed about showing me the scars but was able to do so without much difficulty.

Mental Status Examination:

William presented as a small male who looked several years younger than his stated age of nearly 14. There was no evidence of a growth spurt, acne, or other signs of adolescent development, even though both William and his mother reported the presence of pubic hair. Clothing covered most of the scars. William was well dressed, very polite, and cooperative. He had an excellent vocabulary. His affect ranged from calm to anxious. When he was describing the dog bite incident some pressure of speech was noted along with the anxiety. Thinking was logical and goal directed. There was no evidence of delusions or hallucinations. William was preoccupied with the memories of the attack, the trip to the hospital, and the scars. He was oriented as to time, person, and place.

The remainder of the session was spent considering the criteria for various psychiatric diagnoses. Those details will be described in the section on diagnosis.

Review of Records

The Complaint described the attack by the Rottweilers and listed three causes of action—negligence, premises liability, and breach of fiduciary duty.

The records from Children's Hospital confirm that William was treated on [date] for injuries that resulted from multiple, unprovoked, dog bites. Rabies injections were administered. William was seen for several follow-up visits.

Records from a medical group indicate treatment for the dog bites. Posttraumatic Stress Disorder symptoms included nightmares, anxiety, and emotional instability.

William was seen three times by a social worker at a local clinic. A diagnosis of Posttraumatic Stress Disorder was made. William's symptoms were rated in the moderate range. Mother discontinued the treatment because of financial reasons.

Diagnosis

The Diagnostic and Statistical Manual of Mental Health Disorder of the American Psychiatric Association, 4th Edition (in use at the time of the evaluation), is the only widely recognized diagnostic nomenclature in the field. When using it the diagnostician is asked to divide his diagnostic impressions into five subdivisions called Axes. Using that framework I made the following diagnosis.

Axis I: Posttraumatic Stress Disorder, Chronic (lasting more than three months), 309.81

a. "The person has been exposed to a traumatic event in which both of the following were present."

a. "the person experienced, witnessed, or was confronted with an event or events that involved actual or threatened death or serious injury, or a threat to the physical integrity of self or others."
b. "the person's response involved intense fear, helplessness, or horror." The attack by the two dogs clearly meets the criteria for this diagnostic requirement.

b. "The traumatic event is persistently re-experienced in one (or more) of the following ways:

a. "recurrent and intrusive distressing recollections of the event, including images, thoughts, or perceptions."
b. "recurrent distressing dreams of the event."

William recalls one vivid nightmare that occurred shortly after he was bitten. "I was in a car with my mother. The Rottweilers were chasing us." The nightmare caused William to wake up.

William also recalled three other dreams. In one dream he was in a car and saw a boy being attacked by two black dogs (the same color as the Rottweilers). In a second dream he was in prison and trying to escape from dogs that were chasing him. He jumped on a car (as the woman at the scene of the actual attack told him to do) and the dogs jumped up on the car and bit him. In a third dream he is walking up the hill where the actual incident occurred and two Rottweilers and two Pit Bulls are attacking him. The last dream occurred during the week before the evaluation. He mentioned that pit bulls are more vicious than Rottweiler.

c. "acting or feeling as if the traumatic event were recurring (included a sense reliving the experience, illusions, hallucinations, and dissociative flashback episodes . . .)"

William has flashbacks frequently, particularly in school. The teacher is talking and suddenly he is reexperiencing the dog bite. The last one occurred the day before our diagnostic session.

d. "intense psychological distress at exposure to internal or external cues that symbolize or resemble an aspect of the traumatic event."

"I'm feeling that right now."

e. "physiological reactivity on exposure to internal or external cues that symbolize or resemble an aspect of the traumatic event."

William's heart races and his palms sweat. This was occurring as we talked.

c. "Persistent avoidance of stimuli associated with the trauma and numbing of general responsiveness (not present before the trauma), as indicated by three (or more) of the following":

a. "efforts to avoid thoughts, feelings, or conversations associated with the trauma."

William makes constant efforts to avoid thinking about the dog bite incident because the thoughts are so painful. Most times he is unsuccessful.

He also tries to avoid talking to anyone about what happened.

b. "efforts to avoid activities, places, or people that arouse recollections of the trauma."

William avoids the spot where the incident occurred. During the last school year he refused to walk by the spot on his way to school. Mother had to drive him. This year when he does walk home from school with friends and his brother, never alone, they go "the long way" to avoid the site. William avoids going by the home of the dog owner and avoids dogs in general.

c. "inability to recall an important aspect of the trauma."

William feels that he has forgotten details of what happened when he was on the ground and on the way to the hospital.

d. "markedly diminished interest or participation in significant activities."

William doesn't like to go outside, particularly when alone. "I'm scared. People walk their dogs a lot."

e. "feeling of detachment or estrangement from others."

William has a strong sense that because of his scars he is not like other boys. He is also aware that his need to stay inside makes friendships difficult.

f. "restricted range of affect."

Fear permeates his life on a daily, nearly constant basis. He also has significantly lowered self-esteem.

g. "sense of a foreshortened future."

This is not present.

d. "Persistent symptoms of increased arousal (not present before the trauma) as indicated by two (or more) of the following:

a. "difficulty falling or staying asleep."

William has trouble falling asleep. He thinks about what happened and his scars. He also worries that he will have a nightmare.

b. "irritability or outbursts of anger."

Mother and William both describe him as being much more irritable and angry.

c. "difficulty concentrating."

William describes considerable difficulty in concentrating, particularly in school, because of intrusive thoughts.

d. "hypervigilance."

William is extremely hypervigilant. He is constantly on guard that something bad will happen to him or to his mother or brother.

e. "exaggerated startle response."

If William hears an unusual noise, particularly if it sounds like the noise of a chain around a dog's neck, he has a marked startle response. "Even in my own house."

The symptoms have been present for more than one month and "the disturbance causes significant distress or impairment in social, occupational, or other important areas of functioning."

Treatment

William is in need of a course of individual psychotherapy, two times per week for one to two years. An experienced child psychiatrist or child psychologist in [your city] would charge [fee per session].

During the late teen years, or in his early twenties, William would benefit from an additional course of individual psychotherapy, once per week for one year to help him deal with the psychological consequences of the scarring on relationships and sexuality.

Prognosis

The prognosis, if the course of treatment just described is instituted, is good.

Discussion

This young man had an extremely unfortunate experience of being severely bitten by two vicious dogs. He was unable to defend himself from their attack and suffered considerable injury despite the heroic efforts of two adult women to protect him

The experience has resulted in a significant psychiatric disorder, namely a Posttraumatic Stress Disorder, and some disfigurement. The scarring is particularly traumatic to a boy on the verge of becoming a teenager when thoughts and feelings about the changes that are taking place in the body are so prominent and sensitive.

From all indications William was an emotionally intact child prior to being attacked. There is no evidence of significant psychopathology in his history. Further, he appears to have been a calm, happy individual who had friends and was doing well in school. The parental divorce clearly had an effect on him that continues to the present but was not producing marked symptoms or difficulty in day-to-day functioning.

With treatment, the significant emotional consequences will be diminished to the point that they should not interfere with his adult development. The scarring may require surgery in the future to minimize the psychological consequences resulting from the disfigurement.

Calvin A. Colarusso, M.D.
Clinical Professor of Psychiatry
University of California at San Diego

In chapter 5 we'll delve into the experience of having your deposition taken, discuss how to prepare for the deposition, and how to manage the interaction with the opposing attorney who will be asking the questions. In addition, the case of Robert Rose will continue to be presented with excerpts from the actual deposition transcript.

FIVE

The Deposition Transcript

The Case of Robert Rose

Deposition—a proceeding in which a witness is questioned or "deposed" out of court, usually by an opposing party. The deposition is transcribed for use both in preparation for trial and at trial itself, where it may be entered in evidence in the witness's absence or used to impeach the witness if he or she testifies.

—Melton et al., 2007, p. 694

Subpoena—a legal writ requiring appearance in court to give testimony.

American Heritage Dictionary, 1969, p. 1283

The opposing side takes your deposition to discover your opinions and the bases for them. Depending on what you say and other aspects of the case, your testimony may push the case toward settlement or trial. If the case goes to trial your deposition testimony, taken down word for word by the court reporter, will be used to attempt to impeach your conclusions at trial.

The first indication you will get that your deposition will be taken in a particular case will most likely come from the retaining attorney who will notify you that the opposing side wishes to take your deposition. He will ask for your availability within a window of a week or two and will ask if you need anything further in order to prepare. On occasion, a subpoena from the opposing side may appear in your mailbox, often out of the blue, indicating that you need to appear on such and such a date at such and such a time. Neither the date nor the time is written in stone. Call the referring attorney and he will contact the opposing side and set a time, and place, of your convenience.

I prefer, if possible, to have the deposition in my office where I am most comfortable and in control of the environment. This happens more often than not. If either side insists on taking my deposition in either of their offices, agree without hesitation, since the setting does not change the basic nature of the deposition process.

I begin serious preparation for the deposition approximately two weeks before the actual date. Preparation consists of organizing my file and preparing a *summary sheet* (written in longhand) of the major details of the case and the names of the individuals involved including mental health professional and others. I summarize the information gathered during the review of records and the diagnostic interviews and my diagnosis, treatment recommendations, and prognosis. Last, but not least, in all probability you will be asked at the deposition details of billing information and payment received.

Then, usually on a daily basis, I spend a few minutes reviewing the summary sheet, essentially memorizing the important information about the case. In the day or two before the deposition, I spend an hour or so going over the complete chart for the last time. Here is an example of a summary sheet.

SUMMARY SHEET

The case being summarized is a wrongful death case following a terrible accident. Even though this case, and all the other cases in this book are part of the public record, changes have been made to insure confidentiality. The plaintiff-wife of the deceased was the subject of the evaluation.

Complaint: Road blocked by farm vehicle.
Police report: Husband at fault.

IME, 7/10/08, 90 minutes (2 years and 10 months after husband's death)
7/17/08, 70 minutes
Report: 7/20/08
Janet Jones, born, 2/10, 1974, age 38.
Husband—Thomas Jones, born 5/22/66. Died 9/26, 2006, five years ago.
Accident: Route 67, 9/26/06

Symptoms: Weight loss, sleep, energy, concentration, absent social life, drinking, lost religion, lonely.
Mental Status: Depressed
Developmental History: Intact family, no major issues, college grad.
Psych Testing Diagnoses: PTSD and Dysthymia
My diagnoses: Bereavement Depressive Disorder and Anxiety Disorder. Present from October 2006 to March 2008.
Therapy: Psychotherapy two times per week for one to two years with medication.
Prognosis: Good with Rx.

Update report, 22 months after first interview (6/25/11), seen 4/10/11, 55 minutes

Working, no psychotherapy. Symptoms: sleeping pills, antidepressants, no relationship, fear of commitment, depressed, drinking less, not remove husband's clothes. Mental status—not depressed. Dx.: some PTSD symptoms. Rx.: psychotherapy one to two times per week for one to two years. Antidepressants.

Update interview: April 21, 2013, 70 minutes. Met last two years ago. Moved. In a relationship for six months. Off antidepressants, occasional sleeping pills. Husband's picture out of bedroom when began having sex. Not plan marry. Many new friends. Active. Mental status: euthymic. Dx.: few symptoms of PTSD, not depressed.

Defense psychiatric expert: Saw 2011 Dx: Dysthymic Disorder; on Axis IV, death of husband Axis V, good. Not make DX of PTSD His RX: group, no individual psychotherapy. Continue meds for 12–24 months. Prognosis—quite good.

Billing: 6 statements, spent 15.64 hours. Paid $8,040.

Sometime during the week or so before the deposition arrange to meet with, or talk on the phone, with the retaining lawyer. Go over what you have reviewed and your diagnoses, treatment recommendations, and prognosis. Ask how much time you should set aside for the deposition. Most depositions last one to three hours but others may last six to eight hours or more. I suggest that you ask to begin either first thing in the morning or after lunch. If you agree to begin early in the morning, make it clear that you have a certain number of hours and will have to stop at such and such a time. This is particularly important if you have patients or other obligations scheduled in the afternoon. If your attorney expects the deposition to last several hours or more, clearing your calendar for either an entire afternoon or a day eliminates the possibility of rescheduling. You want to be able to focus all of your attention, without distraction, on the deposition interaction itself.

Ask your attorney how he sees the case in terms of the possibilities for settlement or trial. Also, ask him what he knows about the attorney who will be taking your deposition. What is his style? Is he straightforward, tricky, or hostile, etc. What will he try to get you to say? Although I'm using the masculine pronoun for both sexes the attorney taking your deposition is just as likely to be a woman as a man.

It is important to analyze the interaction between yourself and the referring attorney during the predeposition meeting. Brodsky (1991) talks about "the pull to associate." As referring lawyer and expert meet to discuss the deposition it is not unusual "to observe an exchange of cooperative actions and warm feelings." These affects may compromise impartiality if not recognized. "The expert may want the attorney to win in order that the expert's findings be validated in the judge's or jury's findings. These influences are sufficiently powerful that they may be the single greatest threat to expert integrity" (p. 9).

Relax the evening before the deposition and get a good night's sleep.

The deposition is a formal legal procedure. You are under oath and required to give the opposing attorney the opinions that you will give at trial. In addition to your attorney and the opposing attorney, a court reporter is always present. After swearing you in, she (it is usually a woman) will take down every word spoken by all parties.

In most instances the referring attorney will ask opposing counsel if he has a check to pay you for your time. Sometimes the check may already be written out for the cost of an hour or two. If the deposition runs longer, you may be asked to prepare a bill for the remaining time. In other instances the lawyer taking the deposition has the discretion to pay you for the entire time. Then, the deposition usually begins with a perusal of your chart to see how it is organized. Then often, but not always, referring to your curriculum vitae, the attorney will review your credentials. Either bring a CV with you to the deposition or ask the retaining attorney to e-mail one to the opposing side in advance of the deposition. The original records that were sent to you should be in the room. Most attorneys will want to see them to look for notes or other indications of how you used the records. I always summarize each record and have those notes in my file. I never write anything on the original records other than the date I review them and how much time I spent doing so.

Your chart should be organized in a manner of your choosing that allows you to quickly, without fumbling, get to any aspect of your data or opinions. I organize mine as follows: summary sheet, telephone communications (since you will always be asked when you were first contacted and who contacted you), handwritten notes from diagnostic interviews, my formal report or diagnostic summary, psychological testing report, notes taken while reviewing records, written communications, e-mails, and finally billing information. In regard to billing, have each month's bill available as well as payment stubs and totals of what you billed and have been paid.

Every lawyer has a different approach to taking a deposition. Some are pleasant and straight forward with their questions, others can be distant or sarcastic and hostile, challenging your responses with distain. Regardless of how the lawyer taking the deposition presents himself, your response is always pleasant, thoughtful, and serious. Be sure to limit your response to questions to what was asked. *Volunteer nothing more!* The longer you talk, and the further away you get from the subject matter of the question being asked, the more likely you are to provide the opposing side with information to attack you with at trial.

Although the opposing lawyer is free to examine your file, you are entitled to have it in front of you for reference throughout the deposition. Unlike being on the stand when it is best to have your chart practically memorized, in deposition you can take your time to find whatever information in your file you wish to locate.

The lawyer taking the deposition is interested in determining if you are appropriately credentialed, what is the basis for your opinions (in other words your interview notes, records reviewed, and psychological testing), and what are your diagnoses, treatment recommendations, and prognosis. Some lawyers simply elicit the information. Others challenge every aspect of your work, both trying to undermine your opinions and testing your capacity to stand cross-examination.

Toward the end of the deposition you will be asked some form of the following question: "Dr. Colarusso, I'm entitled to all of your opinions that you plan to present on the stand. Have you given me all of your expert opinions?" If you answer yes any additional opinions you have will be objected to on the stand since you indicated that you had given all of your opinions in the deposition. A better response is as follows: "I have given you all of my major opinions. I have withheld nothing from you. However, if I am asked to comment in ways that you have not asked, I may have other opinions." If not all the records on the case have been sent to you, for example, the opinions of the opposing expert, you may state that you have been asked to review these reports when they become available and that you will have opinions on your observations and conclusions at the time of trial.

At the end of the deposition ask that the total time of the deposition and the money due you be placed on the record in case there is any disagreement later on. Also, be sure that it is determined how your chart will be handled. Usually it is given to the court reporter who will copy it and attaches your file to the deposition transcript, returning your chart and the transcript to you. Always ask for the reporter to return the transcript with a stamped envelope addressed to the lawyer who will receive it. This saves you the time and trouble of taking the signed copy to the post office. If copies of your chart have not been made and the reporter is taking the original with her, state that at the moment this is the only existing copy of your file. In the thirty-plus years that I have had my deposition taken, the original chart was only lost once.

In a period of days, or weeks, the full transcript of the deposition will be sent to you for your scrutiny. Read it carefully, make any corrections that are apparent, sign the deposition on the last page in the space provided for your signature, and return it to whomever the lawyers have agreed should receive the signed copy. Try to make as few changes as possible. Multiple changes indicate that you were not clear and firm in your opinions and will be used against you at trial. You are entitled to charge for the time you spend reviewing the deposition transcript.

THE CASE OF ROBERT ROSE: EXCERPTS FROM THE DEPOSITION

Q Will you state your name for the record, please, Doctor?

A Calvin Anthony Colarusso, M.D.

Q Now, Doctor, my name is [name]. I've already announced and introduced myself, but I am here in connection with a lawsuit brought by Robert Rose against my clients, to take your deposition. You've had your deposition taken before, I would imagine, many times?

A Yes, I have.

Q I think you've provided something that indicated maybe two hundred times or more.

A That's correct.

Q All right. I am going to try to ask you direct questions. Can I—can I ask you to please try and answer only the question that I ask you. Take as much time as you need to answer that, but confine your answers to the questions that I directly ask you. Can you do that?

A I can.

Q Okay. And I am going to try to move fairly quickly. What is your specialty?

A I am an adult and child psychiatrist.

Q Have you ever been disqualified by any court in California or any other state, for any reason, for giving any parts of your expected testimony in a litigated case?

A No.

Keep your answers to questions as short as possible.

Q Have you ever had your testimony stricken, as far as you know, in any lawsuit?

A Not as far as I know.

Q Okay. What does your practice consist of now? Do you still treat patients?

A Yes, I do.

Q You also do a good bit of legal practice, correct?

A I do.

Q You've—I think I saw some records that indicated—well, how much—what percentage of your time spent working, at this point in your career, is in the legal aspect? I mean, as an expert witness in a lawsuit?

A It's probably about 60 percent seeing patients and about 40 percent legal.

Q Okay. Has that evolved—the ratio—over the years?

A Oh, yes. Until about five to seven years ago, I was seeing fifty to sixty patient hours a week and maybe ten hours a week of legal work.

Q Okay. So is it fair to say now you are becoming more of an expert witness, as far as your career path?

A No. What I can say is that now I am moving closer to retirement and so I am seeing fewer patients.

Q Are you still going to be doing the expert witness work when you retire?

A I don't know.

"I don't know" is a perfectly fine answer to questions. So is "I don't remember."

Q And when do you think you are going to quit seeing patients?

A Within a year or two.

Q Can I ask you how—what your age is? How long you've been practicing?

A Sure. It is on my deposition [*sic*]. I am seventy-five years of age. I've been practicing in San Diego since 1973.

Q Okay. Thank you. And about what percentage of your income is from the medical—excuse me—work as a paid expert witness doing evaluations in connection with lawsuits or claims?

A It is probably, at this point, fifty/fifty.

Q Okay. How much have you been paid—well, strike that. What were you asked to do in connection with the Rose lawsuit?

A I was asked to do a psychiatric evaluation on Mr. Rose and be prepared to come to conclusions based on my evaluation and to be prepared for deposition and trial.

Q Okay. And to be clear on this, you have not been a treating physician for Mr. Rose, have you—

A No, I have not.

Q You've never been asked to treat Mr. Rose?

A I was not asked to treat Mr. Rose, and if I had been asked, I would have said no, since I don't mix the two.

Q Okay. That would have been my question. Do you feel it would be a conflict if you were actually treating the patient and acting as an expert witness in doing an evaluation for purposes of trial?

A Well, if I was first asked to serve as an expert witness and then treated, I would see that as a conflict. There have been situations where I've been treating people, and I was then asked to serve as an expert witness. That's different.

Q Now, why is there a conflict in those circumstances, in your mind?

A Because I don't think you can adequately perform both functions. As a therapist, you need to have confidentiality, you need to have a clean *history* of no involvement with the *patient* in the past. When you serve as an expert witness, there is no confidentiality, and quite easily the two roles can be confused, to the detriment of the patient.

Q And so having—having met with him without confidentiality, you can never go back and treat him in a confidential physician/patient relationship?

A That's my opinion.

Q Okay. And how much have you charged Mr. [plaintiff attorney] for your services as an expert witness in this case so far?

A I am looking through my chart here to find that.

Feel free to refer to your chart anytime that you choose.

Q Being an expert, you are not being paid on any sort of letter of protection, right? Your fees are being paid by the attorney?

A Yes, they are.

Q And not contingent on the results of the lawsuit?

A No, not contingent on the results of the lawsuit at all. I am paid for my time and my expertise

Q Okay.

A In December, I billed Attorney [name] $2,433. In February, I billed him $1,916. And I got an original retainer of $3,000. I have not rendered a bill for this month. I also believe that I did some work in September, but I could not find that bill.

Q What have you done this month? Just preparing for the depo?

A This month, mainly preparing for the depo and listening to some videotapes.

Q What videotapes did you listen to?

A I listened to the videotapes that were taken by Mr. [name] of the family members; the wife and children.

Q Do you have the copies?

A Yes, I do.

Q Since you rendered your report have you gotten any additional records—treatment records, from any other providers for—from any of his treaters, for Mr. Rose?

A Yes. From Dr. [name], who is the psychologist who was treating him. I got a copy of his summary up through September. And then just recently, I got an update from September to November.

Q Is that from Dr. [name]?

A From Dr. [name], yes.

Q Anybody else's records you reviewed?

A No.

Q No, I mean since the ones—other than the ones you had reviewed for your report.

A No, I understood you.

Q And is Dr. [name] a treater, in your mind?

A Dr. [name] is a treater.

Q Well, now, who retained Dr. [name] to—strike that. Did you hire Dr. [name] to perform a battery of tests on Mr. Rose in connection with your psychiatric IME examination of him?

A I didn't hire him. He's an independent contractor. I did ask him to do a psychiatric evaluation on Mr. Rose and send the report to me, which he did.

Q Well, was Dr. [name] treating Mr. Rose at the time you asked him to do a psych evaluation?

A No.

Q So was Dr. [name] paid by you?

PLAINTIFF ATTORNEY: No.

BY DEFENSE ATTORNEY:

Q To do a psych—a battery of tests in—in connection with your paid examination and evaluation?

PLAINTIFF ATTORNEY: Objection. Misstates his testimony.

THE WITNESS: He was not paid by me.

BY DEFENSE ATTORNEY:

Q Who was he paid by?

A I assume he was paid by Mr. [name].

Q Well, how—did Mr. [name] determine to hire Dr. [name] to do the testing or did you?

A I made the determination that I needed psychological testing done, and made the decision to use Dr. [name].

Q Okay. And did you ask Mr. [plaintiff attorney] to pay Dr. [name] to do that testing for you?

A Yes.

These are basic questions. I'm thinking that either the defense attorney was not well prepared for the deposition or he has something up his sleeve.

Q And at that point, how did Dr. [name]—if you know, how did Dr. [name] then come to be a treating—or providing therapy—psychotherapy for Mr. Rose?

A After my evaluation, Mr. Rose needed a therapist. He apparently enjoyed his contact with Dr. [name] and worked with him.

Q Okay. So Dr. [name] played some part in your initial independent evaluation as an expert witness to begin with; is that right?

A Yes.

Q And then subsequently became a treating psychologist?

A That's correct.

Q Are you saying that Dr. [name] had nothing to do with the actual neuropsychological or psychiatric testing, that battery of testing that you ordered?

PLAINTIFF ATTORNEY: Objection; misstates his testimony.

THE WITNESS: No, Dr. [name] did the testing.

BY DEFENSE ATTORNEY: Okay. Then I misunderstood what you said just a minute ago. So he did the testing, but at the time that was before he was a treater. He was doing the testing in connection with your order or request in connection with your retention as an expert witness?

A That is true.

Q All right. By the way, you provided a CV, I think, or plaintiff attorney did, a list of—a partial list of attorneys that—I guess it's in your CV—that you did work for in the last year?

A Yes, that's correct.

PLAINTIFF ATTONEY: Objection; argumentative.

BY DEFENSE ATTORNEY:

Q I'll withdraw that. It's not a question. And you,—by the way, I think you tell us in your CV that you've testified—no—that you've been a professional expert witness in more than one thousand civil cases in your career.

PLAINTIFF ATTORNEY: Objection; argumentative.

BY DEFENSE ATTORNEY:

Q Is that correct?

A Yes, it is

Q And so would you consider yourself a highly skilled, qualified, professional expert witness?

A I consider myself to be highly skilled and qualified.

Q And you know how litigation works, correct?

A I am not sure what you mean by that.

Feel free to ask for clarification if you do not understand a question.

Q Do you know how litigation works, as far as evaluations and elements of proof for trial?

A I know what I do. I am not a lawyer. Beyond that, what happens is up to the lawyers, not me.

Q You've been to trial over one hundred times, correct?

A Yes.

Q Okay. Have you worked ever for [plaintiff attorney] or any of his partners? I am not sure he has partners actually, but anybody in his firm before?

A I've worked with [plaintiff attorney] before.

Q How many times?

A Over twenty years, probably somewhere between five and ten cases.

Q Okay. Have you gotten good results for him—Do you get good results for the attorneys you work for?

PLAINTIFF ATTORNEY: Objection; argumentative, calls for speculation.

Clearly trying to trick me into saying I'm a hired gun. The plaintiff attorney, who is very experienced, objects immediately.

THE WITNESS: It is not my job to get good results for the attorney. It is my job to do a thorough evaluation.

BY DEFENSE ATTORNEY: Well, would you agree with me that if your testimony helps or—helps or potentially results in a big number verdict for plaintiff, that generally speaking, the plaintiff's attorneys are happy with the work you did for them?

PLAINTIFF ATTORNEY: Objection; calls for speculation, lacks foundation. Argumentative.

THE WITNESS: No, I wouldn't agree with you, and I usually don't know that is the result of the case.

The opposing attorney asking if you agree with him is another common attempt to diminish your independence.

BY DEFENSE ATTORNEY:

Q The attorney never calls you and says, "Hey, we got a big number in this case; thanks for your help?"

A No, they don't.

Q Okay. Do you agree with me that it's logical, though, that if you work on a case that results in a big verdict for plaintiff, and you are an expert for that plaintiff, that it is likely to help with your future business prospects as a witness?

A No, I wouldn't agree with you on that. I think that I am hired by attorneys because I do a thorough, competent, and fair job.

Q Okay. And I am not questioning that, but are you aware of an incentive for an attorney that acts as an attorney for the plaintiff to make a contingency fee based on how big a recovery his client gets?

PLAINTIFF ATTORNEY: Objection; argumentative, lacks foundation, calls for speculation. Irrelevant.

BY DEFENSE ATTORNEY:

Q Are you aware of plaintiff's attorneys being paid a percentage of the result they get for their clients in a verdict?

A Yes. I am aware of that.

Q And—but you feel—is it fair to say—and tell me if I am wrong. Are you telling the jury that you don't feel that the plaintiffs' attorneys are more pleased with you and more likely to hire you again if you participate in a trial as an expert witness and the result is a big verdict?

PLAINTIFF ATTORNEY: Objection; calls for speculation, lacks foundation, argumentative.

He's still bating me. I deflect the question.

THE WITNESS: You'd have to ask the attorneys that question, not me.

BY DEFENSE ATTORNEY:

Q So as you sit here today, you are telling the jury you don't have any idea whether that would motivate—that would be a motivational factor or a good marketing ploy for you with attorneys for plaintiffs?

PLAINTIFF ATTORNEY: Objection; argumentative, lacks foundation, calls for speculation.

THE WITNESS: I don't use marketing ploys.

BY DEFENSE ATTORNEY:

Q By the way, modern psychiatry—let me ask you this. Is psychiatry becoming more a practice of not prescribing medications for the body as opposed to therapy and psychoanalysis of the mind?

A I would say that both exist and both are prominent in the field.

Q Do you agree with me that a lot of psychiatrists don't do psychotherapy or psychoanalysis?

Again attempting to get me into a discussion that is not relevant to my testimony as an expert in this case.

A You will have to talk to them about that.

Q Well, what's your knowledge of the field, or do most psychologists actually do therapy or psychoanalysis on patients?

A I told you that my analysis of the field is: that psychiatrists both prescribe medication and do psychotherapy.

Q You didn't do any psychotherapy for this patient, correct?

A True.

Q Do you do psychotherapy/psychoanalysis for patients that you treat?

A Yes.

Q What percentage of the patients that you treat actually come to you for any therapy or psychoanalysis?

A Well, all the patients who come to me come for some form of therapy.

Q But are they generally also seen by a therapist or a psychologist in that field?

A The patient—

Q —from your treatment?

A No. The patients who come to see me, I treat them.

Q Okay. So if they need psychotherapy, you provide that?

A Yes.

Q Now, let's talk about what you've done. You reviewed some records, I believe. And I think you note that in your report, correct?

A Yes, I did.

Q And other than—other than what I've asked you about and you've told me about, that you've reviewed since then, the records that you've reviewed in connection with your evaluation of Robert Rose in this lawsuit were the ones that you listed in your report?

A I have a complete list here. Would you like me to read it to you? That way we'll be sure you got everything.

Q What I think I'd like to do, just to save time—here's what we'll do. Let me start marking. Let me mark your entire chart—which would include all the records you've reviewed, correct?

A Yes.

Q Let me just mark that as a composite Exhibit 1.

(Exhibit 1 was marked for identification.)

The identification of the various exhibits to the deposition was then identified. This activity covered a number of pages of the deposition. This necessary process, that doesn't offer any further understanding of the deposition process, is not presented here.

Q I don't know what you'd call it—an interview? You actually examined or met with Mr. Rose for a couple of hours on [the date]?

A No. I met with him for the first time on [date] for two hours and thirty-five minutes.

Q Okay. Is that the only time you've ever met with Mr. Rose?

A No, it's not.

Q When did you meet with him again?

A I had a follow-up interview with him on [date] for one hour.

Q Okay. And where are your notes from that follow-up interview?

A They are all in the file in front of me that was marked No. 1.

Q Okay. But they are not in—I guess they won't be in the records that I received from—well, they wouldn't be in the records that I received before September, obviously? September of this year, correct?

A I don't know what you are talking about there.

Q All right. What I am talking about is I don't have your entire set of records, but okay. Let me just go through here. So you met with him, and this was just an interview. There was no physical examination of any type, even though you are a medical doctor, correct?

A I am a medical doctor, but I am a psychiatrist, and there has been no physical examination of Mr. Rose on my part at any time.

Q Okay. As a psychiatrist, is that the field with which you plan to testify as an expert in this field, limited to psychiatry?

A Yes.

Q You will not be testifying as to any physiological injuries, as to diagnoses or prognosis for any physiological injury, such as nerve injuries, broken bones, erectile dysfunction, urological issues; is that fair to say?

A I will be talking about the consequences of those injuries, but not about the injuries themselves.

Q Will you defer to the urologist as to the diagnoses of the specific physiological injuries claimed?

A Yes.

Q And same as to the neurologist or orthopedist, as to physiological injuries claimed to the lumbosacral spine or to the nerves—nerve roots exiting the spine, to the pelvis—those injuries?

I'm not qualified to give an expert opinion on any aspect of physical injuries or diagnoses. To do so would result in appropriate questions about my expertise and credentials to do so. Give opinions only on what you know as an expert in your field based on your evaluation of the individual.

A Correct. As long as you understand that those injuries are part and parcel of the reasons why I made the psychiatric diagnoses that I did.

Q I am with you, Doctor. Thank you. Now, so in your meeting, this was just conversation between the two of you?

A I wouldn't call it just conversation. I was doing an update, diagnostic evaluation, yes.

Q Right. But it was verbal communication?

A Correct.

Q All right. You didn't have him complete any forms or testing that day—either of those days you met with him?

A I don't do psychological testing. I'm not a psychologist. I did not ask him to complete any forms. All the information I took by myself.

Some psychiatrists give objective, paper and pencil tests that are scored by a computer. I do not. I'm not trained as a psychologist. If I think that psychological testing is indicated, I ask a qualified, forensic psychologist to do a full battery of tests.

Q Do you consider this psychoanalysis that you did with this patient, or was it merely an in-depth consultation and inquiry to him as to his current state?

A I don't think you have a very good understanding of what psychoanalysis is. It is a form of treatment. I did a diagnostic evaluation.

Q Okay. You've helped me on that. Thank you. Now, you didn't do any hypnosis, anything like that?

A I did not.

Q Did you have—is this like the classic—he's lying down on a reclining furniture and you are talking and asking questions and taking notes?

A Are you asking is that what I did?

Q Yes.

A No. He sat in a chair and I sat behind a desk and took notes.

Q Did you record any of your conversation with this gentleman?

A No audio recording or video recording, no, just my notes.

Q And the plaintiff's attorney did not have a videographer there to record your expert examination of his client?

A He did not.

Q Okay. By the way, would that generally—is that something you have any problem with, to have a videographer there when you are trying to find out from an individual his psychiatric issues?

A Yes, I would have a problem with that, because that may make the individual uncomfortable and less likely to talk openly with me. However, if a video record was ordered by a court, so be it.

Q Right. You wouldn't have any choice then, right?

A Correct.

Q Other than to say, no, I won't do it?

A Well, I guess I would have that choice, yes.

Q Right. But you would consider that intrusive, as far as your examination? Your evaluation, I should say?

A I would prefer not to have it that way.

Q Okay. And no one else was present during that—the conversations with Mr. Rose?

A No one else was present.

Q He gave you some—he gave you some detailed history as to the accident itself, correct?

A Yes, he did.

Q Now, did he—I am looking at your notes. Is the information that you include, of the accident, in your notes essentially a summation of what you got—what you understood directly from Mr. Rose as to what happened?

A When you say "my notes," I am not quite sure what you are referring to.

Q Oh, I'm sorry. I don't mean notes. Actually, I am talking about your report. You corrected me. You are right. I am talking about the first page of your report.

A Yes, I have that in front of me.

Q Okay. Where you are talking about the accident there, that's information you got from Mr. Rose?

A All of the information in "The Diagnostic Interview" is information that I got from Mr. Rose.

Q Okay. So he told you that he saw the car driven by the valet get out and inspect the damage, then get back in and put the car in reverse and run into him?

A That's what he told me.

Q Okay. Now, did you look at the surveillance? Do you know if that is accurate, what he told you?

A I did not look at the surveillance.

Q Okay. No problem. Now, you note in your report that Mr. Rose told you he apparently had fears for his life. He was in great fear for his life at the time of the collision.

A Yes. That's on the top of page two.

Q But I think—I am not sure exactly where, but okay. And, now, is it your understanding that he fairly shortly afterward probably became aware that his life was—that he didn't have life threatening injuries, when he got to the hospital?

A No. I don't think he felt that when he got to the hospital. I think that he was very uncertain for some time as to whether he was going to live or die, and he was also very concerned about how severely injured he was.

Q Right. But I am talking about life-threatening injuries. So it is your understanding or your belief that he was—even after he had gotten to the emergency room, he was, for some time, still in fear of a life-threatening injury?

A Yes.

Q Okay. Now, you understand that he didn't have life-threatening injuries, do you not? As a medical doctor?

A I think that life-threatening injuries, in the physical sense, you are going to have to ask some of the—some of the experts. Psychologically, he definitely felt that he had life-threatening injuries.

Q Well, you know that he had fractures of the pelvis and of his sacrum and an L5 fracture, correct?

A Yes.

Q Are you aware he did not have any sort of paralysis, like paraplegia?

A He did not have paraplegia.

Q Okay. Are you aware of anything that was life threatening about the fractures that he sustained?

He's clearly attempting to get me to provide him with an expert opinion about Mr. Rose's physical injuries.

A Well, as I told you, in regard to the physical aspects of that, you'll have to ask the other experts. Psychologically, this man clearly felt his life in danger.

Q Well, as a medical doctor, do you have the expertise to tell me whether or not the injuries were life-threatening? The fractures he suffered?

A We went through that before when you asked me if I was going to have any expert opinions in those areas, and I'm not.

Q Okay. Fair enough. Now, Mr. Rose told you that he has been told by doctors it might take him up to two years to recover from the injury?

A Yes, I remember that.

Q It's been about a year and a half so far now, hasn't it?

A Excuse me?

Q It has been about a year and a half so far now, since the accident?

A Yes. Just about

Q Okay. Oh, with regard to "Physical Symptoms—" I see—I am looking at your report here. I believe you indicated that he told you his entire right leg was numb. Is that what he told you?

PLAINTIFF ATTORNEY: Vague as to time.

THE WITNESS: He said that by the end of the day, he had no feeling in his right leg.

BY DEFENSE ATTORNEY:

Q No. I am looking at the beginning, under "Physical Symptoms." And you say, "His right leg below the knee is numb."

A Yes.

Q Okay. So below the knee?

A Yes.

Q Did he tell you that his right leg was entirely numb below the knee?

A I don't remember the word, "entirely."

Q You didn't qualify. You said that—you indicated his right leg below the knee is numb.

A That's what he told me.

Q What does that mean? So did you get the last question? What does that mean, his right leg below the knee is numb?

A Meaning that he didn't have full feeling in it.

Q So you don't intend that to mean it was completely numb? You are saying that it is less than completely numb? That it had some numbness?

A I don't know the answer to that.

Q Okay. Now—by the way, do you know whether or not the pelvis—his pelvic fractures have healed, or is that an area you are not going to opine on?

A It is not an area that I am going to opine on.

Q Okay. Thank you. Now, you are aware that he claims erectile dysfunction as a result of this accident, correct?

A Yes.

Q Now, would you agree with me that there is often a psychological aspect of—that's a component of any erectile dysfunction, even on occasions where there is an organic component?

Always clarify whether the attorney is asking you to make a general comment or one specific to the individual that you have evaluated

A That's too general for me to answer. If you want to talk in general and not about Mr. Rose, I can tell you that there certainly can be psychological aspects of erectile dysfunction, even when there are physical problems.

Q Would you agree that psychological aspects may tend to magnify any actual physiological problems of erectile dysfunction?

PLAINTIFF ATTORNEY: Objection; overly broad, lacks foundation, calls for speculation.

THE WITNESS: We are talking in general now?

BY DEFENSE ATTORNEY:

Q In general.

A That's possible.

Q It is possible? You think it is possible, but you don't agree that it is probably true?

A You are speaking in a very, very general way, and without specifics, it is hard for me to say more than that.

Q Okay. As to Mr. Rose, is there—I know you are deferring to the urologist as to the diagnosis of any physiological problem creating erectile dysfunction, correct?

A Yes.

Q Is there a psychological component that may be also affecting his ability to produce a spontaneous erection?

A Not that I am aware of.

Q So you feel that even though he has suffered trauma to his genitals in the collision, and has been treated and tested, I guess, or evaluated as to whether or not there was a physiological problem, that you don't feel at this time that there is any psychological component that needs to be considered?

PLAINTIFF ATTORNEY: That is argumentative and misstates his prior testimony.

THE WITNESS: Not in terms of his physical capability to get an erection. My understanding

BY DEFENSE ATTORNEY:

Q I am not talking about—I am talking about his functional ability to get an erection. Whether he can get it or not. Would you agree with me that there may be psychological factors that play into his claimed inability to get an erection when he wants to have sex with his wife?

A No, I do not agree with you. And you cut me off— What I was trying to say was I have—my information from the urologist is he cannot get spontaneous erections because of physical reasons, and that that is now a permanent condition. I, therefore, based also on the fact that he never had any problems getting an erection before the accident, I see no significant psychological factor here. What is very psychological is the way he feels about himself and the way in which his manhood has been affected because of the inability to get an erection.

Q Okay. I want to get to those issues. But now is it your experience in your practice that men are very psychologically sensitive with regard to erectile function, such that a man may have difficulty, as he ages, in getting an erection once or twice, and that may then create the basis for a psychological buildup of concern and anxiety and also inhibit his ability to obtain an erection?

A. That's possible.

Q You are saying that's possible. Is that not—is that not, in your mind, the true state of things?

He is persistent. I understand his aim so my response is always the same.

PLAINTIFF ATTORNEY: Objection; argumentative as phrased.

THE WITNESS: You'd have to give me specifics and we'd have to talk about specific people and specific circumstances before I could answer that any more.

BY DEFENSE ATTORNEY:

Q Okay. Let me just be clear. So as we sit here; today, without specifics, you—you will not agree with me—you do not agree with me that generally there is a psychological component to an inability—or at least to a continuing inability to get an erection in a man of Mr. Rose's age?

PLAINTIFF ATTORNEY: Objection; argumentative, vague.

THE WITNESS: Well, now you are not talking about Mr. Rose; you are talking generally. And as I said, without talking about a specific individual, all I can say is that that is possible.

BY DEFENSE ATTORNEY:

Q Okay. Now, psychological symptoms. You have a section in there, Mr. Rose told you that he has a fear of being hit again, or of this accident—type of accident happening again?

A Where are you referring to, there on the list?

Q I don't know where in the report, but it is in your report under "Psychological Symptoms," I believe.

A Yeah, well, I have that right in front of me, but I don't specifically see that on this list; that's why I am asking you where you are referring to.

Q Well, I am going through the list, too, but, I mean, it's your report here. It says—well, what's your recollection? I mean, you treated him and evaluated him. Does he have a fear of a recurrence of this type of accident? Is that one of the fears that he's suffering from that forms the basis of your diagnosis?

PLAINTIFF ATTORNEY: Objection; misstates his testimony.

THE WITNESS: I did not treat him. I evaluated him. I think that there is a fear that he might be hit again.

BY DEFENSE ATTORNEY:

Q Is that a rational fear, in your mind?

A That is a fairly typical response to a trauma like this, and it is part and parcel of a posttraumatic stress disorder response.

Q And a posttraumatic stress disorder response generally mitigates or lessens over time, in your experience with this diagnosis of the patient?

PLAINTIFF ATTORNEY: Objection; overly broad.

THE WITNESS: Are you talking now about Mr. Rose or are you talking in general?

BY DEFENSE ATTORNEY:

Q No, I am talking about in general. Does posttraumatic stress disorder generally lessen the symptoms of that condition? Generally lessen over time?

A Sometimes, yes.

Q Usually?

A No. I can't say usually. It depends on the circumstance and the severity of the trauma.

Q Exactly. It would depend on—now, for instance, a combat victim who's in battle and is in constant fear of his or her life and witnesses horrible mutilation and death of comrades, that level of severity, with that type situation—have you ever treated a combat—former combat soldiers?

A Yes, I have.

Q Have you diagnosed posttraumatic stress disorder in patients that have been through circumstances like that?

A Yes, I did.

Q Now, would you consider that to be a very severe stressor?

A I would.

Q You would not tell the jury that the incident that Mr. Rose suffered is, in degree of trauma and stress, comparable to, as I said, a combat soldier that has been living for a long period of time in fear for his life in combat and has seen death and mutilations?

PLAINTIFF ATTORNEY: Objection; incomplete hypothetical, argumentative, speculation.

BY DEFENSE ATTORNEY:

Q Or would you? Would you consider those to be roughly comparable levels of trauma and stress?

A It is a different kind of trauma. This is a profound trauma because of the effect that it's had on his physical and psychological well-being. I think it is as severe as what I've seen in Vietnam veterans who have been through combat.

Q So you find, let's just be clear on the record. Do you find Mr. Rose's trauma that you evaluated him for, as an expert witness, to be as severe as the trauma of Vietnam vets that you've evaluated and treated, who lived for months in combat situations, under threat, obviously, of injury or death, and who witnessed carnage and were injured themselves, wounded themselves?

A I just answered that question very directly.

Q Well, I am asking you to have the question in a way that—the way that I would like to ask it. Would you please answer that question?

PLAINTIFF ATTORNEY. No. It is—objection; asked and answered. Move on, Counsel.

BY DEFENSE ATTORNEY:

Q Answer the question, please.

PLAINTIFF ATTORNEY: No, he's not going to repeat his answer. You can restate—

DEFENSE ATTORNEY: I asked him a different question. Are you instructing him not to answer the question?

PLAINTIFF ATTORNEY: No. No. I am asking you to be ethical and honest and listen to the answers and restate a question. If you've got a different question, move on.

DEFENSE ATTORNEY: Are you instructing him not to answer the question?

PLAINTIFF ATTORNEY: No. I am saying, for the record, it's been asked and answered.

BY DEFENSE ATTYORNEY:

Q Okay. Answer the question, please, if you can.

A Okay. I'll be glad to answer the question, and I can. What I said was that there are two different kinds of trauma. And the trauma that the Vietnam veterans—the Vietnam combat individuals experienced was obviously a profound trauma. I am saying that the trauma that Mr. Rose experienced is also profound but in a different way, because of the effect that has had on his physical and psychological mentality and ability to function in all kinds of ways. So, in other words, he lives with the consequences of his injury every single minute of every single day. And in that way, his trauma is every bit as profound as the psychological consequences that the Vietnam veterans live with.

Q Do most of the Vietnam veterans you've treated not also live with the trauma every day?

A They do.

Q Okay. I think I understand what you are telling me to mean that for Mr. Rose, this trauma, where he was hit by a car, has equal or comparable effects—psychological effects—as traumas to patients you've seen who have been in Vietnam combat situations?

A Comparable.

Q Comparable. Okay. But to the person—you are not saying that the event that Mr. Rose went through, the one isolated event, is comparable, in general, to the average person—to being a year in combat and seeing carnage and being injured and wounded in combat?

PLAINTIFF ATTORNEY: Objection; calls for speculation, lacks foundation, incomplete hypothetical.

BY DEFENSE ATTORNEY:

Q Are you—are you competent to answer that question, Doctor?

A I can answer the question. I—I've already answered it twice. But what I said was that the consequences of the injuries that Mr. Rose sustained in that single event have had just as profound and severe effects—if not more so, because they are physical as well as psychological as what I've seen in Vietnam veterans.

Q You are skirting the question. Or are you hearing? My question is yes or no, is it comparable trauma? I am not talking about the consequences to this individual. Do you believe that the trauma that Mr. Rose suffered when a car hit him is comparable to those suffered by Vietnam veterans who were, for 365 days or more, in combat, under the threat of death, and were wounded in combat?

I have the sense that he is getting frustrated because I am not allowing him to bully me.

PLAINTIFF ATTORNEY: Objection; argumentative, incomplete hypothetical, asked and answered.

THE WITNESS: I have nothing else to add to that.

BY DEFENSE ATTORNEY:

Q You can't give me an answer whether it is or is not comparable, yes or no?

You do not need to respond to a demand for a yes or no answer.

A I've given you an answer three times.

Q No, you've answered as to Mr. Rose, but that's fine. Leave it at that. Now, Mr. Rose told you that he was working at the time you saw him, correct?

A That he was working at the time I saw him, yes.

Q All right. And he was working when you filled out your report, was he not?

A Yes.

Q And, in fact, he was working for several months more before he finally quit the job, correct?

A He didn't quit the job. He couldn't perform the job.

Q Well, you are assuming he couldn't perform the job. He stopped going to work, correct?

A He did stop going to work.

Q All right. And up until that time, he had worked approximately seven months at that job?

A Something like that, yeah.

Q In fact, you don't make any note in your report anywhere, do you, that Mr. Rose told you that he had any concerns about being unable to continue to perform his job, OK?

A Well, he was having difficulty at work because he had a drive to get there, but he was doing it.

Q Sir, do you note anywhere in your report that he was—he felt he was unable to continue working at his job when you saw him?

THE WITNESS: As I said, he did not say that he could not perform his job. He did say the hours were long and stressful, so yes, he was having difficulty performing his job.

BY DEFENSE ATTORNEY:

Q And you don't note in your report any information from Mr. Rose that he could not continue his job

A Not that I recall.

Q —is that accurate?

A Not that I recall.

Q Well, you can look at your report if you are not sure.

A Well, I'll be glad to look at my report if you'd like me to.

Q I just want to make sure I get your testimony, but if you don't need to . . .

A I'll look.

Q You don't remember?

A I'll look. I gave you an answer. You weren't satisfied with it. I see no evidence of that in the report.

Q Okay. And he gave you no indication of any intention to stop working at that position at that time you saw him for your evaluation?

A No.

Q He very much wanted to continue working. In fact, he loved his job, didn't he?

A He did.

Q He was pretty much dying to get back to work when he was out of work, before he went back?

A He wanted to work.

Q And did he tell you he was fairly thrilled to be back at work?

A I don't remember those words, but I know he was anxious to get back to work.

Q Okay. And was it true that when you talked to him during your evaluation, as reflected in your report, his main concerns were not as to work but that he had no time after work for any social life? He notes—I think he notes, "All I do is work and come home. I don't have a life beyond that. I want to golf with my guy friends. I don't want people to feel sorry for me." Is that what you indicated in your report on page three, under "Psychological Symptoms"?

A On page three? Would you repeat that, what you are reading from, so I can look at it?

Q "Psychological Symptoms," about—well, about halfway down the page. It starts out, "All I do is work and come home. I don't have a life beyond that. I want to golf with my guy friends. I don't want people to feel sorry for me." Is that what he told you?

A Yes, he did.

Q Did it appear to you that his main concern was that he was not able, with the schedule of working and whatever strain that caused—he was unable to have any social life or any fun at home?

A No, that's not what he was saying. What he was saying was he couldn't do those other things because of his physical injuries and pain, and that he was no longer able to go golfing with his friends or to be as social. That all he could manage was to go to work and come home.

Q In that "Physical Symptoms" section—"Psychological Symptoms" section, does he ever complain to you that he has problems that prevent him from doing his work, that you note in that "Psychological Symptoms" area?

A Not in that "Psychological Symptoms" area. We covered that before, though.

Q Do you make any note that he was unable to perform the work or felt he might be unable to or was having problems at work?

A Not there, no.

Q Okay. Now, how many hours—or strike that. Do you know how many hours the gentleman was working before his accident, at that job? How many hours, how many days a week? Did you talk to him about that?

A I know it was a lot. I don't know precisely how many hours or how many days a week.

Q Does twelve to fourteen hours a day, five days a week sound about right, according to what you recall?

A I don't recall.

Q That's what his testimony was. I am going to ask you to assume I am being honest and accurate in telling you that he has testified that he worked twelve to fourteen hours a day at that job, and that he also drove an hour each way. Okay? Assuming that's true—

PLAINTIFF ATTORNEY: Vague as to time.

BY DEFENSE ATTORNEY:

Q And I am talking about his job as general manager before the accident. Assuming that it's true, that would equate to between fourteen and sixteen hours per day between driving and being at work, and which he would have been away from his home. Does my math sound right—sound right?

A It does.

Q Okay. That would only leave him, then, somewhere between eight and ten hours a day for everything else, including family time, meals at home, his kids, his wife, his intimate relationship, and sleeping; is that right?

A That sounds right.

Q Now, that type of a life, a work life, would be pretty stressful on anybody, wouldn't it?

PLAINTIFF ATTORNEY: Objection; overly broad.

THE WITNESS: Again, you are talking generally.

A It would depend on the person.

BY DEFENSE ATTORNEY:

Q Okay. If he told you, when you saw him, that he was contemplating quitting his job or stopping working for whatever reason, would you have noted that in your report?

A I would have.

Q Okay. Do you make any reference in your—in our evaluation of him in that report, the only report you've issued, that you felt he was not going to be able to continue working at his job?

A Let me look at my conclusions. What I have is under "Occupational Problems" in Axis IV of my diagnosis: absence from work and limited work schedule due to injuries.

Q Okay. Let me find that. All right. I see that.

A And then in the "Discussion" section, which is on the last page, the last sentence in the first paragraph, "Restrictions in the ability to work and limited social and recreational interactions are contributing to the *significant* depression which is present."

Q Okay. Anything else that reflects on whether or not he's going to be able to work, directly in your report—or in your opinion, as of that time?

A As of that time, he was working, he wanted to work, he was having difficulty working, but he was working.

Q Now, as of the time that you—as of now, since you saw him again in, a number of months later, I am assuming he told you he wasn't working anymore, he was on disability?

A He did tell me that.

Q Did he tell you that his doctors had told him—or advised him that he couldn't return to any employment?

A I don't specifically recall if they said he couldn't return to any employment, but that he couldn't do the job that he had, yes. That I recall.

Q Are you going to give any opinions as to whether or not this gentleman is employable, or is that outside of your area of expertise or your area of retention in this matter?

A No, it is not entirely out of my area of expertise. Based on the severity of his psychological symptoms and what I understand about his physical impairments, it is highly questionable whether or not he can be employed.

Q Now, employment is often a great boost to a depressed mind, is it not? Your experience?

A Depends on the severity of the depression.

Q And by the way, depression can be chemical. It is generally thought to be a chemical issue now, is it not?

A Depression is understood to be a rather complex phenomena. In some depressions there is a very major biochemical basis. In others, there is more of an environmental basis. And probably, in all there is some combination thereof.

Q Okay. In Mr. Rose, is it more of an environmental basis than a chemical basis?

A Yes.

Q If we assume his history is accurate, that he was not depressed before the incident, then that would tend to lead you to the conclusion that it was more environmental versus chemical?

A Yes.

Q And by the way, you don't know anything about any medical history other than—before this accident, other than what Mr. Rose has told you or what you've—well, other than what Mr. Rose has told you?

A Well, what Mr. Rose told me and what was in the records of the physicians who saw him.

Q Right. But you don't have any records of any physicians that saw him before the incident, do you?

A That saw him before *the* incident, no.

Q Okay. Mr. Rose indicated to you that he was having sex and having orgasms at the time you met with him?

A It was very difficult for him to get an erection and orgasms were very rare, and they weren't particularly pleasurable.

Q Okay. Is there a section you are reading from?

A I don't know if I am reading from a section. I'll look again. But my—this report is a summation of the notes that I took during the first interview with him, But certainly, what I have at the bottom of page two is "not able to get an erection. Viagra doesn't help. Mr. Rose had his first orgasm during the week before the interview. Achieved an erection through a self-administered needle injection of his penis. He began to use the procedure six—three weeks ago." At the top of page three. "Mr. Rose doesn't expect to be able to get spontaneous erections in the future, but hasn't asked the urologist for a prognosis. A penile implant is the next step. He had no difficulty with sexual functioning prior to the accident."

Q Okay. And, again, that is all from Mr. Rose himself, correct?

A Yes.

Q You met with him again months later, and he told you what? That he had been told that he would never regain functioning, as far as spontaneous erections, without the injection?

A Yes.

Q Can tragedies—life tragedies cause posttraumatic stress disorder, as far as, like, deaths of loved ones, in the same fashion that Mr. Rose suffered, in your mind, the posttraumatic stress disorder from this trauma?

A That's a kind of confusing question. I mean, if the person dies, obviously, they are not going to have a posttraumatic stress disorder.

Q In the sense of loved ones.

A And so can the surviving person develop a posttraumatic stress disorder if a loved one is killed in a fashion similar to Mr. Rose?

Q No. Well, can—in your experience, can an individual suffer a posttraumatic stress disorder similar to what you've evaluated Mr. Rose with in this case, where an individual is not in an accident, but goes through the grieving process or shock from the death of a close loved one?

A Well, again, that's a pretty general question. First of all, the death of a loved one does not usually produce posttraumatic stress disorder. If the loved one witnessed the death of the loved one in some kind of a violent way, that could produce a posttraumatic stress disorder.

Q As part of the prerequisite for that disorder, the actual witnessing of the—of a trauma, a physical trauma, whether it is to the patient himself or to someone else?

A Yes.

Q Okay. The degree of the trauma in place is a component for this—this—contributory to the—whether or not the disorder develops; is that accurate?

A Yes, it is.

Q So depending on how bad the trauma is that a patient like Mr. Rose experiences, that may affect how bad the posttraumatic stress disorder is?

A Well, I think you are confusing—

Q How long it lasts?

A You are confusing apples and oranges again. Now you are talking about Mr. Rose. Before you were talking about in general and about a person witnessing the death of a loved one.

He continues to make generalizations that he then attempts to apply to Mr. Rose.

Q I was just talking about a trauma like Mr. Rose. I think you—strike the question. He seems to indicate that he thinks about the accident all the time and worries about it. Is that an accurate history from your psychological symptoms?

A Yes.

Q At some point, don't you reasonably expect this gentleman to kind of get over this constant obsession with time? Isn't time the biggest healer for any sort of condition like this?

A I don't expect him to get over it because he is in constant pain and because he is unable to function as he could before.

Q What if he does—what if his pain is assuaged or mitigated by treatment and he starts to regain functionality? Then would you expect him to start to get over this memory?

A I would say that the memory would be less prominent if that happened, but there's no indication it's going to.

Q You are not going to tell a jury that every person who is struck by a car in an accident, suffers some injury that in some way restricts that person's function—that you would expect such a person to become—to suffer from a posttraumatic stress disorder for the rest of that person's life, are you?

PLAINTIFF ATTORNEY: Objection. Objection; vague, lacks foundation, calls for speculation as phrased.

THE WITNESS: Well, I am not going to talk to a jury about every person at all. If I am called to testify in this case, I'll talk about Mr. Rose.

BY DEFENSE ATTORNEY:

Q Do you think Mr. Rose is overly—is on the higher end of sensitivity, as far as being able to cope with this trauma, than the . . .

A What do you mean by—

Q Is that what we are coming down to?

A What do you mean by "sensitivity"?

Q Does Mr. Rose have a more difficult time in coping, in getting over the trauma than most people?

A No.

Q So you think his—his progress in coping is about the norm? Would that be accurate?

A The norm of what and for what and whom?

Q A person who is in a trauma, like Mr. Rose, who was hit by a car and suffered some fractures and some nerve injury—would you expect that this is about the normal recovery time for a person with such injuries?

A I can't answer that.

Q Would you expect that—

A I don't—

Q It is a question. Just tell me.

A Well, I can't answer the norm because I don't know what the norm is, and again, you are comparing apples and oranges.

Q All right.

A What I can tell you is I don't think Mr. Rose is in any way, shape, or form having more difficulty than one would expect, based on the severity of the accident *and* the consequences.

Q Would you agree with me, Doctor, that this is a one-time trauma that would have been wholly unexpected for Mr. Rose at the time it occurred?

A It was a one-time trauma and it was wholly unexpected.

Q Okay. Would you agree with me that it is highly unlikely that he is ever going to be hit by a car as a pedestrian again?

A I can't read the future.

Q Statistically, would you agree with me?

A I don't know enough statistics to be able to comment.

Q Okay. Is it true, Doctor, that a great number of people who suffer from depression go undiagnosed?

A You know, you are asking me these very general questions. They are not specific at all. Very difficult to answer any of these questions. Do some people who have depression go undiagnosed? I am sure they do.

Q I mean, do you keep up with the current literature, or even in the modern media, with stories and the current thinking on depression? I mean, depression is a big focus of, certainly, prescription medications these days, is it not? I am aware of depression and prescription medication. Depression seems to be—at least based upon the ads we see for prescription medication, antidepressants, it appears to be almost at—an epidemic?

A I have no statistics on that.

Q It—is it the case sometimes, in your experience, that patients who are clinically depressed do not realize they are depressed?

PLANTIFF ATTORNEY: Objection; calls for speculation, lacks foundation, argumentative.

BY DEFENSE ATTORNEY:

Q I'm not asking you to speculate. If you know from your 30-some years of practicing medicine as a psychiatrist, then answer. But if you don't, tell me you don't know.

A No, I can answer your question. Most of the people that I've treated knew they were depressed. There were a few who did not.

Q Mr. Rose apparently didn't think of himself as depressed early on in his treatment; is that accurate?

A That's correct. That's what he said.

Q And he told you that, right? When you met with him?

A He did.

Q And are you aware from [the neurologist's] treatment notes—did you read the neurologist's—treatment notes?

A I did.

Q Are you aware from his notes that throughout his course of treatment [neurologist] indicated—let me find the note here. "No unusual anxiety or evidence of depression."

A I do remember seeing that.

Q And [neurologist] didn't indicate any evidence of depression or anxiety up until the time that he became aware that Mr. Rose was being seen by a psychologist and psychiatrist. Do you recall that?

A I don't recall that, but I do recall the first one.

Q Do you know what Perthes disease is? PERTHES?

A Legg-Perthes disease, I believe—I am not 100 percent certain about this—that that is a disease in children that has to do with the plates in the long bones in the legs becoming vulnerable in some way.

Q Is it a disabling disease?

A I don't know any more about it. Not enough to say.

Q Did Mr. Rose tell you which leg he had that was braced for four years as a child because of that disease?

A I don't recall.

Q PERTHES?

A I don't recall.

Q Did he present to you as overweight? I think you described him as somewhat overweight?

A Yeah. I think he was mildly overweight.

Q You said in the "Mental Status Examination" I am not sure why there—you said that "Mr. Rose presented as a somewhat overweight middle-aged man."

A Well, the reason why it is there is because that's part of what you do when you do a mental status examination.

Q Is the patient's weight indicative in some way of his psychiatric condition?

A No. The patient's appearance and behavior is what you look at.

Q And is his weight indicative of his psychiatric condition?

A It can be, and sometimes it isn't.

Q How would it be? How would being overweight be indicative of psychiatric conditions?

A Well, sometimes depressed individuals eat more. Sometimes they eat less and become anorexic. So it can be related. But what I was doing there was simply describing his appearance.

Q Okay. And would you agree with me that it is more common, in general—again, in your treatment of patients—that depressed patients tend to gain weight than to lose weight?

A I can't answer that question.

Q Why? Because you don't know?

A No, because I don't have a specific answer to that in terms of my patients.

Q Okay. And you didn't find Mr. Rose to be anorexic, did you? Any indication that he was anorexic?

A No.

Q By the way, he lost weight during the course of the treatment, did he not?

A During the course of what treatment? Treatment since this accident?

A I don't specifically recall that, but that wouldn't surprise me.

Q I think . . . do you recall that he was diagnosed with diabetes in the emergency room; that he went on a diet subsequent and lost a significant amount of weight, more than ten pounds?

PLAINTIFF ATTORNEY: Objection; misstates the evidence of the records at the hospital.

BY DEFENSE ATTORNEY:

Q Would you agree with that? Are you aware of that?

A I do know that he was diagnosed with diabetes after the accident. And know that when he came home that diagnosis was determined to be incorrect.

Q Okay. But I am talking about him losing weight based on a change in diet. Are you aware of him having indicated that that was the case?

A I don't specifically recall that.

Q Are you aware that he's lost weight since the accident?

A I don't know.

Q That was not important for you to find out in your analysis of this guy for depression?

A It's—it's one of the factors that you look at in depression. It wasn't the predominant one here.

Q It wasn't one you considered here, was it, since you didn't . . .

A No. I considered it.

Q Let me ask—I can't tell if [plaintiff attorney's] objection is to the form of the question, so let me ask that, just in case. Was that—was the issue of whether or not Mr. Rose lost weight important to you, since you didn't appear to note one way or the other and don't recall?

A I did note, however—

Q Answer my question first if you would, yes or no.

Once again, you do not have to respond to demands for a yes or no answer.

A Well, I am trying to answer your question. I am looking for my notes so that I can answer your question. In my interview with him in September, I went through the criteria for major depressive disorder and for posttraumatic stress disorder. And certainly one of the things I would have asked about at that point was weight. And what I have in here is—as I went through the criteria for major depressive disorder, "depressed mood all the time. Two, diminished pleasure. Three, lost thirty pounds since last [several months], due to diet and exercise and physical therapy."

Q Okay. So you knew?

A I knew that.

Q You didn't know that when you wrote that first report, your evaluation report for this case?

A No, I can't answer that either way. I am not sure.

Q Well, you didn't note it, and you would have noted it as important, would you not—strike that. That was important enough to note in the follow-up visit, correct?

A It was.

Q And you did testing. Your Structured Clinical Interview Test, is that a standardized test?

A I did not do any testing.

Q You are right. I am sorry. Dr. [name] did that?

A Correct.

Q Okay. Did you look at the results that he got?

A I looked at the report he sent me.

Q You didn't score any of these tests, by the way, did you? Have any involvement in the interpretation or scoring?

A I am a psychiatrist. I am not a psychologist. I am not qualified to do that.

Q Okay. You don't find any deficit as a result of trauma, organic brain injury, do you?

A No.

Q But if he's got some—if he is only average in IQ, did you feel that was because of the depression or the psychological issues?

A You'd have to ask that of Dr. [name].

Q Okay. You don't have an opinion as to whether or not Mr. Rose's premorbid IQ was above average?

A I don't have any IQ earlier than the one that was taken by Dr. [name].

Q Okay. You don't have any opinion as to whether or not Mr. Rose's premorbid IQ was above average?

A I don't have any IQ earlier than the one that was taken by Dr. [name].

Q Did you call for the Rorschach Inkblot Test to be used?

A Did I call for it?

Q Did you request—did you specifically request the test in this battery?

A No. I don't have the competence to do that. The psychologist determines what tests to give.

Q Okay. Do people still use this Rorschach Inkblot Test very much, to your knowledge?

A Obviously. It was used here.

Q Do you see it used often these days, in the last ten years?

A I have seen it used often, yes.

Q Okay. Okay. And we've talked about your diagnoses, I think.

A Actually, we haven't talked about my diagnoses at all.

Q Okay. I beg to differ, but let me see what else I've got. I am almost done here.

PLAINTIFF ATTORNEY: You aren't trying to avoid his diagnoses are you, Counsel?

DEFENSE ATTORNEY: No. I think I've heard most of—

PLAINTIFF ATTORNEY: No, you actually haven't.

DEFENSE ATTORNEY: To great lengths, over and over again. I am trying to avoid hearing it over and over yet again.

PLAINTIFF ATTORNEY: You haven't asked him his current diagnoses yet.

BY DEFENSE ATTORNEY:

Q In fact, you told me before, I think, you didn't have a diagnosis because you were the evaluator, you were not a treater. Do you consider your opinions and your evaluation a diagnosis?

PLAINTIFF ATTORNEY: Objection; misstates his prior testimony.

THE WITNESS: I didn't say anything remotely like that. The purpose of doing a diagnostic evaluation is to determine whether or not a diagnosis and treatment are indicated and what the prognosis is.

BY DEFENSE ATTORNEY:

Q Okay. And the prognosis—you diagnosed him with posttraumatic stress disorder, correct?

A That was one of the diagnoses.

Q I am starting with that one.

A Okay. And what is his prognosis for recovery—and what is his prognosis for recovery—and by that I mean what is the likelihood that he will begin to recover from the symptoms related to the posttraumatic stress disorder, over time?

A Guarded to fair.

Q Well, does that mean that he probably will gradually improve his symptoms?

A No. It doesn't mean that. It means that more likely than not he's not going to improve very much.

Q So your—you're a little pessimistic, aren't you, Doctor?

A No, I wouldn't call me pessimistic. I'd call me realistic.

Q You think this fifty-five-year-old man is never going to be able to recover from his symptoms from when he was hit by the car?

A I think that because of the seriousness of his physical injuries and the likely permanent nature of them, he will continue to manifest symptoms of posttraumatic stress disorder, as well as the other diagnoses that I gave him.

Q You don't see Mr. Rose as a gentleman with the ability and the resilience and strength to be able to gradually cope with this and move on in his life.

A Only if he were able to get back to some reasonable degree of the life that he had before, which was being able to work, being able to play, being able to be social, and being able to have intimate relationships with his wife.

Q Okay. And this opinion is based on the what—approximately three hours and forty-five minutes you spent with him on two different occasions?

PLAINTIFF ATTORNEY: Objection; misstates his testimony.

BY DEFENSE ATTORNEY:

Q And your review of medical treatment records?

A And the psychological testing.

Q Okay. And you've diagnosed him with major depression—

A Major depressive disorder. Single episode.

Q Okay. And what about his prognosis there? Do you think that he's going to be able—he's going to have enough resilience to gradually cope with and accept whatever permanent restrictions he may have and to become a happier person again?

A I don't think he's going to become a much happier person, and the prognosis there is guarded to fair.

Q Okay. Do you think he's going to be on antidepressant medication and need psychotherapy for the remainder of his life?

A Well, I made specific recommendations there under "Treatment."

Q Certainly, then you disagree with Mr. Rose's own assessment to you that he was not depressed.

PLAINTIFF ATTYORNEY: Objection; misstates his testimony.

THE WITNESS: I do. I think Mr. Rose now, based on the diagnostic interviews and his therapy, knows he's depressed.

BY DEFENSE ATTORNEY:

Q Okay. Did you tell him he was depressed?

A No, I didn't tell him he was depressed.

Q You indicated in your report that he was, though, before you saw him a second time?

A Yes. I don't know if Mr. Rose ever saw this report. I did not send the report to him.

Q Okay. You sent it to his attorney?

A Correct.

Q The gentleman who hired you?

A Correct.

Q And you diagnosed—you also included the male erectile disorder due to pelvic trauma, which is the physiological injury that played a part in the psychological and psychiatric injuries you've opined on?

PLAINTIFF ATTORNEY: Objection; misstates his testimony.

THE WITNESS: The fact that the urologist says that he's not ever going to be able to get a spontaneous erection due to the pelvic trauma is an integral part of that diagnosis.

BY DEFENSE ATTORNEY:

Q And pain disorder, based upon pain from the physiological injuries?

A Yes.

Q Does depression magnify pain symptoms in a lot of patients?

A It can do that.

Q Does pain, physical pain—tend to feed depression?

A Does physical pain tend to what depression?

Q Feed depression systems. In other words, increase depressive symptoms?

A That can happen.

Q Okay. Is that happening, are both of those situations likely happening with Mr. Rose?

A Well, let's go back over them one by one and I'll talk about them with regard to Mr. Rose.

Q Okay. With Mr. Rose, do you believe his depression is magnifying his pain symptoms?

A No. I don't think so.

Q You don't feel that his depression is in any way affecting the degree to which he feels the physiological symptoms?

A There is a very clear physiological basis for his pain. I think his pain is partly responsible for his depression, not the other way around.

Q Okay, Doctor and nobody is denying that there's a physiological basis for his pain. But in his circumstances, with the facts as you know them, you don't believe, even though it is possible with—in general, you don't believe that Mr. Rose's depression is causing him to in any way experience the physiological pain more intensively? Is that an accurate statement?

A I just answered it. I said I see it the other way around.

Q Okay.

A The pain is increasing his depression.

Q As far as his social issues, his concerns that he's not able to get out with his buddies—his male friends to socialize, do you think that it is—that would be a good thing for Mr. Rose, to the extent that he can tolerate it, to get out and socialize more that he's not working now?

A Definitely.

Q And, in fact, he's not expending all those hours and effort in work and driving. He would appear to have a lot more time to get out and try and socialize and try and get back some sort of a social—a functional social life?

A Yes.

Q And would that be helpful, also, to his self-esteem, confidence?

A Yes, it would.

Q So that might be something that in the future we would hope Mr. Rose would try to do to assuage the symptoms of depression that he's feeling?

A Yes.

Q You give him a GAF score I think 41 to 50; is that correct?

A Correct. Yes, I did.

Q Now, you disagree with Dr. [psychologist], correct?

A In what way?

Q Didn't Dr. [name] give him a GAF score of 60?

A Hang on a second and I'll tell you. Dr. [name] gave him 50 to 60, moderate to serious impairment.

Q Okay. A higher score than what you gave him?

A Yes, he did.

Q Now would you agree with me that Dr. [name] spent a lot more time with this patient than you have?

A Dr. [name] did the psychological testing, which probably took somewhere between four to six hours.

Q Has Dr. [name] been giving psychotherapy to Mr. Rose?

A Yes. We already talked about that.

Q Okay. So he spent more than just the time in testing with him—with Mr. Rose. Mr. Rose is his patient, correct?

A Yes, but at the time he did the testing, Mr. Rose was not his patient.

Q Okay. But he is now?

A He is now.

Q Would you agree with me that Dr. [name] may have a little better knowledge of Mr. Rose's psychological condition than you, having been treating him now for some time?

A No, I don't agree with that. I did a thorough evaluation. When Dr. [name] made this report and made his comment, he had just done the psychological testing. He didn't have the breadth of the information that I had, and so, therefore, at the time of the evaluation in his report, I am in a better position to make a determination than he is. However, at this point, since he's been treating Mr. Rose for some time, I am sure he'll have an opinion on the severity of his symptoms that you can ask him.

Q Okay. And just to follow—if I can finish up here, you've given your opinions, in this report, of what his future care needs are for treatment, on page seven, correct?

A Yes, I did.

Q As of the date of the report, anyway?

A Yes.

Q And you say he needs psychotherapy, beginning immediately, two to three times per week for two to three years, first of all?

A Correct.

Q And then he also needs an antidepressant medication, correct?

A Yes.

Q And that it's to be decided in the future as to whether or not he's going to need, then, further psychotherapy into the future?

A Yes.

Q But—that's something he may need, but as of now, you can't say whether he will or he wouldn't?

PLAINTIFF ATTORNEY: Objection; misstates his testimony.

THE WITNESS: I do say what I think he's going to need in the future. I say an additional course of once to twice per week psychotherapy for one to two years is indicated to help Mr. Rose continue to deal with sexual issues, relationship problems, pain, and physical injury consequences, and the relationship between physical and psychological consequences of the accident and the aging process.

BY DEFENSE ATTORNEY:

Q Does that mean to say that he's going to need one course of one to two years of that—of psychotherapy once or twice a week, sometime during that ten-year period?

A Yes. That's what that says. And, of course, it also says that he'd have to be evaluated to determine what else would be needed.

Q Right. Okay. And by the way, are you—tell me if you can agree with what I am saying, based on your knowledge of Mr. Rose and his function, because I am not sure what you know and as far as what his restrictions are. Is he able to drive? Is Mr. Rose able to drive his own car?

A I think he does drive, yes.

Q Without any modification to the vehicle?

PLAINTIFF ATTORNEY: Objection; calls for speculation.

THE WITNESS: I don't know the answer to that.

BY DEFENSE ATTORNEY:

Q And is he able to walk?

A He can walk, yes.

Q Is he able to walk in a normal fashion?

PLAINTIFF ATTORNEY: Objection; calls for speculation.

THE WITNESS: After.

BY MR. GILBERT:

Q I am asking you based on what you know from your conversations with him or what you observed. You indicate he has a limp, somewhere in your report, I think.

A Yes, I did indicate that. Based on what I know, he can walk for a while, but soon he experiences pain. It is difficult for him to walk for any period of time.

Q Did he tell you that he always limps?

A I don't think I asked him that question.

Q You just indicated in your report that he limps. Now let's go back and look at the exact verbiage on this. You say—

A It's probably in the "Mental Status Exam."

Q Well, "Physical Symptoms"—let's see. No. "Mental Status Exam," you say?

A That's where I think it would be.

Q You say he—how he presented, we talked about being somewhat overweight, and then you say he walked with a limp—

A Right.

Q When you saw him the first time?

A Correct.

Q Did he walk with a limp when you saw him again the second time?

A He had a slight limp.

Q Okay. On the right leg right?

A Yes.

Q On the right leg?

A Yes.

Q Okay. Does his wife still love him, from what he tells you?

A From what he tells me, his wife loves him, although he's very concerned about her falling out of love with him.

Q Okay. But did he give you, do anything to give you any indication that there is any reason for him to believe, at this point, that she is falling out of love with him?

A There's no rational reason to believe that.

Q Okay. And does he still love his wife?

A Yes, he does.

Q The kids still love him?

A Do his kids still love him?

Q Yeah.

A As far as I know, yes.

Q Does he still love his kids?

A He does.

Q Does he still have a good relationship with his children?

A Yes. As far as I know.

Q Have his children turned on him and do they love him less now that he's not as physically active as he was before?

A I didn't evaluate his children, so I can't answer that definitively. From the DVD, they appear to love him.

Q Do you have any reason to think, from anything you've seen or what you've heard from Mr. Rose, that his children love him any less because he was in this accident?

A No.

Q And do you have any new opinions—let me just—as a result of seeing him a second time, that are not noted in this report? I think you answered that, but I just want to be sure.

A Basically, my conclusions from the second interview were that he was unable to perform sexually and he was more aware of his limitations. He was worried that he would not be able to work again. He was more aware of his limitations. He was worried about becoming addicted to medications. He couldn't play any sports. Quote, he expected to be disabled for the rest of his life, end of quote. He was worried that his wife would leave him. He expects to end up in a wheelchair, and he was still having nightmares about being crushed. And on "Mental Status Examination," there was strong evidence of depression, and the new factor was he was realizing at this point the he would be permanently disabled.

Q Are these new opinions you are giving me?

A These are the opinions I am giving you from the second interview.

Q These are new opinions you are expressing in what you are telling me about what he told you?

A Well, basically the diagnoses are all the same.

Q Okay.

A The opinions—the opinions are—

Q Any new expert opinions in this case, as an expert psychiatrist, other than what you've already expressed in your report, as a result of seeing him again? That's what I am trying to find out.

A Yes, and that's what I was just giving you.

Q You are telling me what he told you. Are those your opinions?

A They are my opinions that I am telling you; that he's coming to the realization that he's permanently disabled, that he can't work, that he is very troubled about his relationship with his wife, and that he can't get an erection. And because of all these things, the diagnoses that I made in the initial diagnostic evaluation remain valid, and his symptoms continue to be as serious as they were before, if not more so.

Q Okay. Are you hopeful that Mr. Rose can have some further improvement psychiatrically, psychologically, and physiologically?

A Yes.

DEFENSE ATTORNEY: That's all the questions I have for you, sir. Thank you.

EXAMINATION BY PLAINTIFF ATTORNEY:

Q Okay. Doctor, I am going to start with the current curriculum vitae that will be marked as exhibit next in order. And this has a date of July 2010, correct?

A Yes.

(Exhibit 5 was marked for identification.)

BY PLAINTIFF ATTORNEY:

Q All right. And would you tell the jury briefly about your *background*, as it relates to the opinions you are giving in this case?

A Yes. I am an adult and child psychiatrist. I am board certified in adult and child psychiatry. In 1969 in adult psychiatry; in 1972 in child psychiatry. I am a clinical professor of psychiatry at the University of California at San Diego. I am the author of approximately fifty professional articles and seven professional books. And throughout my career I have taught at the University of California in San Diego. For twenty years I was the director of the child psychiatry residency training program. I am also an adult and child psychoanalyst and teach at the San Diego Psychoanalytic Institute. I've lectured in various places, nationally and internationally. And currently I am involved with professionals in Korea and Argentina.

Q In the few cases that you have worked in matters that I've been involved in, have I ever asked you to do anything specifically, other than to perform a fair and open evaluation of the patient?

A No.

DEFENSE ATTORNEY: Form, relevance, speculation, improper hypothetical, and predicate and foundation.

BY PLAINTIFF ATTORNEY:

Q You indicated that you had available to you Dr. [psychologist] records, as well as the testing report that he did, correct?

A I had the records of his psychotherapy sessions with Mr. Rose yes.

Q And he reported to you his test results, as well?

A Yes.

Q Okay. Briefly, is Dr. [psychologist] an experienced therapist and psychologist in the San Diego community?

A He is.

DEFENSE ATTORNEY: Object to the form; relevance. Improper boosting of the credibility of another expert.

BY PLAINTIFF ATTORNEY:

Q What did you glean from the more recent records of Dr. [psychologist] concerning how Mr. Rose is doing, given the care that he's undertaken with Dr. [psychologist]?

A Dr. [psychologist] notes and conclusions are almost exactly the same as mine from my follow-up diagnostic interview. Mr. Rose continues to have the diagnoses that were made earlier. He's coming to terms with the fact that he is going to be permanently disabled, and it is deeply affecting his mental and emotional state.

Q As part of your file, do you have the treatment summary prepared by Dr. [psychologist]?

A I do.

Q Okay. And he there lists his opinions and his diagnoses, using the DSM IV, relating to Mr. Rose?

A He does.

Q What is the DSM IV?

A *The Diagnostic and Statistical Manual* of the American Psychiatric Association, the fourth edition. It is the only widely used diagnostic nomenclature in the field. And when using it, the diagnostician is asked to codify his diagnoses according to the criteria that are listed in the manual for each diagnosis.

Q Do you have in your file that you are producing for defense counsel the DSM IV sections that you believe are relevant to the opinions that you are giving in this case relating to Mr. Rose?

A I do, and they came from this diagnostic manual.

Q Okay. And that's the standard in the field of psychiatry and psychology for diagnoses such as what you are rendering in this case?

A It is.

Q Okay. With respect to the treatment summary that Dr. [psychologist], do you disagree with any of his findings in that summary?

A No. As I mentioned, his findings are very, very similar to what I found in my diagnostic evaluation.

Q Okay.

DEFENSE ATTORNEY: I didn't want to break in, but I wanted to get my objection on the record: hearsay, predicate, foundation, and form.

BY PLAINTIFF ATTORNEY:

Q Okay. And then since that time, you've had additional information such as the depositions of Mr. and Mrs. Rose that were taken by defense counsel Dr. [psychologist] ongoing evaluation and treatment notes, and the videotapes that you've already identified, correct?

A Yes.

Q And with respect to the opinions that you are going to present to the jury, is it going to be based on all of that information, up to the time you testify at trial?

A Yes, it will.

Q Okay. And from the standpoint of everything that you've done, at this point could you provide for the jury a brief summary of the opinions that you believe relate to Mr. Rose's psychological injuries, and identify whether or not you believe they are permanent and whether or not those opinions are given to a reasonable degree of medical probability?

A My opinions are based on the idea that his injuries are permanent, and that is to a degree of medical and psychological certainty.

Q You made four diagnoses which we have talked about: posttraumatic stress disorder, major depressive disorder, erectile disorder due to pelvic injury, and pain disorder.

A I feel that all of those diagnoses are based on the criteria in the manual of the DSM IV. I—on the basis of that, they are all directly related to the accidents and the physical injuries, and very importantly, to the consequences of how his life has been changed as a result of those injuries, I made treatment recommendations for psychotherapy and antidepressant medication in the present, two to three times a week for two to three years, with antidepressant medication. And within the decade after the completion of that, individual psychotherapy one to two times a week for one to two years. And an evaluation at that time would determine future needs. The prognosis is guarded to fair. Meaning that it's not likely there is going to be much improvement, and that is because of the severity of the physical injuries and the consequences thereof, meaning that Mr. Rose is not able to work at his former profession, cannot play golf and be involved in the other activities that he was. And there has been a serious change in his ability to perform sexually with his wife.

Q From the standpoint of the erectile dysfunction, what is your view or opinion as to how that affects him individually?

DEFENSE ATTORNEY: Format and answer predicate. Speculation.

THE WITNESS: That has a profound effect on his self-esteem, on his masculinity, on his sense of himself as a man, and it very much undermines his relationship with his wife.

BY PLAINTIFF ATTORNEY:

Q Anything further, Doctor, in the way of general opinions that we have not covered at this point?

A I think we've covered all of my major opinions.

PLAINTIFF ATTORNEY: All right. Thank you. I have nothing further.

FURTHER EXAMINATION BY DEFENSE ATTORNEY:

Q One quick follow-up, Doctor. You are talking about the erectile dysfunction undermining the relationship with his wife. I think you told me a minute ago that there's nothing that you know of to indicate that the wife is falling out of love with the husband, but this is Mr. Rose's perception.

A That's correct.

Q In other words, if—to the extent that undermines the relationship between the husband and wife at this stage and what you know, it is based on Mr. Rose's concerns and worries and perception?

A Yes.

DEFENSE ATTORNEY: Okay. That's all I have. Thank you.

THE WITNESS: His wife—his wife also is very aware of how the relationship between the two of them has changed across the board, including sexually. But as far as I know, at this point, she's determined to live with that and make the best of it.

BY DEFENSE ATTORNEY:

Q Well, wait a minute now. Have you ever met with Mrs. Rose?

A No, but I listened to her DVD and I read her deposition.

Q Okay. So what you just told us was based upon what you heard in a—in a DVD of a—well, strike that. You read her deposition and you've also watched the DVD, a brief interview, provided by counsel, with Mrs. Rose?

A Correct.

DEFENSE ATTORNEY: Okay. I guess read or waive?

PLAINTIFF ATTORNEY: Well, just one last point.

FURTHER EXAMINATION BY PLAINTIFF ATTORNEY:

Q Doctor, from your evaluation of the materials in this case and your meeting with Mr. Rose, is there any indication, from your standpoint, of any evidence of malingering or faking on Mr. Rose's part?

A No.

DEFENSE ATTORNEY: Form, speculation, relevance, predicate.

BY PLAINTIFF ATTORNEY:

Q And is that something you typically would look for in the evaluation of a patient such as Mr. Rose?

A In the evaluation of any patients in a lawsuit.

PLAINTIFF ATTORNEY: Thank you. I have nothing further.

This is a fairly typical example of a deposition. My impressions of this attorney are that he was persistent, occasionally confrontational, and not particularly organized. The plaintiff attorney followed the course of the deposition closely, intervened when necessary, and saw to it at the end of the deposition that all of my diagnoses, treatment recommendations, and prognosis were on the record.

In chapter 6 we will discuss testifying in court. My direct testimony in the case of Robert Rose will be presented, thus providing a comparison between testifying at deposition and trial.

SIX

Testifying in Court

Direct Examination in the Case of Robert Rose

In my opinion, the most important variable in testifying is your attitude and degree of comfort with your *controlled* aggression. Remember, the court system is adversarial—plaintiff verses defense, attorney against attorney, attorney against expert witness. If you like intellectual sparing, debating of a sort, you will enjoy testifying. As we will discuss in chapter 7 on cross-examination, you are far from helpless on the stand. In fact, during cross-examination I believe you have more "guns" and "ammunition" than the attorney examining you.

Having been in psychotherapy or psychoanalysis, where you examined your aggressive impulses and fantasies and the past experiences that shaped them, will help you distinguish between the past and present experience on the stand. The reality of the present is that testifying is not mortal combat. No one dies. No one gets injured. The worst thing that can happen is a sense of embarrassment and momentarily diminished self-esteem; but you are just as likely to feel a sense of triumph and excitement after successfully matching wits with opposing counsel.

It is just as important to be aware of, and analyze your narcissistic stance on the stand, as it is to be aware of your aggressive feelings. A certain degree of healthy narcissism is as essential for this work as is tempered aggression because of the certainty of being attacked. Narcissistic pitfalls include the effect of flattery, the will to win, narcissistic excitement, rage, and injury. The goal, never completely realized, is an egoless state (Gutheil and Simon, 2005).

Once the attorney agrees to the direct outline, I become familiar enough with its contents that I do not bring it into the courtroom with me. The retaining attorney will have a copy that he will use as the basis for the questions he will ask. Only once, early in my career, did I have to deal with a plaintiff attorney who did not want to meet before a trial or prepare a direct outline. He said he preferred to "wing it," suggesting that the presentation of my opinions would be more natural and less formal that way. Due to lack of experience, I reluctantly agreed. I attempted to follow his disjointed questions with apprehension that I'm sure was evident to the jury. After about fifteen minutes, during which he only asked about a few records I had reviewed and my diagnosis, he abruptly ended the direct examination. The opposing lawyer who was much more organized wisely did not ask me on cross-examination about my interviews or treatment recommendations which were never heard by the jury. The jury made no award for emotional damages or treatment.

Scheduling

If testifying locally, ask the attorney if he wants you to set aside a half or full day. The minimum charge is for a half day whether or not you are on the stand for thirty minutes or four hours since you will need to clear your calendar for the entire morning or afternoon. Since neither you nor the retaining attorney can predetermine the length of the cross-examination, clearing your calendar of therapy sessions or other commitments for several hours beyond the time formally set aside is advisable. As was also described in chapter 5, "The Deposition," this ensures that you will be able to comfortably focus your full attention on the task at hand and not be distracted by concerns about being late for subsequent commitments.

If you are called to testify in a distant city or state, hours spent in travel during typical workday hours are charged at a fee commensurate with what you would be earning on an hourly basis seeing patients or in other professional activities (Gutheil et al., 1998).

The progress of a trial is not predictable. You may be scheduled to testify on a particular day or hour but due to factors beyond the control of the retaining attorney long hours may be spent in the hallway outside the courtroom since experts are excluded from the courtroom except when they are testifying. For example, the judge may remain in chambers longer than expected, or the direct or cross-examinations preceding your testimony lasted longer than predicted or there were multiple sidebars.

The Day Before

Exercise and a good night's sleep are excellent preparations for testifying. Much of the detailed study for testifying is over by this time. Prolonged focus on the details the night before, or in the corridor outside the courtroom, is likely to produce anxiety.

Proper Attire

A dark business suit for men and a dress or business pantssuit for women is always appropriate. The courtroom is a formal place where the reverence for the law is evident at all times. Proper attire demonstrates your respect. I have a "testifying suit" which I wear when I appear in court. It is dark blue and always worn with a white shirt and a solid colored tie. Bright colors and stripped shirts and ties are less formal. Attorneys will almost always be dressed in a similar fashion although the occasional flamboyant litigator may appear in a light colored suit or wear a flower on his lapel.

Visiting the Courtroom

If possible, visit the courtroom before being called to testify. That way, when you are called and stand before the judge and jury, and sworn in by the judge's deputy, you can focus on responding in a firm, composed voice and then confidently stride to the witness box without appearing uncertain about where to go.

Most courtrooms are arranged as follows: the judge is seated at a raised platform in the middle of the head of the courtroom. The witness stand and the jury box are located near each other on either the right or left of the judge. The court reporter sits in front of the witness stand and records all spoken words. The lawyers from both sides are seated in the middle of the room facing the judge and the witness. Spectator seats are on either side of the entrance to the courtroom.

Waiting to Testify

As just mentioned, because of the rule of sequestration, namely the exclusion of expert witnesses from the courtroom other than the time spent on the stand (Slovenko, 2004), you may spend minutes or hours in the hall waiting to testify.

Ask to be the first witness of the day, that way you will be fresh and avoid any anxiety while waiting to be called. Being scheduled as the first witness of the day does not mean that you will be. As previously described, the retaining lawyer cannot dictate the speed of the trial. A witness may take the stand ahead of you to complete testimony or cross-examination begun the previous day.

Upon arrival at the assigned courtroom in the morning or at the beginning of the afternoon session, it is likely that the jury will not yet have been called into the courtroom. Without exception, the retaining attorney will ask you not to sit by, or talk to jurors, plaintiffs, defendants, or members of their families. If the retaining attorney wishes to converse with you he will ask you to walk with him away from the immediate area of the courtroom.

I try to be prepared for a situation in which the jury has been called into the courtroom and I have been told that I will not be called to the stand immediately, or for some time to come. I bring a newspaper or magazine with me to help pass the time. Doing crossword puzzles or playing games on your cell phone serve the same purpose. Last second cramming has little benefit and tends to heighten anxiety.

A full bladder is an enemy of an expert witness. Restrict fluid intake prior to testifying and use the courthouse restroom before going on the stand. Heightened urges to urinate are common in stressful situations. If the urge to urinate while on the stand becomes very strong and is distracting ask the judge for a brief recess. He will understand. You are not the only one with such biological urges. Hence, every morning and afternoon session is punctuated by a fifteen- to twenty-minute recess halfway through the usually three-hour-long session.

Entering the Courtroom

A deputy will come for you when it is your turn to testify. He will direct you to stand outside the railing separating the spectator seats from the courtroom proper and ask you to raise you right hand so that you can be sworn in and then direct you to the witness stand. Proper attire, a confident voice, and erect posture are the attributes that allow you to make a positive initial impression on the jury. As I stride toward the witness stand I attempt to convey an attitude of confident humility. A seeming contradiction, I'm trying to say through my body language that I'm confident, but humble, before the majesty of the law and the power of the judge and jury.

The Witness Stand

The witness stand is your space. Take possession of it! You will find a comfortable swivel chair, a microphone, a pitcher of water, and often a notebook containing documents that have been admitted into evidence. Either lawyer may ask you to refer to it as you testify. Bring your case file to the stand with you but not the original records that you reviewed. They were admitted into evidence at your deposition. If you can testify on direct examination without referring to your file (having committed the important information to memory) do so. When necessary, usually on cross-examination, feel free to refer to your file as needed. The attorney conducting the cross-examination will often refer you to various documents in your file. Know the organization of your file by heart so that you will not need to fumble as you locate the document requested.

Throughout the time you are on the stand look at, and speak to, the jury. Eye contact indicates confidence and comfort on your part. Also direct your gaze toward the lawyer questioning you.

Lawyers may not approach the witness stand without permission from the judge. When permission is granted it is usually to present a document for your consideration. Only once in my experience was the witness stand invaded in a particularly effective way. I had not been provided with all of the records reviewed by the opposing expert. As the examining lawyer asked me, one by one, if I had reviewed a particular record and I answered no; he walked to the witness stand and placed the record on the desk in front of me. By the time he had made the trip six or seven additional times, the stack was so high the jury could no longer see me. Lesson learned! Always insist on reviewing *every* record seen by the opposing mental health expert.

I have been frequently asked during direct to teach the jury about the *Diagnostic and Statistical Manual* or aspects of normal and pathological development. In such instances visual aids, prepared by the attorney at my request, are projected onto a screen. With the court's permission, I have been allowed to leave the witness stand and use a pointer or laser light to elaborate various points.

DIRECT TESTIMONY

Before we begin to talk about the direct examination let me state a hard and fast rule about testifying in court. *Do not talk unless addressed by a lawyer or the judge.* I learned this lesson the hard way very early in my career. After being called to the stand the opposing side objected to my being allowed to testify. After listening to the lawyers argue back and forth for more than thirty minutes I said, "Your honor, may I say something? I may be able to help." After an awkward silence he said, his voice dripping with sarcasm, enunciating every word, "Dr. Colarusso, when I need you to tell me how to run my courtroom I'll ask you!" It never happened again.

The Direct Exam

Since you and the retaining lawyer had already agreed on the outline of the questions he would ask you and you had memorized the sequence of questions to be asked, the direct examination is a calm, relatively anxiety free, procedure. Remember to speak clearly and confidently, looking at the jury frequently as you talk. The goal of the direct examination is to present you as a likeable, credible witness who has opinions that will be helpful to the jury in their deliberations.

The likeability of expert witnesses has been found to be significantly related to jurors' perception of their trustworthiness (Brodsky et al., 2009). Women rated highly likable witnesses as more credible witnesses than less likable ones. Men did not differentiate between the two types.

Sidebars

The term refers to the not infrequent occurrence during trial of a conference in the courtroom between the judge and the lawyers, recorded by the court reporter, but out of the prevue of the jury and the expert witness, during which procedural issues or points of law particular to the case are discussed and resolved by the judge.

If you are on the stand when the judge calls a sidebar some aspect of your testimony is being discussed. The sidebar can be very brief or last several minutes or more. During that time sit quietly, look ahead, and occasionally glance at the jury. You and they have something in common at that moment; both are excluded from knowledge of what is being discussed. You are bonded to each other in that sense.

Do not use the time during a sidebar to review your notes. To do so may give the impression of anxiety or uncertainty about your knowledge of the case.

When you come to the phase of the direct in which you give your diagnoses, treatment recommendations, and prognosis (whether testifying for the plaintiff or the defense), you will be asked over and over if your opinions are "to a reasonable degree of medical certainty," the standard of evidence accepted by the court. You will also hear the term "trier of fact." The trier of fact is the jury or the judge in a bench trial, when the judge serves as both judge and jury at the request of both sides. The trier of fact weighs the evidence and makes the decisions as to guilt or innocence or what financial rewards will be given in a civil trial.

Criticizing the Opposing Expert

Toward the end of your direct testimony you will be asked to evaluate the opinions and conclusions of the opposing expert. This is a highly uncomfortable situation for many mental health experts but need not be if approached thoughtfully and maturely. It has been referred to as fouling one's own nest (Gutheil, Schetky, and Simon, 2006). Criticizing the opposing expert's opinions is an integral, unavoidable aspect of your role as an expert witness in this adversarial environment.

Either attorney may ask you if you know the opposing expert. If the answer is yes the next question is what is his reputation in the community. If I know that he has a good reputation I say so. In those instances when I know the opposing expert but see him as someone whose reputation is that of a gun for hire, whose opinions can be bought, I avoid a direct answer but comment that on those occasions when we were on opposing sides I've felt that his opinions were often skewed and based on incomplete information. To strenuously attack a fellow expert on his reputation may come across as pompous and narcissistic, and could be examples of un-modulated aggression and un-tempered narcissism.

A thorough study of his deposition and report will allow you to clearly define the areas of disagreement. These opinions should have been incorporated into the direct summary outline that was agreed upon by the retaining attorney and yourself prior to trial. The direct summary outline in the case of Robert Rose is presented later in this chapter.

Research has been done on the degree of agreement among experts on the same adversarial side and those on the opposing side. Mental health experts on the same adversarial side had good agreement about the presence of a mental disorder (K = .74) but only fair agreement about a specific psychiatric diagnosis. Reports of mental health experts on the opposing side had poor agreement about either the presence of a psychiatric diagnosis or a specific one (Large and Nielssen, 2008). I find this data to be particularly interesting because I believe it reflects the degree that expert bias toward the side that is paying is a conscious and unconscious factor in the formulation of opinions by mental health experts.

In those situations in which there are ethical professionals on both sides who are aware of the tendency toward bias based on the understandable desire to be paid, there should be considerable agreement about diagnosis, as well as treatment recommendations and prognosis. In my thirty years of forensic experience this kind of agreement has been present less than 50 percent of the time.

THE DIRECT EXAMINATION OUTLINE

The order of presentation on the direct examination is fairly standardized but can be modified as you wish. Here is the usual order of presentation. First, your credentials: this includes education beginning with college, medical school, internship, residency, and any additional postgraduate training. Next comes licensure to practice, board certification, and clinical experience, followed by faculty appointments, teaching experience, research, and publications. Psychologists would list college, graduate school, post-doctoral experience, licensure, clinical experience, faculty appointments, teaching experience, research, and publications.

The following is the direct testimony outline that I prepared in conjunction with the plaintiff's lawyer before taking the stand in the Robert Rose case.

DIRECT TESTIMONY OUTLINE
ROBERT ROSE CASE

Credentials:

Graduate of Jefferson Medical College in Philadelphia, PA, 1961
Internship, York General Hospital, York, PA, 1961–1962
Adult Psychiatric Residency, Eastern Pennsylvania Psychiatric Institute, Philadelphia, PA, 1962–1964
Child Psychiatric Residency, Albert Einstein Medical Center, Philadelphia, PA, 1964–1966
United States Air Force, 1966–1968
Board Certified in Adult Psychiatry, 1969
Board Certified in Child Psychiatry, 1972
Clinical Professor of Psychiatry, UCSD, to the present
Private practice: of adult and child psychiatry in San Diego since 1973
Forensic expert in more than 1,000 civil cases

What asked to do?

> A psychiatric evaluation of Mr. Robert Rose and serve as an expert witness.

What did you do?

> Independent Medical Examination lasting 2 hours and 35 minutes
> Psychological testing performed by Dr. B.
> Review of records:
> Three follow-up interviews with Mr. Rose

What did you ask about in your Independent Medical Examination?

> Identifying information
> The accident
> The hospitalization and return home
> Physical and psychological symptoms resulting from the accident
>
> > Physical:
> >
> > > Can't run or jog
> > > Numbness in right leg, below the knee
> > > Pain and soreness in the back
> > > Inability to get an erection
> >
> > Psychological:

On edge
"I think about it all the time. I try not to."
"I worry about getting hit again."
"Now I know how people give up and die. I'm so fortunate I'm alive."
"Internally I'm disabled, not to mention my sexuality."
"My wife has been patient. On my anniversary I couldn't get an erection."
"I'm jumpy. If people come up to me I jump."
"I love my job. I never missed except for this accident." (Had to stop work due to pain and fatigue.)
"I can't sit through a football game."
"I want to golf with my guy friends. I don't want people to feel sorry for me."
"I'm frustrated, tired, and disappointed."
"Before the accident I was friendly, had best friends, was active and jovial."
No emotional problems or treatment prior to the accident.

Developmental History:

Intact happy family
Mother full-time caretaker
Excellent student in elementary school
Adolescence: Heterosexual orientation, no problems with police, good grades
Ages 20–30: Working. Earned AA degree.
Ages 30–40: Married. Child born.
Accident occurred when Mr. Rose was 55 years of age.

Mental Status Examination:

Walked with limp
Good vocabulary
Emotionally labile, crying
Depressed affect
Logical and goal directed thinking

Why did you order psychological testing?

To obtain additional information and understanding that cannot be obtained in clinical interviews.

What did the testing show?

DSM IV diagnoses of Major Depressive Disorder, Single episode. Posttraumatic Stress Disorder, Chronic. Pain Disorder Associated with a General Medical Condition. Symptoms in the moderate to serious range.

Did you make psychiatric diagnoses?
What is DSM IV? (Three pages from DSM IV projected before the jury. DSM V not yet published)

- Major Depressive Disorder (one page from DSM IV projected before the jury)
- Pain Disorder
- Posttraumatic Stress Disorder (two pages from DSM IV projected before the jury)
- Male Erectile Disorder Due to Pelvic Trauma (one page from DSM IV projected before the jury)

How did you rate the severity of Mr. Rose's symptoms?

- Axis V: 41–50, serious.

Did you recommend psychiatric treatment for Mr. Rose?

- Individual psychotherapy, two to three times per week for two to three years to help him cope with the ongoing physical and psychological consequences of the accident.
- Cost in San Diego: $225–$250 per session.
- Antidepressant medication may be indicated: up to $100 per month.
- In the decade following the completion of the first course of therapy—an additional course of once to twice per week psychotherapy for one to two years to help Mr. Rose continue to deal with sexual issues, relationship problems, pain, and physical injury consequences of the accident and the aging process. Medication may be needed at that time.

Has Mr. Rose received any psychotherapy to this point?

- Seeing a therapist once per week. Describes his pain, inability to work, can't play the way he used to, less social, quality of life is negative and pessimistic, inability to function sexually without injections. Requires psychological treatment indefinitely.

What did you find during the three follow-up diagnostic interviews you had with Mr. Rose during the two years following your initial evaluation?

- Constant pain, spinal injections to attempt to relieve the pain.
- Had to stop working within a year after the accident.
- Will need injections into his penis for the rest of his life. (Very limited sensation.)
- Worry will become addicted to medication.
- No sports, socially withdrawn.
- "I expect to be disabled for the rest of my life."

Worry that his wife will leave him or cheat.
Expects to end up in a wheelchair.
Nightmares of being crushed.
Depressed affect.

Any final comments?

This was an emotionally healthy, functional man living a full life who suffered a tragic accident that resulted in a life of constant pain, inability to work, loss of hobbies, and sociability and a severe and permanent interference with sexual functioning.

As he ages his physical impairments and limitations are likely to increase, leading to the probability of intensified psychological symptoms and emotional impairment.

Notice that the direct testimony follows the outline to a fair degree.

DIRECT TESTIMONY OF CALVIN A. COLARUSSO, M.D., IN THE CASE OF ROBERT ROSE

All of the material that follows was taken from the court reporter's transcript of the court proceedings. Information that identified the plaintiff has been altered to protect confidentiality. As is evident from the speech of all of the individuals involved, the spoken word is not always as polished as the written word, particularly under a stressful situation.

MR. B. (plaintiff attorney): We'd like to call Dr. Calvin Colarusso, Your Honor.

THE COURT: All right.

(Dr. Colarusso enters the courtroom.)

THE COURT: Dr. Colarusso, if you would come up there and stand by that chair, please, sir, and raise your right hand. Swear the witness, please.

—CALVIN A. COLARUSSO, M.D., having been produced and first duly sworn as a witness, testified as follows:

THE WITNESS: I do.

THE COURT: Thank you very much, Dr. Colarusso. If you would have a seat. If you need to adjust that microphone, please feel free to do so, all right?

THE WITNESS: Thank you.

THE COURT: You're welcome. You may inquire, Mr. B

MR. B: Thank you, Your Honor.

DIRECT EXAMINATION BY MR. B:

Q Would you state your full name for the record, please.

A Calvin Anthony Colarusso, M.D.

Q And what is your profession, sir?

A I'm a physician with a specialty in adult and child psychiatry.

Q And would you share with the jury your credentials and your field of expertise?

A I graduated from Muhlenberg College in Allentown, Pennsylvania, in 1957, Jefferson Medical College in Philadelphia in 1961. That was followed by two years of full-time training in adult psychiatry at the Albert Einstein Medical Center in Philadelphia, followed by two years of full-time training in child psychiatry at the Albert Einstein Medical Center in Philadelphia. And following that I served in the United States Air Force for two years as a psychiatrist. And I was board certified in adult psychiatry in 1969 and in child psychiatry in 1972.

Q Have you served as an expert witness before?

A Yes, for the past thirty years.

Q And in civil cases, approximately how many cases have you evaluated and been retained on for that period of time?

A Approximately a thousand.

Q And in this case, before I get into the substance of your testimony, you've asked that I have Mr. Rose excused, correct?

A I did.

MR. B.: With the court's permission?

THE COURT: Yes, he may be excused.

(Mr. Rose leaves the room.)

Q Do you have a University affiliation?

A Since the early eighties I've been clinical professor of psychiatry at the University of California at San Diego.

Q Do you have any professional publications?

A I've written six books and fifty book chapters and various articles on various aspects of psychiatry and development.

Q Okay. And you've been practicing medicine for approximately how many years now?

A Well, I graduated fifty years ago this month.

Q And you have been called as an expert witness in all types of cases over those fifty years?

(Inclement weather causes lights to dim in the courtroom.)

THE COURT: If y'all don't mind, we'll keep on going, if you don't mind. Is that all right? Nobody's afraid of lightning? Ms. C. [defense attorney], are you okay?

MS. C.: (Nods head.)

MS. F. (defense attorney): Just tornadoes. I grew up in Tennessee, so . . .

BY MR. B.:

Q Approximately when were you first contacted concerning Mr. Robert Rose, sir?

A [Date first contacted.]

Q Okay. And what were you asked to do at that time?

A I was asked to do a psychiatric evaluation on Mr. Rose in connection with his lawsuit and serve as an expert witness.

Q Okay. And what did you do, in fact, as a follow-up to that request?

A In December—on December 16 I saw Mr. Rose for a two-hour-and-thirty-five-minute diagnostic interview. I requested that psychological testing be done. In addition I reviewed multiple records having to do with his experience in the hospital, his medical care after returning home, the depositions of Mr. Rose and his wife, and other documents.

And that's basically what I did. And then I had three follow-up visits with Mr. Rose, one of them in later in the year of the evaluation and two the following year.

Q Okay. What did you ask about Mr. Rose when you conducted your independent medical review?

A I went through the basic ingredients of a standard psychiatric evaluation. You ask about identifying information, about the issues that led to the injuries, any physical and psychological symptoms which relate to the injuries. Then I took what's called a developmental history, which traces an individual's life from birth to the chronological present, did a mental status examination, and considered various diagnostic possibilities.

Q Okay. And what identifying information did you obtain from Mr. Rose that was pertinent to your assessment of his mental health condition?

A Mr. Rose was a married man in his fifties. He had been married for twenty-three years. The couple has one grown child. Mr. Rose has worked in management all of his adult life.

Q And did you obtain from him information about the trauma that he had sustained related to this particular case?

A Yes. In shorthand form, basically he told me that he was standing at the valet of a restaurant when the valet inadvertently put the car into reverse, slammed into him, and pinned him against the wall. He was crushed and experiencing intense pain for approximately fifteen minutes, until the car was able to be removed from him. At that time he thought he was going to die and did not black out, so he has very vivid and very painful memories of what happened. After that he was taken to the emergency room, and from there was life-flighted to the hospital where he spent five days, then ten additional days in rehab. He returned home on an airplane, having to carry a urinal bottle with him on the airplane because he could not stand to get to the bathroom. And for the first four months after returning home he had numerous doctor's appointments having to do with his injuries and his pain.

Q Okay. And did you identify in your notes some of the important factors from the standpoint of his physical limitations at that time that were relevant to your mental health assessment?

A Yes. He described intense nearly constant pain in his pelvic area. He described that his right leg below the knee was numb, and as the day went on became painful and difficult for him to function. He had trouble walking. He was no longer able to play the sports that he had before. He was an avid golfer. He played soccer with his daughter. He was unable to do any of those functions. And very importantly to him, because of the injuries sustained from the accident he was unable to get an erection or to have intercourse with his wife without injecting his penis in order to become erect.

Q And in addition to the physical symptomatology, did you ascertain from him any relevant psychological symptomatology that you identified given your background and experience?

A Yes. He was working at the time that I first saw him, but was having great difficulty in work because he didn't feel that he could handle the load easily. He was distressed because of his relationship with his wife and his great concerns for her. But they had been a very close couple, and the loss of a sex life between them without injecting his penis was very difficult for him, very much lowered his self-esteem. He very much missed the full social life that he had with friends and family. And he was—although he didn't state this specifically, it was very clear that he was depressed and anxious much of the time.

Q Okay. Did he tell you how he was dealing with his frustrations and his emotional problems at that time?

A He was trying the best he could. This was a man who before the injuries had a very full, very happy life. He was a very outgoing person. That was evident from the way he presented himself in the face of these great difficulties. So he tried to have a stiff upper lip, he tried to look on the bright side, but it was quite clear that he was being taken down emotionally by the enormous limitations and pain.

Q Okay. Now, within your field is there a tool that you use called the developmental history?

A Yes.

Q Okay. Did you obtain that from Mr. Rose?

A Yes. The developmental history, as I mentioned, follows an individual's life from birth to the chronological present and compares that person's experience against the large body of knowledge about normal and pathological development. And this is what we call a clean developmental history, meaning there was no evidence of any psychological problems. He was born into an intact family. His parents were married forty-something years before his dad died. His father worked at several different jobs and so he and his family spent time living in different states. After high school he—he was an athlete. After high school he got an AA degree in business management. Mr. Rose married in his early thirties and the couple has a grown daughter. Throughout his adult years he basically managed the offices of businesses.

Q Okay. As another tool, did you perform a mental status examination on Mr. Rose?

A Yes. Mental status examination is a standard way that a mental health professional assesses an individual's mental and emotional state. And you look at appearance and behavior; characteristics of speech; affect, or feeling tone; thinking; and orientation and memory. Mr. Rose presented as a slightly overweight adult man who walked with a slight limp. He had a good vocabulary. His affect was—there was evidence of emotional lability. There was considerable tears as he described the accident and its consequences. There was evidence of him trying to appear bright. He was clearly depressed as I experienced him. I saw no evidence of any impairment in his ability to think or to reason.

Q All right. And based on that mental status exam, what did you do?

A Based on the mental status exam, the next thing I did was to consider various diagnostic possibilities towards the end of the diagnostic interview.

Q Okay. And how did you go about doing that?

A I utilized the Manual of the American Psychiatric Association, which is the cookbook, if you like, the bible. It is the book which describes all of the recognized psychiatric diagnoses and the criteria that have to be present for a diagnostician to make a diagnosis.

Q Okay. Before we get into the diagnostic DSM-IV manual, did you order psychological testing?

A Yes. As I mentioned earlier, a complete psychiatry evaluation includes psychological testing. I'm a physician, I'm not a psychologist. I'm not qualified to do the testing. The man that I asked to do the testing is a highly qualified psychologist. He did a full battery of psychological tests and wrote me a report. It's the equivalent if someone had a broken bone, as a physician, you would ask the radiologist to do an X-ray or CAT scan. Dr. B. did his testing, sent me a report. I incorporated that with my clinical interview and all of the information from the records before arriving at my opinions.

Q Okay. I'm going to go to Exhibit 282 just for a minute. We've seen this briefly in the trial. This is a treatment summary from Dr. B. who began treating Mr. Rose in psychotherapy, at your request, after your evaluation ended.

(Treatment Summary from Dr. B. is presented to the jury.)

"Mr. Rose has been treated in weekly individual psychotherapy [date]. Initial diagnoses included Major Depression, Posttraumatic Stress Disorder and Pain Disorder associated with a general medical condition. All diagnoses are still fully present by DSM-IV criteria.

"Mr. Rose suffers from significant physical difficulties and limitations combined with intense and frequently debilitating chronic pain. It requires very strong pain medication on a continual basis. He also takes nightly medication for sleep difficulties.

"Mr. Rose is typically a quite positive, optimistic and hopeful individual. Unfortunately, his ongoing chronic pain and physical difficulties have left him dysphoric, frustrated, discouraged, and depressed. He also continues to experience significant signs symptoms of sustained psychological trauma. Every aspect of Mr. Rose's existence and psychosocial functioning continue to be greatly diminished and negatively impacted by his injuries, pain, and compromise emotional functioning. He remains unable to work or to enjoy most of the social activities he engaged in premorbidly. He is unable to participate in nearly all activities involving physical movement or exertion. His general mood and sense of life quality is decidedly negative and pessimistic. He spends much less time with friends. Intimacy and sexual relations are still extremely limited and a source of profound frustration and difficulty. It is necessary for Mr. Rose to inject medication directly into his penis to achieve an erection. Unfortunately, even with such drastic measures, he feels almost no pleasurable stimulation in his genital region. Mr. Rose's physical limitations and erectile dysfunction have been devastating to his self-image and view of himself as a masculine, productive, successful father and husband.

"Mr. Rose will require ongoing psychological treatment indefinitely depending on the outcome of his treatments and procedures to address his physical injuries and chronic pain. If he significantly improves physically, then such psychological treatment can be tapered back appropriately. If his condition and functioning remains significantly unchanged, appropriate ongoing psychological care will remain necessary."

Q Did you also have this treatment summary available from Dr. B. at some point in time?

A I did. It's dated approximately seven months after my report. And in addition to that, Dr. B.'s office is in the same building as mine, and so I've talked to him periodically over the months about his treatment with Mr. Rose.

Q Okay. I just want to focus briefly, before we get to your ultimate opinions here, was there anything about the findings of Dr. B. during his treatment of Mr. Rose that you thought were incorrect or inaccurate in light of the evaluation that you performed as a psychiatrist?

A His findings were very similar to mine in this treatment summary and in one that he also wrote up just last month in June. Basically he finds Mr. Rose as struggling with all of the areas that I talked about. And as time has gone on, the time since my evaluation, and in the more than sixty sessions that Dr. B. has had with him, there's been a growing realization on Mr. Rose's part that he's not getting better, but in some ways he's getting worse, and that he's likely to be handicapped for the rest of his life.

Q Okay. And if we look at the last paragraph—

ATTORNEY: Can we highlight that?

Q "Mr. Rose will require ongoing psychological treatment indefinitely depending on the outcome of his treatments and procedures to address his physical injuries and chronic pain. If he significantly improves physically, then such psychological treatment can be tapered back appropriately. If his condition and functioning remains significantly unchanged, appropriate ongoing psychological care will remain necessary." In essence, what is this telling us, sir?

A It's telling us that—he was told in the hospital at the time of his injury that he'd be better in two years. It's telling us that he has not gotten better, that he's not going to get better, and indeed as he ages it's likely that the his condition will deteriorate.

Q And with respect to Dr. B.'s actual progress notes and reviewing those, is he of the opinion that that is going to be required the rest of Mr. Rose's life?

A Yes. Yes, psychiatric treatment and medication for the rest of his life.

Q And is that based on not only the testing that he did, but the sessions that he conducted over sixty-six—or approximately sixty-six visits and then the evaluation that you did?

DEFENSE ATTORNEY: Objection, Your Honor. This is a different doctor.

THE COURT: The objection's overruled. Go ahead.

DEFENSE ATTORNEY: This is one expert commenting on another expert, Your Honor.

PLAINTIFF ATTORNEY: No, this is the foundation.

Q And can you explain why Dr. B. believes that?

A Basically, he has been treating Mr. Rose on a weekly basis. The notes repeatedly demonstrate the symptoms of posttraumatic stress disorder, in particular, multiple nightmares about the crash or other crashes; great pain as he deals with his sexual limitations and the extraordinary procedures he has to go through in order to be able to have sexual relationships with his wife; the realization which gradually dawns on him that he's not going to get better; great suffering over the fact that he was not able to continue working at the job that he loved; and a deepening sense of depression from the time Dr. B. started with him up to the present. And that's very similar to what I found during the three follow-up sessions I had, the last one being just last month.

Q You mentioned the word "suffering." Can you distinguish from a mental health standpoint how that differs from just dealing with pain?

A Well, in this instance, because we know that he's in a great deal of physical pain, I would distinguish it that way. This man is experiencing nearly continuous physical pain. Psychologically, there's enormous suffering. We could use "pain" for both situations because he is obviously in great emotional pain as well.

Q Now, before I get into the actual testing that you did, is it fair that you asked that Mr. Rose be excused?

A I did.

Q And can you tell us why?

A Well, because what I have to say is not very pleasant to listen to and he's had enough pain as it is without having to hear me state it all over again.

Q Okay. With respect to the psychiatric diagnoses that you are going to share with this jury, you mentioned that you used the DSM-IV.

A Correct.

Q Now, just tell us a little bit about the background of DSM-IV. Why is that a tool that psychiatrists use in their practice?

A Well, this was formulated by a group of psychiatrists who are members of the American Psychiatric Association. It is actually the fourth edition, because over the years it has been updated and changed. And as I said, it contains all of the diagnoses that are recognized in the field. It's also used by psychologists, social workers, mental health workers of all kinds. And it gives you specific criteria which have to be present in order to make the diagnosis.

Q All right. Let's go to Exhibit 332. And Doctor, you have a pointer there, and we can blow this up a little bit, but do you recognize the first page of Exhibit 332?

A I guess—oh, it does work.

Q And come on down center if you would, that's fine.

THE WITNESS: Is that okay, Your Honor?

THE COURT: That's all right. I'd just ask you to make sure you speak up loudly enough for the jury to hear you, please.

(The Multiaxial Assessment page of the Desk Reference to the Diagnostic Criteria from DSM-IV-TR [page 37] was projected onto a large screen in front of the jury.)

A Okay. This is the first page, basically, in the manual. And it describes the five subdivisions that are—you must look at when you make a diagnosis. The first one has your major diagnoses. The second one is where you would place any character disorders, personality disorders, patterns of long-standing maladaptive behavior. The third one asks you to list or describe any physical conditions which directly relate to the psychiatric diagnoses on Axis I. The fourth one from a list in the manual asks you to describe what are called psychosocial and environmental problems. And these are things which help the diagnostician understand more about the diagnosis on Axis I. And the Global Assessment Scale of Functioning, Axis V, in the manual there is a chart, and you have to rate the severity of the patient's symptoms from 1 being profound to 100 being absent. So that's what this page describes.

Q All right. Let's go to the next page.

(Page 47 in the Desk Reference, the Global Assessment of Functioning [GAF] Scale, was projected onto the screen.)

A That doesn't look like it's—can be seen very well. There we are. This is the upper end of the Global Assessment scale, and it describes the criteria that have to be present for you to make an assessment in—from the 51 to 60 range and all the way up to 100. As I said, that's the upper end of the scale where the symptoms are not very pronounced.

Q Let's go to the other page, if we can.

(Page 48 from the Desk Reference is shown to the jury.)

A This is going from 1 to 50. And 41 to 50 is important in this case because that's where I listed Mr. Rose's symptoms in terms of severity. And if you look at the second part of it, any serious impairment in social, occupational, or school functioning. And that's where I placed Mr. Rose's symptomatology in terms of severity.

Q Okay. Next page.

(Page 173 from the Desk Reference, Major Depressive Disorder, comes up on the screen.)

A It's not very clear.

Q There we go.

A Okay. This—these are the criteria for major depressive disorder, which is one of the diagnoses that I made. And I don't know if you're able to read that. I have a tough time reading—

Q We can blow it up a little more maybe. Oh, that's much better.

LAWYER FOR DEFENSE: Judge, can we object? I—I think it's improper for the doctor to be reading a test to the jury. I don't think that's appropriate.

THE COURT: I understand the objection, but I'm going to overrule it. He's just giving his opinions at this point.

BY PLAINTIFF ATTORNEY:

Q Okay. Now, so you have the elements set forth for major depressive episode, correct?

A Yes.

And what I'd like you to do is to share the elements and the facts that apply to Mr. Rose.

A Yes. Mr. Rose has depressed mood and lack of interest in pleasure all of the time. And so he clearly meets A, which is the first of the criteria in order to make this diagnosis.

Q Let's go to B.

DEFENSE ATTORNEY: Judge, could we approach on this?

THE COURT: You may.

(Whereupon the following sidebar conference was had out of the hearing of the jury.)

Sidebars occur when an attorney wants a ruling from the judge that is made outside the prevue of the jury and the witness. The transcript of that sidebar is presented here.

DEFENSE ATTORNEY: I was trying to give counsel some leeway, but I think it's entirely improper for this witness to be bolstering his opinion by referring to a text from—you know, that he relies upon. He can testify about his opinions but he cannot bolster it by saying, "Oh, look, here's a book that agrees with my diagnosis." He's supposed to testify that—

THE COURT: That's not what the book is doing.

DEFENSE ATTORNEY: But it is. He's utilizing the book to say, "This is the criteria you're supposed to use"—"that I use and you're supposed to use, and based on that criteria Mr. Rose is suffering from X, Y, and Z." He can testify to what Mr. Rose is suffering from, but he can't rely upon a book and have it open in front of the jury while he's doing his testimony, that's the part I'm objecting to. It is bolstering. You're only supposed to use an authoritative text like this in cross-examination, not to bolster your direct testimony.

PLAINTIFF ATTORNEY: It's not to bolster, it's to lay down the criteria or the elements. But I can speed it up and just have him read the key elements if looking at it bothers you.

DEFENSE ATTORNEY: No, I think he can testify what he thinks the key elements are, but I don't think he's entitled to rely upon a book and say, "These are the key elements." That's my objection, Your Honor.

PLAINTIFF ATTORNEY: Well, that's the whole basis of the psychiatric diagnosis. You've got to rely on the foundational—

THE COURT: Okay, okay. Every case that I've dealt with where we go with psychological evaluations based on either Axis I or Axis II the witnesses have come in, have used what the definition of the axis is and testified about it. They do that because it's the only recognized standard in terms of psychiatric medicine. I'm going to allow it to go forward with the understanding that we're going to move this thing along.

DEFENSE ATTORNEY: But do we need to have the book opened while he's testifying?

THE COURT: He just told you he wouldn't do that if that was offending you.

PLAINTIFF ATTORNEY: Yeah, I told you I'd just move on and just have him read the key elements. I don't have to post it.

DEFENSE ATTORNEY: All right.

THE COURT: That's what he said.

(The following proceedings occurred in open court, in the presence of the jury.)

BY PLAINTIFF ATTORNEY:

Q Now, Doctor, moving forward with the DSM-IV you can pull that down for now—let's focus on the key elements for depression. We talked about A. What's the next element that we have to consider?

A The next one is markedly diminished interest or pleasure in all or almost all activities most of the day. And that is certainly true of Mr. Rose. He's not able to live the life that he did before. Because of the depression and the pain involved, he has less interest in doing so. He does not meet the third factor, which is a significant weight loss or gain, which you often find in depression. The reason for that is because he was encouraged to lose weight by his physicians because he was overweight and because of the pressure on his pelvis. The fourth one is insomnia or hypersomnia nearly every day. Mr. Rose has insomnia very frequently. It's a result both of the pain and his depression and worry about his life. The next one is psychomotor agitation or retardation. What that means is either talking too fast or your thoughts being slowed down. There are times when Mr. Rose has what we call pressure of speech because he's experiencing anxiety in relation to whatever the current stressor he's dealing with: a doctor's appointment, the end of work, whatever. Fatigue or loss of energy nearly every day. He indeed has that. And I think it's both physically and psychologically based. This one he has in spades, feelings of worthlessness or excessive or inappropriate guilt. This is a man who was fully active in life, working, making a good living, happily involved with his wife and his family. Now he is unable to support his family or to do the kinds of things that he could. He is unable to have the kind of intimate life that he had with his wife before, and there are intense feelings of worthlessness. Diminished ability to think or concentrate. There is some of that to a mild degree, which is related to the depression and the pain. And recurring thoughts of death. Recurrent suicidal ideations. Mr. Rose has not had any suicidal ideations. There are many times he tells me that he wished he were dead because he sees no end to the situation that he's involved in. So that's the criteria in the manual for major depressive disorder and for how Mr. Rose meets the criteria.

Q Based on the initial evaluation that you conducted, including the input from Dr. B.'s testing, did you form an opinion at that point in time that Mr. Rose was suffering from major depressive disorder?

A I did.

Q And did you rate the severity?

A I rated all the diagnoses together on Axis V and I address the severity of the diagnoses after considering all of them.

Q Okay. And then let's go to the next diagnoses that you came up with after reviewing the evidence and looking at the DSM-IV. That would be what, sir?

A The second one is pain disorder associated with a general medical condition. And a general medical condition has a major role in the onset, severity, exacerbation, or maintenance of the pain. And pelvic is specifically listed as one of the parts of the body that can cause the pain disorder. In this case, the pain disorder is obviously due to physical causes, but there is also a psychological element attached to it because the pain stirs up in him continual feelings of inadequacy and of not being able to have the life that he had before. And there are no specific criteria beyond that listed in the manual for that diagnosis.

Q And then what is the next diagnosis relevant to Mr. Rose that you assessed?

A The next diagnosis is posttraumatic stress disorder. And post-traumatic stress disorder, in the manual there's very specific criteria, so I'll go through them. First, it's broken down into three groups of symptoms. The first one is the mind's attempt over and over again to try and deal with the trauma and master it. The second one is exactly the opposite. The mind tries to shut it off and push the awareness of the injury out of mind. And the third one is a sense of hyperalertness, that you're expecting something bad to happen again, and so you're constantly on guard. So that's the general criteria. The first thing that has to be present is that the person has been exposed to a traumatic event in which both of the following were present: the person experienced, witnessed, or was confronted with an event or events that involved actual or threatened death or serious injury or a threat to the physical integrity of self and others. That certainly happened as a result of the injuries that he suffered. Two, the person's response involved intense fear, helplessness, or horror. And I think he experienced all of those at the time of the accident. Now, in terms of part B, the event being persistently re-experienced, he has recurrent and intrusive thoughts on—multiple times a day, stimulated by the pain, stimulated by what he can't do, stimulated by his awareness of how his life has changed. The second one is recurrent distressing dreams of the event. Mr. Rose continues to have nightmares up to the present dealing primarily with his own accident and with similar accidents in which someone is being severely traumatized. The third one, what are called flashbacks, acting or feeling as if the traumatic event was reoccurring. And he has this to a degree. But he doesn't have full-blown flashbacks that overwhelm him, but very frequently he has the feeling of being back in the situation at the restaurant. Intense psychological distress and exposure to internal or external cues that symbolize or resemble an aspect of the traumatic event. This happens if he hears about an accident on television. This happens when he experiences pain. There are constant stimuli that he experiences which stir up very painful psychological feelings. And the last one in the section is physiological reactivity. His heart races sometimes, his palms get sweaty, he gets anxious, his stomach gets tight. Those are examples of physiological activity. The third subdivision is persistent avoidance of stimuli associated with the trauma and numbing of general responsiveness. He tries to avoid thinking about what happened and to, as he calls it, put on a happy face and get on with his life. It's very difficult and impossible to do for any length of time. He tries to avoid activities, places, and people that arouse recollections of the trauma. Driving by the restaurant is very painful. He doesn't like going by restaurants because they're a reminder. He doesn't like to be around people the way he did before because people inevitably want to know what happened, and he finds that very painful. The third one is inability to recall an important aspect of the trauma. There's no repression here. He is fully aware of what happened to him. Next one is markedly diminished interest or participation in significant activities. He has that in spades, both because of his physical limitations and his depression. Feelings of being detached or estranged from others. He at this point considers himself to be very different from his wife, his family, his friends, his coworkers. He describes himself as a handicapped person who's going to end up in a wheelchair. Restricted range of affect. He has that. He's mostly depressed and his affects are not as comfortable and easy as they were before. And sense of a for-certain future; does not expect to have a career, marriage, children or a normal life span. He can't work anymore. He's worried about the future of his marriage, although that's based on his fears, not on anything that has actually happened in regard to his wife. And he certainly is concerned about how long he's going to live and also that he's going to live in a wheelchair or as an invalid. And then the last subsection are symptoms of increased arousal. In other words, you're on guard that it doesn't happen again. He has difficulty falling asleep and staying asleep because of the nightmares. He can be quite irritable and have outbursts of anger about which he feels quite guilty. He finds it difficult to concentrate because of the pain primarily. Marked hypervigilance. He is terrified around any kind of a vehicle that something similar will happen again. And exaggerated startle response, which certainly occurs to loud noises. So he meets almost every one of the criteria listed in the manual. And you don't have to have all of them to make the diagnosis. And because it has lasted longer than three months, it is considered to be chronic.

Q Okay. Now, Doctor, backing up a step, what experience have you had in dealing with posttraumatic stress disorder?

A I was in the United States Air Force at the time of Vietnam. I was a psychiatrist in California. We treated all of the individuals with psychiatric situations coming back from Vietnam. They almost all had posttraumatic stress disorder. And since that time, as a result of my expert testimony work and in my practice, I've probably dealt with fifty to a hundred other individuals with that diagnosis.

Q Do you still see patients?

A I do.

Q And approximately what percentage of your work is forensic work versus working with patients?

A Well, at this point it's about fifty/fifty. But for decades I saw fifty to sixty patient hours a week.

And do you work on behalf of both plaintiffs and defendants in cases of PTSD?

A Yes, I do.

Q Do you evaluate them any differently?

A No.

Q Okay. What's the next diagnosis after that.

A The last one was erectile dysfunction, which is a specific diagnosis in the manual which is very short and basically says if erectile dysfunction is present, you make the diagnosis and try and determine what the factors are that are responsible for it. And in this instance, there are clear physiological factors related to his difficulty in getting an erection, and there are also psychological feelings of embarrassment and shame associated with that.

Q Okay. Now, once you've analyzed and made these basic diagnoses, then how do you deal with that from the standpoint of the standardization protocol that you're required to follow?

A Well, you do what I just did. You list all the criteria that are present in this individual which serve as the basis for your diagnosis, and that then leads to considerations of treatment and prognosis.

Q Okay. And based on the initial work-up that you did with Mr. Rose, would you describe to the jury what—what opinions did you form with respect to the severity of Mr. Rose's symptoms at that time?

A I said that immediately he needed individual psychotherapy two to three times a week for two to three years and antidepressant medication and that at some point in the decade following the completion of the first treatment, individual psychotherapy one to two times a week for one to two years.

Q And then beyond that?

A At the time of my initial evaluation, I did not make a comment on that. However, seeing Mr. Rose over the course of the time that followed, and talking to Dr. B., it's become clear, as I mentioned, that his condition has gotten worse instead of better and is not likely to change. So it's likely that he's going to need continued psychotherapy and medication for the rest of his life.

Q And in the future, do you anticipate—first of all, is it your understanding that what Dr. B. has done for Mr. Rose has been of benefit to him?

A Mr. Rose describes it as very helpful. I've talked with Dr. B. about it. Dr. B. feels that he has been helpful in stabilizing Mr. Rose and that the main task of the therapy to this point has been to help him slowly accept and recognize the limitations and the fact that he's not going to get better.

Q From a mental health assessment standpoint, as we look into Mr. Rose's life as he begins to age with these injuries, what is the medical prognosis from a psychiatric standpoint?

A I think the depression is likely to stay the same or get worse because as he ages and becomes more incapacitated, he's going to feel worse.

Q All right. How about the PTSD?

A Well, as we know from experience with Vietnam veterans and many individuals, posttraumatic stress disorder in profound traumas like this can last a lifetime.

Q And how about the diagnoses of the pain disorder?

A I think you'll have to defer that to the physicians who are treating that. But from everything I've read, there is no cure for his pain, there's only management.

Q And with respect to the erectile dysfunction that's permanent, what is your assessment in that regard from a mental health standpoint.

A From what I've read, he's been told he's going to need injections in order to get an erection for the rest of his life. That's highly traumatic.

Q And what is the cost of psychotherapy?

A Approximately $250 per forty-five minute individual psychotherapy session.

Q And is Mr. Rose—you understand he's taking antidepressant medication?

A Yes.

Q And what is your recommendation in that regard in the future?

A He's likely to need that indefinitely. And the cost is approximately $100 per month.

Q Okay. And with respect to—in the decade following the completion of the first course of therapy that you mentioned, given Mr. Rose's status based on your review of his current treatment and assessment, to a reasonable degree of medical probability, what is your opinion as to whether or not he will require lifetime psychotherapy care and treatment, given what we see now?

A The fact that since I did my evaluation his condition has become worse physically and he's been told that it's not likely to change for the better, he's going to need supportive psychotherapy indefinitely for the rest of his life. He's being seen now once per week. But he needs more treatment than that. I don't know if he is not being seen more often than that because of financial reasons.

Q Dr. B., in his deposition, said that Mr. Rose was keeping up but not quite there. But as far as needs of Mr. Rose, based from now into the future, until the Good Lord takes Mr. Rose, what do you foresee will be the amount of medical psychotherapy treatment he should have if he's going to do the best to contain his mental health issues?

A Well, my second recommendation was in the decade following the first course of treatment, one to two times a week for one to two years and antidepressant medication, and as best I can estimate, I would say probably once a week after that for the rest of his life.

Q After a decade out?

A After a decade out.

Q And that's what he's getting right now?

A That's what he's getting now.

Q Will you summarize for the jury what you feel is relevant for them to understand concerning your assessment in these interviews, sir.

A I can summarize them quite easily. It's slowly been dawning on Mr. Rose that he's not going to get better, that he's not going back to work at the job that he loved, that his life is going to be highly limited in terms of the sports and activities that he played before, and that his relationship with his wife and their intimacy has been severely compromised and will continue to be. And he certainly hopes that she's able to tolerate that and stay with him.

Q Has he expressed any concerns about his potential for addiction to pain medication?

A He did. He doesn't like taking medicine because he's afraid he's going to be addicted. But it's quite clear that life would be unbearable without the pain medication.

Q Okay. One final just to conclude, any final comments or reflection on Mr. Rose from the standpoint of his mental health status as you see it now and into the future, sir?

A Well, this—this is a man who was living a full, happy life. He's one of these very unfortunate individuals who had an act of fate that could happen to any one of us that absolutely brought him to the point of enormous pain, injury, and the loss pretty much of the life that he had before. He—the fact that he was an intact individual emotionally before the accident is what I think allows him to function as well as he is.

PLAINTIFF ATTORNEY: Okay. Thank you, sir. That's all I have, Your Honor.

THE COURT: All right. Thank you.

This is an outstanding example of how a plaintiff attorney conducts direct testimony with a psychiatric expert witness. He gave me latitude to express my opinions during the first part of the direct testimony in as much detail as I wished and made sure that the last thing the jury heard before I left the stand was a restatement of my credentials and my major diagnostic impressions and treatment recommendations.

In chapter 7 we'll discuss undergoing cross-examination and read the actual cross-examination in the Robert Rose case.

SEVEN

Testifying in Court

Cross-Examination in the Case of Robert Rose

> Cross Examination—The Questioning of a Witness by an Opposing Party.
>
> —Melton et al., 2007, p. 694

Why is there such a thing as cross-examination? The life of the mental health expert witness would certainly be much easier if cross-examination did not exist. But cross-examination does exist and is at the very heart of the American judicial system. The following description, taken from *The Mental Health Professional and the Legal System* (Committee on Psychiatry and the Law, Group for the Advancement of Psychiatry, 1991) explains why. Our legal system is based on the resolution of disputes based on the presentation of evidence within the procedural rules of the law. The adversarial nature of plaintiff versus defense insures that there will not be an unsubstantiated rush to judgment. It is the duty of the advocate (both to his client and to the law) to make a vigorous presentation of the plaintiff case. It is the role of the defense to critically challenge that presentation.

> No feature of the legal system embodies the principles of conflict and advocacy more clearly than reliance on cross-examination as a tool in the search of truth. The rule against admitting out-of-court statements (hearsay) is based on the belief that no evidence should be admitted that cannot be tested by cross-examination. *The techniques of cross-examination threaten mental health witnesses who are afraid that they will be unable to defend their opinions and be made to appear foolish.* The properly prepared witness need not fear either of these possibilities. His resolve to participate in the legal system is heightened by the awareness that he

is playing a vital role in the search for truth and justice within the best legal system in the world. (p. 13)

Now that we have an understanding of the vital, indispensable need for cross-examination let's deal with the fear. In my opinion this is not a situation in which the lawyer has the upper hand, all the power, and the expert is relatively helpless. The expert's power derives from the thoroughness of his evaluation and preparation and the reasonableness of his opinions. You know more about your field and your opinions than he does. Further, you have the ability to respond as you choose, not as he demands. Varying the time before responding to a question, and varying the length of your answer allows you to challenge the attorney for control of the pace of the cross-examination. Think of yourself as a counter-puncher in a prizefight. Mohammed Ali used this technique to great advantage. In addition, during your pretrial meetings with the retaining attorney you were told about the style of cross-examination that would be utilized and the areas of greatest interest and concern to the examining lawyer.

Obviously, I cannot cover all of the possibilities of what you will encounter in cross-examination; however, the following information about attitudes, responses, and often-encountered questions and approaches will provide a foundation on which to build your experience.

THE CROSS-EXAMINER'S EMOTIONAL TONE

Pay attention to the tone of the voice of the attorney as he introduces himself to you. More than likely he will greet you cordially and will maintain that demeanor throughout the cross-examination. The emotional tone for your interaction has been set. You respond in kind. Do not be fooled by this attempt to get you to relax. He will attempt to disturb your equilibrium and undermine your opinions through his questions, not his attitude. He is no less dangerous than the lawyer whose introduction is cold and emotionally hostile. This often means that he feels he is in a weak position, vis-á-vis you, and will attempt to unnerve you through sarcasm and hostility. There is pleasure, and great effectiveness, in maintaining your cool and responding to his aggression calmly and cordially.

QUESTIONING OF YOUR CREDENTIALS

If you are relatively inexperienced the examiner may question your credentials. The answer to lack of experience is evidence of having done a thorough evaluation and clear and concise opinions and recommendations. Talking to the jury in plain English, as you look them in the eye, quickly overcomes this approach.

RESPONDING TO QUESTIONS

Listen closely to each question. Remember, all the attorney is allowed to do is ask questions. *Answer only what is asked.* However, if you feel that you need to expand your response to get your point across, do so. If the question is about an opinion of yours that you do not feel you were allowed to fully present in prior questioning, bring up your additional thoughts here, recognizing that the cross-examiner may object, leaving the decision if you may continue to the judge.

CONTROLLING YOUR ANSWERS

If the lawyer demands a yes or no answer to a question and you feel a fuller response is needed to reply to the attorney's attempt to limit or skew your opinion, simply say that you cannot answer the question with a yes or no. *The lawyer controls the questions. You control the answers. In other words, stick to your guns.* If you have done a thorough evaluation and substantiated your diagnoses by enumerating the criteria from DSM V he has little ability to criticize you.

Do not change your opinions on the stand. To do so under the pressure of cross-examination would destroy your credibility.

AVOIDING THE "WAFFLE"

If confronted with a difficult or unanticipated question you may find yourself attempting to overwhelm the questioner with words, sometimes evasive ones, as you attempt to formulate a response to the question. This is called a "waffle" (Gutheil, 2007). In such a situation you may ask the examiner to restate the question or say that you do not understand it—giving you time to organize your thoughts. A long pause as you thoughtfully consider an answer is another useful technique.

DO NOT GENERALIZE

Resist attempts by the lawyer to get you to generalize. For example, he may ask how other individuals with diagnoses you gave might respond differently than the individual that you evaluated. Answer—"I can't make any comment and certainly have no expert opinion on an individual whom I have not evaluated personally."

"DON'T YOU AGREE, DOCTOR?"

Another common technique used by lawyers at both deposition and trial is to attempt to circumscribe and limit your opinion by asking "Don't you agree, Doctor?" after making a definitive statement about an aspect of the case. Do not hesitate to disagree and explain why. Always remember the basic distribution of power in deposition or on the stand—the lawyer controls the questions, indeed that is all he controls, but you control your answers.

REQUEST FOR TAX INFORMATION

Although I have never personally experienced this cross-examination technique it has been reported in the literature. In an attempt to impeach your testimony the opposing lawyer may request a copy of your tax returns. This is an attempt to portray you as a "hired gun" whose opinion has been strongly influenced by the party that engaged you and paid your fee (Gutheil, Simon, and Simpson, 2006).

If such a request is made at trial the retaining lawyer would certainly object. Even if the judge granted the request, which is highly unlikely, it would require days or weeks to gather the information and the trial would likely be over. It is a technique aimed at embarrassing and unnerving you on the stand.

HAVE YOU BEEN PAID FOR YOUR TESTIMONY?

A much more likely question, along the same line and with the same intention in mind is "Doctor, how much are you being paid for your testimony?" Answer—"I'm not being paid for my testimony. I'm being paid for my expertise and my time."

WHAT ARE YOUR HOURLY RATES?

You will undoubtedly be asked at deposition and/or trial about your hourly rate and how much you have billed and been paid in this case. Be sure to have totals of what you have billed and been paid prior to deposition or trial. *Do not* take the stand without having been paid for your work up to the time of trial. If you have not been paid in full the cross-examiner may suggest that your opinion is influenced by your desire to be paid. In addition, if you are working for an individual lawyer, or a small firm, if the verdict goes against the retaining lawyer, you may have difficulty getting paid for your prior work and trial testimony.

When I'm asked about my hourly rate or how much I've billed, I'm always concerned that the jury will react negatively to the rates, considering them to be high which they certainly are when compared to what the vast majority of people earn. Answer these fee questions calmly and without embarrassment. Your attorney will ask the same questions of the opposing experts. By the end of the process the jury will understand that your fees are not unusual or out of the ordinary for experts in court.

THE "PERFECT PHANTOM"

A technique used by some lawyers on cross-examination is described in the literature as the "Perfect Phantom" (Brodsky and Heller, 2008). The term refers to an individual who has experienced the same difficulties, traumas, and consequences as the individual you evaluated for the trial but did not develop symptoms or psychopathology. The question put to you directly or indirectly is "How do you explain that, Doctor?" The answer is twofold. First, and I return to this idea over and over again, you have a detailed explanation of why the individual you evaluated warranted the diagnosis you gave and the treatment recommendations you made. Your opinions have a solid, reasonable basis to them. Second, you cannot make any statement as an expert witness about an individual that you have not personally evaluated. This highly ethical stance not only applies to your forensic practice but to your clinical work as well.

CROSS-EXAMINATION: THE CASE OF ROBERT ROSE

As with the direct testimony which was presented in chapter 6, what follows is taken directly from the court reporters transcript. Changes have been made to ensure confidentiality. It is interesting to compare the tone of the defense attorney at trial as opposed to his somewhat rambling, confrontational approach at deposition.

CROSS-EXAMINATION BY DEFENSE ATTORNEY:

Q Dr. Colarusso, let me just ask you a few questions that we can go through I think fairly quickly. You're not a treating psychiatrist or psychologist in this case; is that fair to say?

Q You were retained by Mr. (name) to serve as an expert witness, what you're doing here today testifying in a courtroom; is that fair to say?

A Yes, it is.

Q Thank you. Now, you generated a report—and let me just back up for a second here. You're the—you brought in Dr.—you brought in Dr. B., the jury saw his videotape deposition, but you're the one that, through [plaintiff attorney] brought him in; is that fair to say?

A I asked Dr. B. to do the psychological testing, yep.

Q Okay. And, in fact, Dr. B. turned from somebody that did psychological testing into somebody that has been seeing Mr. Rose I think you said one time every—one time a week; is that fair to say?

A Yes.

Q Now, you generated a report dated [date]; is that correct?

A True.

Q And your practice is now in La Jolla, California?

A Yes, it is.

Q Okay.

DEFENSE ATTORNEY: And what I'd like to do is, Denise, if you can bring that up.

PLAINTIFF ATTORNEY: Give us an exhibit number for it, Counselor. I couldn't find it.

DEFENSE ATTORNEY: I don't have it.

PLAINTIFF ATTORNEY: Well, let's mark it.

DEFENSE ATTORNEY II: What are you looking for?

DEFENSE ATTORNEY: Colarusso's report.

DEFENSE ATTORNEY:

Q Doctor, do you recognize that as your report?

A I do, and I have it in front of me.

DEFENSE ATTORNEY: Okay. So—let's see. You—Denise, why don't we, if you could, highlight the upper one-third above the diagnostic interview part. That's good enough. We can stay—that's fine, Denise. You can bring that back. Thank you.

BY DEFENSE ATTORNEY:

Q Doctor, you interviewed, [date] Mr. Rose; is that correct?

A Yes.

Q And you also had the benefit of reviewing those items that were identified in that list; do you recall that?

A Yes.

Q Okay. And the last item you see there, you see [neurologist's] name?

A Yes.

Q And you had his records as well?

A I did.

Q Okay. And I think if my notes are correct, you—when you met with Mr. Rose, you indicated that he was, I think from a psychiatric standpoint, severely depressed; was that your opinion?

A That was the conclusion I came to, yes.

Q Okay. And that was based on at this point you had met with him (date), correct?

A That was when I wrote the report.

Q Just one second, Doctor.

(Inclement weather causes buzzing in the court room.)

Q Okay. But when you met with him on—

THE COURT: Hang on a minute, Doctor. That's the first time that's happened.

A When I wrote the report I also had Dr. B.'s testing report.

Q On [date of interview], it was your impression that there was severe depression?

A No, I did not make a diagnosis on [date of interview]. I considered various diagnostic possibilities. I made my diagnoses after I received Dr. B.'s report and reviewed the records.

Q But did you get any impression when you met and spent the couple hours that you spent with him on that date?

A I got a number of impressions, yes.

Q And was one of the impressions having to do with depression?

A Yes.

Q And what was that impression or—that you got on that date?

A That he appeared to be depressed.

Q Okay. So—

DEFENSE ATTORNEY: Denise, if you can bring up Dr. [name] report [date] which would have been eight days before you saw him, Doctor.

BY DEFENSE ATTORNEY:

Q You recognize that, The Neurology Center, [name] practice?

A I don't specifically recall it, but I did review his records.

DEFENSE ATTORNEY: And Denise, if you can bring up the next page. And if you could highlight under psychiatric.

BY DEFENSE ATTORNEY:

Q So this would have been eight days before you saw Mr. Rose. And you had this record; did you not?

A I did, yeah.

Q And do you see next to psychiatric "no unusual anxiety or evidence of depression"? Do you see that?

A I see, yes.

Q Was that consistent or inconsistent with your impression eight days later?

A That's inconsistent.

Q Okay. He's a neurologist, isn't he?

A Yes, but he's not a psychiatrist.

Q Is he also trained in psychiatry?

A Not in the way I am, no.

Q I know he's not a psychiatrist, but don't all doctors receive training in psychiatry?

A better prepared lawyer would have known the difference between the training of a neurologist and a psychiatrist.

A All medical students receive some exposure to psychiatry but do not take a full-time, three-year residency in psychiatry that is required to become a psychiatrist.

DEFENSE ATTORNEY: It's L0035, Denise. If you could highlight the date of it. Just enlarge that so the doctor can see it.

By DEFENSE ATTORNEY:

Q You can see, this is now [date], right around the same time frame as you're doing your work, Doctor; is that fair to say?

A Yes, it's a month later.

Q Okay.

DEFENSE ATTORNEY: And Denise, if you could jump to the next page, 0036. And if you go, again, to psychiatric.

Q [Neurologist name] noted "no unusual anxiety or evidence of depression." Do you see that, Doctor?

A Yes.

Q Is that consistent or inconsistent with the impression that you got from meeting with Mr. Rose?

A Dr. [name] is a neurologist who is focusing on this man's pain and neurological injuries. He's not a psychiatrist. He didn't do a psychiatric evaluation.

Q Do you have any reason to think that Dr. [name] would write that unless he had some reason to write that?

A I have no reason to think that.

DEFENSE ATTORNEY: Now, Denise, let's go back to Dr. Colarusso's report, page one.

BY DEFENSE ATTORNEY:

Q What I'd like to go now down to is the first paragraph under the diagnostic interview where you discussed the issue of no confidentiality. You told him that the usual doctor/patient confidentiality was not present in your relationship with him because you were serving as an expert witness in his law suit. Did you had that exchange with him?

A I did.

Q Okay. So the purpose of this was, again, for you to be able to come in here and testify as a psychiatrist, as a retained expert witness, not as a treater; is that fair to say?

A True. Yes.

DEFENSE ATTORNEY: Denise, if you could bring that up for jury.

Q "Mr. Rose was seen in my office. No one else was present. Mr. Rose was informed that unlike the usual doctor/patient relationship, this evaluation was being performed as a part of his lawsuit and there was no doctor/patient relationship present." Is that accurate?

A Yes.

Q Okay.

DEFENSE ATTORNEY: Now, Denise, if you go to the next page of the doctor's report, page two. First sentence in the second paragraph.

I'm thinking that all this jumping around he is doing is likely confusing the jury and not very effective.

BY DEFENSE ATTORNEY:

Q "After approximately fifteen minutes the car was pulled off Mr. Rose." That was what he told you?

A Yes.

Q Okay. Let's go to the bottom of that page. The last paragraph on that page under symptoms, the last paragraph, Doctor, and correct me if I'm wrong, "He is not able to get an erection. Viagra doesn't help. Mr. Rose had his first orgasm during the week before the interview, achieving an erection through a self-administered needle injection of his penis. He began to use this procedure three weeks ago."

Q Is that what Mr. Rose told you?

A Yes.

Q Let's go to page three.

BY DEFENSE ATTORNEY:

Q "Mr. Rose was an excellent student in elementary school. He was well liked, had lots of friends and was interested in sports. The family went camping and on vacations in Europe, where his father was stationed. From ages five to nine Mr. Rose wore a leg brace because he had Perthes disease." Is that what Mr. Rose told you?

A Yes.

Q Did Mr. Rose tell you which leg he had the Perthes disease problem with?

A I don't recall.

Q You agree with me, sir, that Mr. Rose has strong family support, strong family background?

A Yes.

Q Okay. That would make him less of a candidate or less prone to psychological long-term injury; is that fair to say?

A That—that's a little bit confusing. It would make him less prone to develop a psychiatric illness based on psychological factors.

Q Okay. And we know that Mr. Rose had been through the—maybe normal is too strong a word, but had gone through life experiences that were of disappointments that everybody has to go through, such as the loss of a parent, the loss of both parents, and we also know that he went through a difficult divorce from his first wife, and he was able to—and I'm sure those things are always difficult, but he was able to, with time, go on without the need of outside counseling or outside psychiatric care; is that fair to say?

A Yes.

Q And would you agree with me, sir, that after a trauma, something that is of a traumatic impact from a psychological nature, that as the time grows from the—from—grows from the event, or the distance grows from that event, that the healing processes of the person from that traumatic event take into being and there is coping and other mechanisms that all of us go through in coping with those events; is that fair to say?

A That depends on the individual and the event.

Q Okay. Well, you're not suggesting, are you, sir, that—first of all, there was some comparison between what [names plaintiff] has gone through and somebody in combat out in war. Do you recall that, sir?

A Well, I don't think you meant [name of plaintiff attorney], what he's gone through, but I think you meant Mr. Rose.

He appears somewhat confused and befuddled and I immediately correct his mistake.

Q Mr. Rose.

A Yes.

Q Pardon me. I stand corrected. You are right, sir. There was some comparison drawn between those types of traumatic events?

A Yes. Depends on what the consequences of the accident were. In this case, it's not the accident that is now the problem, it's the injuries that resulted from it and the loss of his life, basically, in an emotional sense and a work sense. That's the problem. And that's ongoing.

Q Okay. Are you suggesting that the number of people that are involved in automobile accidents or serious automobile accidents, that that type of experience is, in fact, comparable to someone who suffers an injury under military conditions during a war?

A It can be, if not the actual circumstance in which the injury occurs, but in the long range effects of the physical and psychological injuries.

We had the same discussion during the deposition.

Q Would it not be beneficial for Mr. Rose to, in fact, have structure in his life? Isn't that something that you recommend to your patients?

A What kind of structure are you talking 'bout?

Q I'm talking about where somebody has a job, whether it's full-time or part-time, to go to, would that be beneficial from a psychological standpoint for Mr. Rose?

A I'm not sure Mr. Rose is going to be capable to do very much of anything. But if he could, sure.

Q That would be helpful. And you had mentioned that—and correct me if I'm wrong, but that you indicated that Mr. Rose would have a fear, I think you said, of—from cars? Is that what you had said?

A Yes, fear of cars, being around cars.

Q Fear of cars?

A Fear of being around cars.

Q Fear of being around cars. Now—and is that going to get better?

A I don't think it's going to get better in this case because every day of pain is a constant reminder of what happened.

Q Okay. And Dr. Colarusso, have you had the benefit of seeing the surveillance tape that was done of Mr. Rose in this case?

DEFENSE ATTORNEY: Denise, the October video.

PLAINTIFF ATTORNEY: Your Honor, there's no foundation for this.

THE COURT: I'll allow the question, see where it goes.

PLAINTIFF ATTORNEY: Your Honor, we are going to post this then?

(A portion of surveillance videotape without audio was played.)

BY DEFENSE ATTORNEY:

Q Do you recognize who's in that video, sir?

A That looks like Mr. Rose.

Q Okay. Tell me whether or not you see any signs of the posttraumatic stress disorder from fear of cars that you're talking about in this video, sir.

A I assume we're going to see some cars?

Q Stay tuned, yes. These valets move very slowly, sir.

DEFENSE ATTORNEY: I might disagree.

BY PLAINTIFF ATTORNEY:

Q You see Mr. Rose, what he was doing there, sir, seemed to be conversing with the valet, laughing just before this?

A Yes.

Q Does that not indicate that he is recovering from posttraumatic stress disorder?

A He is not recovering from the posttraumatic stress disorder. I wish he were.

Q Okay. We can stop it wherever you see the fear, terrified around vehicles that you were talking about.

A Fear is an internal state. Anxiety is an internal state. It's not necessarily going to show on a film like that. But to answer your question, I saw no outward evidence of fear there.

Q And we don't have to play it. If there's another video the jury has seen where Mr. Rose is walking around with [plaintiff attorney] for some time in a parking lot showing no signs of fear, would that be a good sign that perhaps he is recovering from post-traumatic stress disorder that you're talking about?

A No, like fear, the symptoms of posttraumatic stress disorder are experienced as thoughts and feelings, during the day and during sleep.

Q Okay. Did Mr. Rose ever tell you that he could not perform his job?

A He said it was very difficult for him.

Q Did he ever tell you that he was—that it was difficult, where he was contemplating leaving the job? And I'm talking about during the time frame that you saw him.

A No. He wanted to work.

Q Did he tell you that he was thinking about leaving the job in that time frame?

A He wanted to continue working but was not sure he could manage it physically.

DEFENSE ATTORNEY: Doctor, thank you.

I was surprised at the brevity of the cross-examination. Because the same attorney conducted both the deposition and the cross-examination, recalling the length and contentiousness of the deposition, I expected a similar interaction during cross-examination. However, regardless of the reason, from my standpoint, the shorter the cross-examination the better.

THE COURT: All right. [Plaintiff attorney], any redirect?

PLAINTIFF ATTORNEY: Just brief, Your Honor. I'll try to get everybody out of here in time.

THE COURT: Everybody okay?

THE JURY: (Nod heads.)

REDIRECT EXAMINATION BY PLAINTIFF ATTORNEY:

Q Doctor, with respect to the auto issue that we just discussed, is it a fear about being around automobiles or what they might do to you that Mr. Rose has expressed concerns?

A Well, they go together mentally because anytime you're around an automobile, there's a possibility that something like this could happen. Since learning what happened to him, I am much more cautious around automobiles.

Q With respect to your expertise, are you board certified in the field of psychiatry?

A Yes, I am.

Q And how much training did that take?

A Four years of full-time training in adult and child psychiatry and then taking and passing a national examination in each.

Q And when did you obtain that board certification, sir?

A In adult psychiatry in 1969 and child psychiatry in 1972.

Q Okay. Let's go to Exhibit 88. Another psychiatric impairment. Down towards the bottom. This is from [the neurologist]. What was the doctor's assessment at that point of Mr. Rose's mental status?

A As far as I can read that, it says some two years, is it, depression and PTSD, posttraumatic stress disorder.

Q And it says, "Does the patient have a psychiatric cognitive impairment?" And the box is checked. And then it identifies major depression, PTSD, correct?

A That's what I see.

Q Now, in fairness, [neurologist's name] is in there treating this man for his physical conditions, correct?

A Correct.

Q You had the ability to do an assessment using the DSM-IV and the tools that [psychologist's name] provided to you to assess him over what was basically more than two hours of examination plus the testing that took many, many hours, correct?

DEFENSE ATTORNEY: One expert commenting on another expert.

A Yes, and the three follow-up interviews and the records.

Q All right. Now, let's go to your report.

PLAINTIFF ATTORNEY: What is the exhibit number, Counsel?

DEFENSE ATTORNEY: I don't know that we have one.

PLAINTIFF ATTORNEY: We'll call it C1 and we'll give it a trial court exhibit number. (Exhibit C1 was marked for identification.)

Q And I want to turn to the last page, because this was your discussion on page seven following the initial evaluation. And if we go to that last paragraph, if you could read that into the record for us, sir, the last two paragraphs.

DEFENSE ATTORNEY: Judge, we'll object to this, Your Honor. This is just emphasizing the direct examination again, Your Honor.

PLAINTIFF ATTORNEY: This is a report he brought up.

THE COURT: Yeah, gentlemen. Let me see it first. The last two paragraphs?

Q The last two paragraphs, yes, sir, under "discussion."

A "As a result of a cruel and devastating act of fate, Mr. Rose went from being a happy, active individual one moment to being a significantly injured person in great pain and in a life-threatening situation the next. The consequences of the severe injuries he's suffered have been devastating physically and psychologically. Major psychiatric diagnoses have come into being as a direct result of the accident of [date]. They will require intensive long-term intervention. The inability to function sexually without penile injections is devastating to his self-esteem and masculinity and has complicated the marital relationship. Restrictions in the ability to work and limited social and recreational interactions are contributing to the significant depression which is present. Fortunately, Mr. Rose was a high-functioning emotionally intact individual before the accident. With ongoing medical and psychiatric help, likely for the rest of his life, he will persevere but never be able to return to the rich, rewarding life that was present before the accident."

Q And based on what you've seen and the care and treatment of Mr. Rose—let's just look at Exhibit 400 briefly. This is an overview of Mr. Rose's care and treatment.

(Exhibit 400 was marked for identification as Exhibit A15.)

DEFENSE ATTORNEY: Judge—objection, Judge, outside the scope of cross.

PLAINTIFF ATTORNEY: I'm going to go right to the center.

BY PLAINTIFF ATTORNEY:

Q These are the appointments that you had—

THE COURT: If you want to ask him about that you can.

PLAINTIFF ATTORNEY: That's what I want to ask, Judge.

A Yes.

Q And based on the totality of the evidence that you have looked at and your understanding of the current treatment assessed by [therapist] and your evaluations to date, to a reasonable degree of medical probability, do you believe the opinions that you set forth in your report and that you just gave us are accurate and true.

A Yes.

PLAINTIFF ATTORNEY: I have nothing further, Your Honor.

THE COURT: All right. Anything else, [defense attorney]?

DEFENSE ATTORNEY: No, Your Honor.

THE COURT: All right. Dr. Colarusso, you're free to go about your business. I don't know what the weather's like out there, but have a good time.

THE WITNESS: Thank you Your Honor.

THE COURT: You're welcome. Thank you, sir.

PLAINTIFF ATTORNEY: Thank you, Doctor.

(Witness excused.)

Just as he did at the end of the deposition the plaintiff attorney saw to it that the last thing the jury heard was a summary of my credentials and opinions. The jury awarded a plaintiff verdict of multiple millions of dollars for Mr. Rose.

In chapter 8 a child case is presented in its entirety from initial phone call through the deposition. The case settled at that point.

EIGHT

The Case of Evan Doe

From the Initial Phone Call through the Deposition

The case of Mr. Rose was presented throughout the book in relationship to the various themes discussed in the various chapters. In this chapter the case of Evan Doe will be presented in its entirety from the initial phone call through the deposition. The term "Doe" is used to protect the identity of minor children in sexual abuse cases. The case did not go to trial.

INITIAL PHONE CALL

The initial phone call came from a junior lawyer in a firm that had asked me to serve as an expert witness in the past. I had a positive experience in the two previous cases and was inclined to accept the invitation if the case was in an area of my expertise.

I was told that Evan Doe had been sexually molested when he was thirteen years of age by an adult at an outpatient rehabilitation program that he was attending because of drug abuse. The perpetrator had confessed and was in jail. Because of my extensive experience as a clinician and expert witness in child abuse cases I had no hesitation about being able to adequately serve as an expert witness.

I asked for the attorney's e-mail address and emailed my CV, fee agreement, and legal record. I asked that the complaint, police investigation, and any records that were available at the time be sent to me if the senior partner on the case decided to use me as an expert. Two days later I received a phone call informing me that the signed fee agreement and retainer were being sent to me. I mentioned that after I had reviewed the records I would call to begin the evaluation.

THE EVALUATION AND REPORT

After receiving his telephone number from the law firm I called Evan's father. I had asked the law firm to tell him that I would be calling and for what purpose so he would not be surprised by my phone call. I explained that I would like to meet with him and Evan's mother prior to meeting on two occasions or more with his son. We had no difficulty making an appointment. I also asked for Evan's phone number, explaining that because he was an early adolescent and would want to be treated as an individual in his own right, I would like to call him directly to make my appointment with him. Would father please tell him that I would be calling.

The Diagnostic Interview with Mother and Father

When I met father I offered them water, coffee, or tea and explained the outline of the evaluation and went over what I would be asking them. I also informed them that unlike the usual doctor/patient relationship where there was total confidentiality there was no confidentially here since I was a retained expert and would not be treating their son. My entire file, including the information they were about to tell me, would be available to the lawyers on both sides of the case. They seemed a bit surprised but understood and agreed to proceed.

I first obtained Identifying Information:

Father was fifty-six-year-old businessman.

Mother was a fifty-year-old teacher.

The couple was married for fifteen years before they separated and divorced.

Evan was fourteen years and six months old at the time of the evaluation. He was a junior in high school.

Evan divided his time between his two parent's homes. His relationship with both parents was described as excellent.

The Sexual Abuse

Evan returned to his mother's home, drunk, shortly after his thirteenth birthday. Apparently, the boy had drunk an entire fifth of whiskey. His parents took him to the hospital where he tested positive for alcohol and marijuana. As a result, he was referred to an intensive outpatient program that he began almost immediately afterward.

Evan met the perpetrator, whom we will call Ben, at the program. Many addicts were attending the program that consisted of individual and group therapy and mandatory attendance at AA meetings. A sponsor was required. A program administrator suggested Ben as Evan's sponsor. Father wondered what a middle-aged man would have in common with a thirteen-year-old boy. He was told that Ben attended the program to remain sober and was a popular sponsor, particularly for teenage boys. Ben told the parents that he was a gay man in a stable relationship. Despite asking, father and mother heard little from their son about his relationship with Ben. The parents heard about the sexual abuse six months after Ben became Evan's sponsor. Evan told a friend who told his parents who then told Evan's parents.

During the six months that Ben served as Evan's sponsor Evan began to fail in school and cut himself. As a result, he was admitted to an adolescent inpatient unit for several days. Evan never told his parents about the details of the abuse. They learned the details, which included at least two experiences of masturbation, at Ben's trial.

Symptoms and Effects

The parents described their son as withdrawn and socially isolated. He had been diagnosed previously with depression and became increasingly depressed during the six months of sponsorship by Ben. Evan was glad Ben had been incarcerated. He was fearful that Ben would be released and come after him.

"Evan is still the walking wounded. He has not begun to heal."

"He's still carrying on open wound."

"He needs long term treatment."

Developmental History

Pregnancy, labor, and delivery were uneventful. Mother breastfed Evan and was home full time caring for him. The terrible twos were mild and Evan was toilet trained by the age of three.

Ages 3–6: Evan attended preschool at age four and did well. He was reading when he went to kindergarten at age five. The school suggested advancing him to first grade but his parents felt that he was not ready socially. The parents were having marital difficulties during these years.

Ages 6–12: At age eight Evan became angry and regressed, likely because of the parents' marital problems. He began seeing a therapist. When Evan was nine years of age, his parents separated. During the elementary school years Evan was an excellent student who was well behaved and had lots of friends. He played various sports. Father remarried when Evan was twelve years of age.

Ages 12–resent: Puberty occurred when Evan was twelve. He had no difficulty accepting the change. Evan had a girlfriend before his involvement with Ben. He wants to be a psychiatrist and specialize in the treatment of addiction. Father was told that Evan had a very high IQ.

The First Diagnostic Interview with Evan

When I saw Evan for the first time I informed him that this was not a doctor/patient relationship and what he told me would become known by the attorneys on both sides. I began the interview by asking about general topics.

School was the first topic we discussed. Evan enjoyed school. He was a good student. He didn't always fit in but had a few friends. He wanted to be a psychiatrist because in sixth grade he saw a lot of kids becoming addicted to drugs. Evan spontaneously described living with his mother and his father. Things were good. He loved music and spent a lot of time listening to rock and rap.

Later in the interview he mentioned that he had gone to the rehab program. He began using alcohol and marijuana at age twelve and after drinking "a lot" of hard liquor went to the emergency room and then was sent to rehab. As a result, he went to see a therapist who made a diagnosis of bipolar and put him on medication. He had been to see the same doctor when he was nine because he was upset about his parent's separation. He was not seeing a therapist at the time of this interview.

Evan had played some sports but wasn't particularly interested at present. Tall and well built, he looked like an athlete. Toward the end of the interview Evan talked about his experience testifying against Ben. He was very nervous. "It wasn't fun."

The Second Diagnostic Interview with Evan

The second interview lasted ninety minutes. Evan was pleasant and cooperative. We talked about school and his desire to be a psychiatrist. I asked him to tell me more about how he got involved with drugs and alcohol at such an early age. He explained that when he was in elementary school he was fat and at the top of his class. Most groups did not accept him but the stoners did. He struggled with the decision to use drugs. "I had an angel and a devil on my shoulder." Evan denied a relationship between his parents' divorce and the drug use.

I asked about his recent experience with his therapist whom he was no longer seeing. The therapist was trying to help Evan achieve an emotionally stable state. They did not focus very much on the sexual abuse. But Evan was aware that it was often on his mind and was keeping him from getting to sleep. Similar thoughts intruded into his masturbatory fantasies "a lot." Evan would think about a girl and "a thought about Ben would intrude into my head."

Evan had been dating since sixth grade. He did not have a serious girlfriend but had dated several girls and had intercourse for the first time last year. Thoughts about Ben interfered with his ability to enjoy intercourse but he had no performance problems.

At this point I asked about the sexual abuse. The leaders at the rehab center had suggested Ben as a sponsor. Ben was a sponsor for several other boys. When Evan learned that Ben was gay he was not concerned. He had no problem with gays.

When Ben took Evan to his house he put on porno and said that Evan would like it. He gave the boy a cigarette. As they watched Ben asked if he could touch Evan's penis. Evan was shocked and scared and didn't know what to do or say. He mumbled OK. Ben unbuttoned Evan's pants, put his hand under the boy's underwear and masturbated him for fifteen to twenty minutes. "I didn't know what to think. I was scared." Then Ben pulled down Evan's pants and continued masturbating him. He asked if he could suck Evan's penis and kiss his butt. Ben told Evan not to tell anyone. "Dude, you're so cool. We're tight. You wouldn't do anything like that."

After being abused Evan cut himself on his upper thighs, near his genitals. "The physical pain distracted my mind from thoughts about the abuse."

The second episode of sexual abuse occurred shortly after the first. As they rode in Ben's car on the way to his home Ben rubbed Evan's penis over his clothes. Once at his home Ben put on porno and took Evan's pants off and began masturbating him. Ben asked if he could suck Evan's penis but decided not to because he was the boy's sponsor. Evan did not reach a climax either time. Shortly afterward, he told a friend who told his parents who told Evan's parents.

Mental Status Examination

Evan presented as a tall, casually dressed adolescent. He did not display any unusual mannerisms. Evan had an excellent vocabulary and was obviously very bright. Affect was calm and stable. There was evidence of both anxiety and depression as he discussed the sexual abuse and its continuing effects on his life. Thinking was logical and goal directed. There was no evidence of delusions or hallucinations. Evan was oriented as to time, person, and place and there was no evidence of memory impairment. Toward the end of the interview I went through the diagnostic criteria in the DSM IV Manual, one by one, before coming to a conclusion about the diagnosis.

Review of Records

Evan testified at Ben's criminal trial. He told the same story about the details of the abuse that he told me. Evan described his shock, bewilderment, and sense of being overwhelmed and threatened and being unable to extricate himself from the situation until he was able to tell his friend what had happened after the second experience of sexual abuse.

The Deposition of Evan Doe

After describing the sexual abuse Evan told about his difficulty urinating in public toilets, becoming anxious when anyone touched him, feeling flat emotionally, and avoiding males. Evan attributed his diminished sexual desire to using marijuana on a regular basis at the time of the deposition.

Treatment Record of Evan's Therapist

The therapist saw Evan when he was in elementary school at the time of his parents' separation. He saw him again after the sexual abuse was discovered. The therapist was aware of the sexual abuse experiences and preexisting problems and rated Evan's symptoms in the serious range.

Plaintiff's Response to Special Interrogatories (Set One)

In this document the rehabilitation center was considered to be negligent because they did not adequately investigate Ben's long history of substance abuse and multiple prior convictions related to sexually deviant behavior.

Psychological Testing

After taking a detailed history and conducting a mental status examination the psychologist administered, at my request, a battery of psychological tests. His findings will be summarized here.

The WASI-11 is a brief measure of intellectual functioning. Evan achieved an overall IQ score of 120, placing him in the superior range of intellectual functioning.

The MMSE-2EV is a quantitative measure of cognitive functioning. "His performance on this instrument, when considered in relation to his reported history, contraindicates an impression of any type of significant cognitive impairment."

"Overall, it would appear that Evan is of superior intelligence. It is likely that he experiences symptoms of anxiety that occasionally interfere with his ability to focus and sustain attention."

The TSCC is a self-report measure of posttraumatic distress and related psychological symptoms. Evan demonstrated "clinically significant elevations on multiple scales, including those of anxiety, depression, posttraumatic, dissociation and sexual concerns."

The PAI-A is a self-report, objective measure of psychopathology and personality functioning in adolescents. "His PAI-A profile is marked by significant elevations across several scales, suggesting a broad range of clinical features and increasing the possibility that he has more than one psychiatric diagnosis." There was evidence of posttraumatic stress, anxiety, and depression.

Based on the psychological testing profile, the psychologist suggested the following diagnostic possibilities: Posttraumatic Stress Disorder, Bipolar 1 Disorder, severe without psychotic features, most recent episode depressed; Cannabis Abuse, and history of poly-substance abuse. On Axis III of the DSM IV he noted the molestation by Ben. On Axis V he rated Evan's symptoms as moderately severe, interfering with social and adaptive functioning.

Diagnosis

The Diagnostic and Statistical Manual of the American Psychiatric Association, Fourth Edition (at the time) was the only widely recognized diagnostic nomenclature in the field. Using DSM-IV I made the following diagnoses:

Axis I: Sexual Abuse of a Child V61.21. Clinical attention on the victim 995.63.

Posttraumatic Stress Disorder 309.81.

The sexual abuse by Ben meets the criteria for a traumatic event that was a threat to physical integrity and was accompanied by intense fear and helplessness.

The traumatic events were persistently experienced through recurrent thoughts, dreams of the abuse, flashbacks, and physiological and physiological reactivity.

Persistent symptoms of increased arousal were evidenced by difficulty falling asleep, outbursts of anger, poor concentration, and hypervigilance.

The Posttraumatic Stress Disorder was present for more than three months and was classified as chronic.

Bipolar I Disorder, severe without psychotic features, most recent episode depressed 296.53.

Based on history and psychological testing.

Cannabis Abuse 305.20, from history.

Polysubstance abuse, by history.

Axis II: No character disorders, long standing patterns of maladaptive behavior, were present.

Axis III: Any medical conditions that are directly related to the diagnoses on Axis I are described here. None were present.

Axis IV: Psychosocial and Environmental Stressors: From a list in the Manual the diagnostician is asked to describe those stressors that amplify an understanding of the diagnoses on Axis I.

Problems with primary support group—parental divorce, acting out.

Problems with social environment—difficult relationships with peers.

Problems related to interaction with the legal system/crime—litigation, victim of crime.

Axis V: Global Assessment Scale of Functioning: Using that system I rated Evan's symptoms, at the time of the evaluation, in the 51–60 moderate range.

Treatment: Evan is in need of individual psychotherapy two times per week for three to four years to deal with the effects of the sexual abuse on his adolescent and young adult development. An experienced psychiatrist in San Diego would charge $250 per forty-five minute session.

At some point in the decade of the twenties and/or thirties, an additional course of individual psychotherapy, once to twice per week for one to two years is indicated to help Evan deal with the effects of the sexual abuse on the young adult developmental issues of intimacy, marriage, and parenthood.

Evan obviously has other problems that preceded the sexual abuse that also would benefit from psychotherapy and medication. I have attempted to separate the treatment required for these matters from the treatment required for the sexual abuse. The treatment needed described in the first and second paragraphs are my recommendations for what is required to treat the sexual abuse.

Discussion

Child sexual abuse by an adult male, particularly during adolescence, has a profound negative effect on all aspects of adolescent development, but particularly on the emergence of a comfortable sense of masculinity. Further, the effects of childhood sexual abuse tend to have lifelong consequences, affecting self-esteem, relationships, and in particular, attitudes toward sexuality, marriage, and parenthood. Coupled with the other significant mental and emotional problems that this young man is dealing with, the road ahead will be difficult but with personal and professional support the prognosis is fair to good.

EXCERPTS FROM THE DEPOSITION

Present at the deposition were one attorney from both sides and the court reporter. The deposition began when the court reporter asked me to raise my right hand and swear that I would tell the truth and nothing but the truth.

The deposition was in my office. I offer everyone water, coffee, or tea. As in earlier chapters, my thoughts about the deposition as it proceeded are in italics.

Examination

BY MS. B (defense attorney taking the deposition):

Q Good morning, Dr. Colarusso.

A Morning.

Q My name is Alice B., and I represent the defendants in this case. Could you state and spell your last name for the record, please.

A Sure. Calvin Anthony Colarusso, M.D., C-o-l-a-r-u-s-s-o.

Q Dr. Colarusso, have you been deposed before?

A Yes.

Q On how many occasions?

A More than two hundred.

Q Is it fair to say that you are familiar with the process such that you can dispense with the normal admonitions?

A Yes.

Q I will remind you, however, that you've just taken an oath to tell the truth, and the oath is the same oath that you would have taken if you were testifying in a court of law. Do you understand that?

A I do.

The normal admonitions, which are always given to a witness if he or she has not had experience with depositions, include an explanation of the court reporter's role, the role of both lawyers, and what is expected of the witness, namely to answer each question as clearly and precisely as possible.

Q How many times have you been retained by Evert and Brown?

A Twice before.

The attorney was trying to determine if I derived a large percentage of my income from this one firm and, therefore, am more likely to slant my opinions in their direction.

Q What percentage of your work as an expert is for the plaintiff?

A Over the years it's been about 60 percent plaintiff and 40 percent defense.

Behind the question, do I work for plaintiffs or defense most of the time, again assessing whether I work for both sides and therefore are likely to be more objective.

Q And what percentage of your professional time is spent doing forensic counseling as opposed to seeing patients as a clinical psychiatrist?

A In the past five years I've cut back on the number of hours I work. At this point, approximately 50 percent is spent seeing patients and 50 percent is spent serving as an expert witness.

Q Ok, I'm going to ask you about your background. Did you bring a CV?

A Yes I did.

(The lawyer then proceeded to ask questions about my education, from college to the present; my university affiliation, board certifications, and publications and presentations.)

Q Do you have license to practice medicine in the state of California?

A Yes I do.

Q Has your license ever been suspended?

A No.

Q Has your license ever been revoked?

A No.

Q Has there been any disciplinary action on your license in California?

A No.

Q Do you understand that you have been designated as an expert on behalf of Evan Doe in this case?

A I do.

Q What is your understanding of the scope of your assignment as an expert in this case?

A To do a psychiatric evaluation on this boy and be prepared to discuss my opinions as to the effect of the sexual abuse on his development.

Q Anything else?

A To be prepared to testify in court if need be and to comment on the defense expert's opinions.

Q Have you seen any information from the defense expert?

(I had. The lawyer asked me to produce the records and designated them as an exhibit to the deposition. She then asked to go through all of my records on the case and chose to designate some of them as exhibits.)

Q Did you rely on all of these records in formulating your opinions?

A Yes I did.

Q Are you prepared to give your full and final opinions today with regard to Evan Doe?

A I'm prepared to give you my opinions. I understand that there may be some additional documents coming, which I will review, but I've done a thorough evaluation. I have arrived at conclusions. I doubt very much that anything is going to change those opinions.

Q So as you sit here today, are you ready to give your full and final opinions that you are going to express at trial with regard to Evan Doe?

If I agree she would try to exclude at trial any opinions other than those expressed during this deposition.

A I am, but that doesn't mean that I won't review whatever additional records are provided to me.

Q (*Insisting and raising her voice slightly, attempting to unsettle and intimidate me.*) And as you sit here today, are you prepared to give your full and final opinions that you intend to express at trial with regard to Evan Doe?

A I've answered it. The answer is yes, with the qualification that I made.

Q Do you need the testimony of the defense expert to formulate your own opinions?

A No. I need the testimony of the defense expert to be able to comment on his opinions.

PLAINTIFF ATTORNEY: (Confronting the attorney taking the deposition.) It's been asked and answered. He said he may have opinions on the defense experts deposition, which he can't give until he sees his deposition.

Q Understood. Did you ask for anything that was not provided?

A The one thing I asked for was the CPS [Child Protective Service] report, which I understand is very difficult, if not impossible, to get.

Q And other than reviewing the CPS report, the defense psychiatric expert's deposition and potentially references from Drs. A. and Dr. B [two treating doctors] with regard to the sexual assault between Evan and his brother—

A (Interrupting) I would not characterize it as a sexual assault; the sexual involvement between Evan and his brother.

When Evan and his brother were twelve and thirteen, nineteen months apart in age, they were involved in sexual experimentation. The defense is trying to say that this incident is on the same plane with the sexual abuse inflicted on Evan by a forty-year-old perpetrator.

Q I didn't mean to put words in your mouth.

A Okay.

Q Other than the records still outstanding do you expect to review anything further prior to trial?

PLAINTIFF ATTORNEY: Calls for speculation. Lacks foundation. He doesn't know what additional documents we are going to provide to him.

Q Have you been asked to do any additional work between today and the time of trial?

A No. But what I would want to do if the case goes to trial is to meet with the attorney who is going to be taking the direct and discuss it.

Q Have you met Evan Doe?

A Yes.

Q How many times have you met him?

A I met him once. He forgot the first appointment, so we had a forty-five-minute phone interview. I met him face-to-face in the office on [date].

Q Have you spoken to his mother?

A No.

Q Have you spoken to his father?

A Yes, I had a diagnostic interview with father on [date].

Q Have you met with or spoken to any other member of the family?

A No.

Q And what information was provided to you by Evan during the forty-five-minute telephonic interview?

A How much detail do you want?

Q Do you have handwritten notes in regard to that?

A Yes. I do.

Q And what was the purpose of that phone interview?

A It was a diagnostic evaluation interview.

Q And when you say a diagnostic interview—I don't have any psychological or psychiatric background, so if you can explain to me what occurs, just in a general manner, in a diagnostic interview and what the purpose of that is?

(I described the components of a comprehensive child psychiatric evaluation.)

Q What is the purpose of the psychological testing you referenced?

A Psychological testing, when performed by a qualified psychologist, is another way of understanding an individual in depth. These tests, which have been standardized through their use with many, in some instances, hundreds of thousands of people, give the data to the psychologist to understand the individual's mental and emotional state. The psychologist then writes a report, conveys that to the clinician—in this case, me—and it's useful information, in addition to what I can gain clinically from face-to-face contacts and involvement.

As mentioned in chapter 6 on direct testimony, the spoken work during a deposition or at trial is not always the best English.

Q And did you rely on Dr. D.'s psychological testing evaluation in reaching your opinions with regard to Evan?

A Yes.

Q How was that information used in developing your opinions?

A I reviewed the report. I'm not qualified to administer the tests or understand the raw data because I'm a physician; I'm not a psychologist. I read the report and integrated what Dr. D. had to say. At the end of his report, he suggests various diagnostic possibilities, based on the data obtained from the testing, and I utilized that also in trying to formulate my own opinions.

Q And did you reach the same diagnostic conclusions that Dr. D. suggested at the end of his psychological testing report?

A Dr. D. did not make diagnostic conclusions. He made diagnostic suggestions. I came to my own conclusions, using his report, the information I gathered during the clinical interviews, and the records I reviewed.

Q Let's back up for a minute. I'm going to ask you what opinions you intend to express at the time of trial with regard to Evan Doe.

A Okay. Again, I've had that question two hundred times or more, [in past depositions] and I'm going to give you all of the opinions that I've arrived at. I will withhold nothing from you. If additional information comes along and I'm asked other questions, I may have other opinions.
These are my diagnoses. Sexual abuse of a child, with the focus on the victim; posttraumatic stress disorder, and, by history, bipolar I disorder, severe, without psychotic features, most recently depressed; cannabis abuse, from his history; and polysubstance abuse, from history.
My next conclusions refer to my treatment recommendations. And as I say in my report, these recommendations are to deal specifically with the effects of the sexual abuse. This young man had multiple problems, which led to his going to Rehab in the first place. And I am not attempting to define the treatment that he would need for that, although I am saying that he needs extensive treatment above and beyond what he needs for the child sexual abuse.
In regard to the child sexual abuse, I recommend now individual psychotherapy with an experienced psychiatrist

or psychologist who is trained to work with children and adolescents, twice a week, for three to four years. An experienced psychiatrist in San Diego would charge $250 per forty-five-minute session.
At some point in the decade following the completion of that treatment—so it would be somewhere in his twenties or thirties—I recommend an additional course of individual psychotherapy, one to two times per week, for one to two years. I would add that he may well need treatment beyond that, because the effects of child sexual abuse tend to be lifelong, but I can't really define the future to any degree where I can say with any certainty how much additional treatment he might need.
The prognosis with the treatment outlined is "Fair to good." Those are my major conclusions.

Q Okay. Let's start with your diagnosis of PTSD.

A Yes.

Q Was that diagnosis based upon your clinical diagnostic interview with father and Evan.

A And with the psychological testing report and with the records that I reviewed.

Q What specific information that you got from Evan supported your diagnosis of PTSD?

She is asking for the basis of my opinion.

A Okay. What I'm doing now is, I'm referring to face-to-face notes that I took during the second diagnostic interview with Evan. And with him, I went through the detailed criteria in the Manual for—the diagnostic manual for PTSD.

Q And what are those criteria, Doctor?

A Do you want a summary, or do you want me to read from the Manual?

Q If you can do it from memory, that's great; otherwise, you can refer to the Manual.

A I can give a summary. The criteria for PTSD are divided, basically, into four parts. First, there must be an experience in which there was a threat or actual injury to the body integrity, which produced powerful feelings in the individual.

Then, there are three differing sets of criteria that have to be met. The first one is, basically, the mind's need to repeat the trauma over and over again in order to master it. And there's a set of individual criteria for that, which we can go through. The second set are exactly the opposite: the mind's attempt to squash, to push out of awareness, to not have to deal with the experience and the thoughts and feelings about it. And the third set have to do with hyper-alertness; in other words, to be on guard that the same thing could happen again. So that's the summary. And when we—we'll go through now the individual criteria, and as we go through it, I will read from the manual and then tell you what the responses were.

The detailed descriptions from DSM-IV that follow provide an objective basis from the only widely used diagnostic nomenclature in the field and are the widely accepted basis for this diagnosis. My use of it greatly strengthens my diagnostic opinion in regard to PTSD. As you may remember, I've used the same procedure in all the earlier cases presented in the book.

Q Okay.

A Is that okay?

Q That sounds great.

A Okay. Posttraumatic Stress Disorder. "A. The person has been exposed to a traumatic event in which both of the following were present: 1. The person experienced, witnessed, or was confronted with an event or events that involved actual or threatened death or serious injury or a threat to the physical integrity of self and others."

THE WITNESS Is my speed okay?

THE REPORTER: Thank you for slowing down.

THE WITNESS: "2. The person's response involved intense fear, helplessness, or horror. (Note: In children, they may be expressed instead by disorganized or agitated behavior.)"

In my opinion, the sexual abuse by Mr. Z. clearly meets the criteria for Axis I, a threat to the physical integrity of the self and, indeed, an invasion of the individual's body. And it certainly led to a sense of helplessness on the part of this boy and to disorganized behavior, following the abuse and during it.

Next—this is part B. "The traumatic event is persistently experienced in one or more of the following ways: 1. Recurring and intrusive disturbing recollections of the event, including images, thoughts, or perceptions." And this boy very clearly had recurrent thoughts, that he told me about, that happened very frequently, sometimes more than on a daily basis.

Q And is that something that Evan told you during his diagnostic interview?

A Yes.

Q And did you get that information from any other source other than Evan?

A No, because I didn't go through the criteria with anybody else but Evan.

Q Did you see anything in his other records or anywhere, any of the materials that you reviewed, that indicated to you that he had recurrent thoughts of his experience with Mr. Z.?

A To answer that carefully—he saw his therapist. I specifically noted that there was very little talk in those notes about sexual abuse. And I asked him about that, and he said that his therapist was interested in getting him stabilized before they talked about it. So no, I do not have specific information from the therapist who saw him, in regard to the recurrent thoughts.

Q Just backing up. What do you mean when you say "disorganized behavior," with regard to that first criteria for PTSD.

A I mean acting up at home, being difficult, withdrawing from individuals, more drug use, those kinds of things.

Q Thank you.

A All right. No. 2 under part B: "Recurrent distressing dreams of the event." What he specifically said to me—and this is a quote—"Too many to count," end of quote. Some of them repeat the abuse, and others—he wakes up before the abuse actually takes place.

Q And these are Evan's reports of nightmares that he is having?

A Dreams.

Q Dreams that he is having?

A About the abuse.

Q About the abuse by [the perpetrator] specifically?

A Yes. Everything that I'm going to tell you here is his specific response to questions by me about his responses to the sexual abuse.
Okay. No. 3. "Acting or feeling as if the traumatic event were recurring"; in other words, a flashback. Flashbacks have occurred with a family friend, who was an obese male, who hugged him. He had a sense of being back in the situation with [the perpetrator] when he was being abused. Another happened when he saw a guy who looked like [the perpetrator] and he had a flashback. He estimated that he's had approximately ten to twenty flashbacks.

Q In what time period?

A Since the abuse to the present.

Q I'm wondering when the abuse of Evan occurred, by Mr. Z.?

A OK. From his father, he reports that the abuse started after he attended rehab and met [the perpetrator]. From the father, it continued at least through January of [year of the abuse].

Q What did father say continued through [year of the abuse]?

A The sexual abuse continued.

Q Did the duration of that abuse, as you understand it, impact your opinions with regard to recommended treatment for Evan moving forward?

A Yes, the fact that there were multiple times, as opposed to a single time.

Q And what is your understanding of how many times Mr. Z. sexually abused Evan?

A There were two significant episodes, both of which consisted of masturbation. Masturbation was Mr. Z.'s hand on the boy's penis. The first one, according to him, lasted approximately fifteen to twenty minutes. I can give you more details if you want, from what he said.
And there was a second one, a few days later that was quite similar, in Mr. Z.'s home. And on this occasion, he very quickly pulled the boy's pants down and masturbated him again for a length of time.

Q Did Evan tell you that he was uncomfortable around Mr. Z. after these two specific instances of masturbation that you've described?

A Yes.

Q What other information did Evan tell you about the first episode with Mr. Z.?

A All right, I'll give you the details. Basically, I'll read to you my notes. I asked him to tell me about the sexual abuse during the second interview. "Bob and Andrew suggested Mr. Z. as a sponsor. Mr. Z. sponsored a lot of guys. When he heard that Mr. Z. was gay, it was no problem because he was okay with gays. In his bedroom, Mr. Z. put on porn. He said, 'You'll like it.' He gave him a cigarette. They watched the porn for forty-five minutes. Mr. Z. asked if he could touch his penis. Evan was shocked, scared and so he mumbled, 'Okay.' Mr. Z. unbuttoned his pants, had his hand under his underwear, was masturbating him."
Quote, "I didn't know what to think. I was scared," end of quote. "The masturbation went on for fifteen to twenty minutes. Eventually Mr. Z. pulled down his pants and continued masturbating him. He asked if he could suck his penis. He didn't. And he kissed his backside, and Mr. Z. told him not to tell."
This is a quote of a boy telling me about what Mr. Z. said: Quote, "Dude, you are so cool. We are tight. You would do"—"You wouldn't do anything like that," meaning tell. He went on to say that he cut himself afterward. Quote, "A physical pain distracted my mind from thoughts about the abuse," end of quote. He mostly cut his thighs, his upper thighs, obviously, the area close to where he was abused. Second time. They were—

Q Can I stop you there, Doctor?

A Sure.

Q When you say "obviously, the area close to where he was abused," what does that mean?

A That means that in my mind, there's psychological significance that he cut himself on his upper thighs because he was in great conflict, embarrassed, ashamed of what happened when Mr. Z. masturbated him.

Q Any other reason why he would have chosen that location for that type of self-harm?

A I don't think we need any other reason. I think that is the reason.

Q I'm just asking, did you consider any other reason why he would have chosen that location?

A Did I think about it? Yes. Did I come up with any other explanation? No.

Q Are you aware of any other instances of self-harm that Evan engaged in prior to meeting Mr. Z.

A I'd say, in a way, his whole history was you know, with the drugs and the alcohol—was an expression of self-harm.

Q Any other—other than the drug and alcohol abuse prior to meeting Mr. Z., are you aware of any other instances of self-injury with Evan?

A Let me check. He was admitted to [a children's inpatient unit] as a result of the cutting. And other than what we talked about before, I'm not aware of any other.

Q And this admission was after the incidents with Mr. Z., correct?

A Yes.

Q Okay. Is self-injury a common symptom or consequence of childhood molestation?

A Yes.

Q Okay. If you wouldn't mind continuing on with what you were told about the second episode.

A Okay. The second time. On a car ride there, Mr. Z. rubbed his penis over his clothes. They got to his house. He puts on porno. And then he takes his pants down and masturbates him. And this lasted about fifteen minutes, as well. He said, "Can I suck you off?" and he—the boy said no, and he said that, well, he wouldn't do it because he was his sponsor. And that's what happened the second time.

Q And did all the information relating to the specifics of the episodes with Mr. Z. come from Evan, verbally?

A Well, there's also the court records.

Q Okay. But the notes that you've just read are all the information that you got from Evan verbally, through the diagnostic interview; is that correct?

A Yes.

Q Did you ever get anything in writing from Evan about what happened?

A No. I didn't ask him to do that.

Q But nothing was ever provided to you that was written—in a written form about Evan's symptoms or the events that occurred with Mr. Z.

A Other than the court records, in which there's a lot of information about it.

Q So just the court records. Have you ever spoken to [his treating psychiatrists]?

A No.

Q Was there additional information about your posttraumatic stress disorder diagnosis that we have not discussed?

A We've gone through the details of the information that I collected, that allowed me to make it, as well as considering Dr. D.'s suggestion that it was a possibility.

Q Okay. Anything else that you can think of that you relied upon or considered in reaching the posttraumatic stress disorder opinion or diagnosis regarding Evan?

A My experience with the diagnosis.

Q Of course. Anything else?

A No.

Q Did you—have we discussed all the symptoms you believe Evan has experienced as a result of the posttraumatic stress disorder that you've diagnosed? Meaning the dreams and flashbacks.

A We've discussed that. Yes. His father, however, describes additional symptoms.

Q Okay. Other than the dreams and the flashbacks, did Evan tell you any other symptoms that you associate with PTDS? We were talking about the flashbacks. Then we moved into the specific instances of sexual abuse, so we may not have completed that. I want to make sure we did.

A We have not completed that.

Q So far, we've discussed the dreams and the flashbacks as symptoms that he has experienced relative to the PTSD diagnosis; is that accurate?

A Yes. And we will go ahead and discuss the rest.

Q Do you believe that the—while you are looking for that, do you believe that the two episodes of sexual abuse by Mr. Z. caused the dreams that you've testified about?

A Yes.

Q And do you believe that there's any other cause for those dreams?

A No. Those dreams are specifically about Mr. Z., about the abuse.

Q And same question with regard to the flashbacks. Have you reached an opinion that the two episodes of sexual abuse by Mr. Z. are the sole cause of those flashbacks?

The attorney is thorough and methodical.

A Yes. We've talked about the flashbacks. Criteria 4 and 5: "Intense psychological distress at exposure to internal and external cues that symbolize or resemble an aspect of the traumatic event." He had certainly had intense psychological distress, both with the flashbacks and the dreams and the memories.

Q Anything else that you would continue in terms of psychological distress, other than the flashbacks, dreams, and the memories of the abuse by Z.?

A Yes, which we'll come to.

Q Okay.

A And No. 5, "Physiological reactivity on exposure to internal or external cues that symbolize or resemble an aspect of the traumatic event." And his heart would race, and he would become sweaty, anxious during the flashbacks.
Section C, which is entitled, "Persistent avoidance of stimuli associated with the trauma and numbing of general responsiveness not present before the trauma as indicated by three or more of the following: 1. Efforts to avoid thoughts, feelings, or conversations associated with the trauma." He tries very hard to avoid thinking about it, talking about it, and he is embarrassed, as an adolescent, to have others know that this has happened to him.

Q And that information came solely from your conversations with Evan?

A Well, his father also told me information, but that's the primary source, and that's the source that's most important to me.

Q How does he try hard to avoid, if he mentioned it?

A How you try to avoid the thoughts? You try and put your mind on something else, and you try not to think about it.

And the same thing with the feelings. You try and push them out of mind, and you avoid talking to anybody about them.

Q Is that what Evan was doing, avoiding talking about it?

A With whom?

Q With anyone.

A Yes. He was. It was difficult for him to talk about it with me, but he was able to do so.
"2. Efforts to avoid activities, places, or people that arouse recollections of the trauma." His response to that was that he avoids men, particularly older men, and he tends to be timid around his peers, quiet around his peers. So there's some social withdrawal that's associated with this.
The third criteria, "Inability to recall an important aspect of the trauma." There is not much loss of memory, so he really—the answer to that one is no.
No. 4. "Markedly diminished interest or participation in significant activities." There's a considerable withdrawal socially and not nearly as involved with peers as he was before.

Q What do you know about his interaction with peers prior to meeting Mr. Z.?

A He was very involved with peers, and that's where he got into difficulty with drugs and alcohol.

Q What kind of involvement did he have with his peers prior to meeting Mr. Z.?

A He was more outgoing. He had friends and was not able to manage his interactions with them particularly well.

Q Did he tell you how many friends he had prior to meeting Mr. Z.?

A He said he was very friendly. He had a lot of friends. A specific number, no.

Q Okay.

A No. 5. "Feeling of detachment or estrangement from others." He has a strong feeling of detachment. He feels he is different now that he's been abused and that he is a victim of abuse, that he is different from the other boys, who have not been. So he feels quite different and detached.
6. "Restricted range of affect." The example I give here is, "Unable to have loving feelings" end of quote. I would say he can have loving feelings toward his parents, but very

definitely his affect is restricted in the sense that it's narrow, it's bland, it tends toward the depressive side. There's not a full range of happiness and outgoingness, that you would expect to see in a person—a normal person.

Q And, Doctor, with regard to the detachment and the "unable to have loving feelings," is there any sort of scientific method to confirm that, or do you need to rely almost exclusively on Evan's substantive reports in that regard?

A Well, you also rely on his parents and his psychological testing, and the psychological testing does address issues like that.

Q Fair enough.

A Okay. No. 7. "Sense of foreshortened future. Example: does not expect to have a career, marriage, children, or a life span." And I see no evidence that there are thoughts about a foreshortened future.

Q Okay.

A The third set of criteria in the manual, is, "Persistent symptoms of increased arousal not present before the trauma as indicated by two or more of the following: 1. Difficulty falling or staying asleep." He's had difficulty falling asleep because of intrusive thoughts about it, and also the dreams have disturbed his sleep.
"2. Irritability or outburst of temper." He describes himself as more irritable and now having a terrible temper.
"3. Difficulty concentrating." He describes his concentration as "very, very bad." I would say that's probably a combination of more than just the thoughts about the sexual abuse. Drug use can certainly contribute to that.
"4. Hypervigilance." This is very definitely there, as, for instance, when he described his discomfort around men, particularly older men, anybody who reminds him of Mr. Z. He, like almost all victims of sexual abuse, are constantly on guard against the possibility of it happening again.

Q Just in general terms, does the psychological testing assist you in confirming a diagnosis of hypervigilance?

A Well, it's not a diagnosis. It's a symptom. Yes. It can.

Q As you sit her right now, without reviewing the report, you don't have a specific recollection of whether Dr. D.'s report helped confirm that symptom?

A I don't.

Q Okay. Fair enough.

A And last, "exaggerated startle response." He does not have a startle response.

Q Okay.

A And "E. The duration of disturbance. The symptoms in B, C, and D is more than one month." That is true. "F. The disturbance caused clinically significant distress or impairment in social, occupational, or other important areas of functioning." That is true. And if the symptoms have lasted for more than three months, the diagnosis is considered to be chronic.

As we proceeded through the criteria in DSM-IV for PTSD I was thinking the more detail in the deposition record about the basis for my diagnosis, the stronger my opinion appears to the questioning attorney.

Q And do you believe the diagnosis to be chronic?

A Yes.

Q When did Evan tell you that these symptoms began?

A His symptoms began during the time of the abuse and have continued since then to the present.

Q And that, again, is based on conversations with Evan and his father?

A And the psychological testing.

Q And what functioning problems, I think was the last thing you mentioned, do you believe Evan has?

A He is withdrawn socially. He is not productive in school. He is kind of isolated. This is a boy who ought to be fully engaged with peers, with school, with planning for his future, and he is not doing that in any kind of a significant way.

Q And you believe that all the symptomatology that we have just discussed relating to PTDS is caused by his interactions with Mr. Z.?

A I connect the PTSD 100 percent to the sexual abuse with Mr. Z. Obviously, this boy had multiple problems before that, and those are clearly something that he also needs to deal with.

Q Why don't we talk about his dad. What symptoms did his dad articulate?

A His father talks about his being withdrawn, which is a symptom. His father talks about him not being involved with peers. He was very involved before. His father says that the sexual abuse has made his preexisting bipolar disorder worse. No girlfriends. "He lives with his guitar," is the way father describes it. So that's isolated. And he is emotionally flat, and certainly I observed that.
He also is concerned about Mr. Z. He has a sense of relief that Mr. Z. couldn't get to him, that he was in jail. He was fearful when he learned that Mr. Z. made bail.
He is erratic. He has nightmares. He felt safe after the trial. Quote, "Evan is still a walking wound that has not begun to heal. He is still carrying an open wound," end of quote. Quote, "He needs long-term treatment," end of quote.

Q Doctor, is drug abuse a common consequence of child molestation?

The lawyer is trying to diminish the effect of the molest and the PTSD by demonstrating that some of the same symptoms were there before the molestation.

A Yes. But in this case, the drug abuse was there before the molestation.

Q And is alcohol abuse a common consequence of childhood molestation?

A Yes.

Q Did Evan have alcohol abuse problems prior to meeting Mr. Z.?

A He did.

Q Is low self-esteem a consequence of childhood molestation?

A Yes.

Q And are you aware whether Evan had issues regarding low self-esteem prior to meeting Mr. Z.?

A Yes he did.

Q Is depression a common consequence of childhood molestation?

A Yes.

Q Do you know if Evan had depression prior to meeting Mr. Z.?

A He did.

Q Is hypersexuality a common consequence of childhood molestation?

A Yes.

Q Do you know if Evan had any symptoms of hypersexuality prior to meeting Mr. Z.?

A No. I don't think he did. You have to remember his age. He is just going through puberty. That's the time of intense interest in sex, intense preoccupation in sex. I have no evidence that his attitude toward sexuality was out of the ordinary.

Q What would you consider an ordinary attitude toward sexuality in a boy of his age at that time?

PLAINTIFF LAWYER: Vague and ambiguous.

THE WITNESS: You really want to talk about that?

Q Sure.

A Constant thoughts about sex, constant preoccupation with your body, spontaneous erections, masturbating, infatuation with girls, looking at *Playboy*, pornography. You are consumed with sex because of the outpouring of testosterone that occurs at puberty.

Q Is an increase in behavioral problems a common consequence of childhood molestation?

A Yes.

Q Do you know whether or not Evan had any behavioral problems prior to meeting Mr. Z?

A He had significant behavioral problems.

Q Such as?

A Well, drugs, alcohol, basically, involved in those illegal activities, not doing terribly well in school, not motivated. And so yes, he had significant problems before. That's why he ended up at the rehab center.

Q Is defiance or oppositional behavior a common consequence of children who have been molested?

A Yes.

Q Are you aware of any defiance and oppositional behavior that Evan exhibited prior to meeting Mr. Z?

She is doing a good job of trying to relate many of his symptoms to preexisting conditions, not the sexual abuse.

A He was defiant and oppositional before.

Q Do you know if Evan had exhibited any anger and irritability prior to meeting Mr. Z.?

A Yes. I would say he was angry and irritable and rebellious.

Q And that's based upon what?

A Based on what father told me and what he told me.

Q And isolation or alienation, reduction of interaction with peers are all common consequences of children who have been molested?

A They are.

Q And do you have any information that Evan was isolated or withdrawn prior to meeting Mr. Z.?

A No. According to his father and he, he was very social before.

Q Same question with regard to being disinterested in friendships. Is that a common consequence of childhood molestation?

A Can be. Yes.

Q Are antisocial behaviors a common consequence of childhood molestation?

A It can be.

Q Would planning violence be considered an antisocial behavior in your professional opinion?

PLAINTIFF LAWYER: Vague and ambiguous.

A Yes. I was going to say, can you be more clear about that, what you have in mind?

Q I'm just wondering if articulating plans of violence would be considered an antisocial behavior in your professional opinion.

PLAINTIFF LAWYER: It's vague and ambiguous. It could be one person's idea of what is violent, you know, hitting a sibling, which is common, or setting a house on fire, which is a little bit different, so—

THE WITNESS: Yeah. It's very general. But can it be? Sure.

Q Are you aware of any articulated plans of violence by Evan prior to meeting Mr. Z.?

A No.

Q Is a sense of hopelessness a common consequence of molestation?

A Yep.

Q Are you aware that Evan had exhibited any evidence of hopelessness prior to meeting Mr. Z.?

A No. I would describe him as troubled but not hopeless.

Q And when you say "troubled," what do you mean by that?

A Drugs and alcohol, rebelliousness.

Q Against—rebellious against what?

Q His parents, authority, wanting to do his own thing, be his own person, which is part and parcel of one of the major developmental tasks of adolescence, but, obviously, he was not handling that very well.

Q Are you aware that he was rebellious against his parents and authority prior to meeting Mr. Z?

A Yes.

Q Is suicidal ideology a common consequence of childhood molestation?

A It happens. Yes.

Q We talked about the sleep issues, the difficulty falling asleep or staying asleep, as a potential consequence of childhood molestation. Is that accurate?

A Well, a specific symptom of posttraumatic stress disorder, which in this case is a direct result of the child molestation.

Q Are temper tantrums a common consequence of childhood molestation?

A Well, temper tantrums, as you may or may not know, are normal between the ages of eighteen months and three. They can occur later than that. The child would have to have been quite young when they were molested: three, four, five, six. Temper tantrums might be a regressive response to molestation in those ages. Adolescents and adults, no. I wouldn't say it's a very common response at all.

Q Are you aware of any temper tantrums that Evan experienced after Mr. Z.?

A You are applying something from age one to three to an adolescent, and it doesn't compute.

Q Did you consider Evan's psychiatric family history in reaching your diagnoses and opinions with regard to his posttraumatic stress disorder or other diagnoses?

A Yes. I would say the major psychiatric history of relevance is the parental separation and divorce, because that directly impacted him.

Q What about his extended family?

Once again, she is looking for evidence to present to the jury that his problems are due to other factors and not the sexual abuse.

A I don't think that information is relevant to my opinions and my diagnoses. In this case, we have an absolutely clear causation. We have a perpetrator who's been convicted of the crime of child sexual abuse. We know that happened. That is, by far, the determining factor in the diagnosis I made.

Q Have we discussed all of your opinions that you intend to present at the time of trial relating to your diagnosis of posttraumatic stress disorder in Evan?

A Yes.

Q Now, you made a separate diagnosis of sexual abuse of child, focus on victim; is that accurate?

A Yes.

Q Why is that a separate diagnosis?

A Because it's a separate diagnosis in the Manual. And, furthermore, that's the first diagnosis I made and the most important one.

Q Okay. Well, then we'll go straight to the most important diagnosis, and we'll go through that.

A Well, there—you are going to be disappointed because all it says is, "Sexual abuse of a child. This category should be used when the focus of clinical attention is sexual abuse of a child. Coding note: Specify 995.53 if focus of clinical attention is on the victim."
In this case the diagnosis is simple and very obvious because we have a perpetrator who's been tried and convicted. We are not dealing with speculation here. We are not dealing

with something that could have happened. And this is the primary diagnosis in this case. And we'll jump ahead a little bit to the defense expert, who didn't make that diagnosis, who ignores the obvious and doesn't make a diagnosis of childhood sexual abuse.

No matter what she says or does she cannot change the basic facts in the case. Nor can the defense psychiatrist, even if he chooses to ignore the diagnosis.

Q We'll get to you assessment of his opinions a little bit later.

A I'm aware of that.

Q Is there any symptomatology of your diagnosis of sexual abuse—and I'm just going to call it your diagnosis of sexual abuse, rather than saying "sexual abuse of child focus on victim." Is that fair?

A Just as long as it's clear that it's sexual abuse of a child. Legally, of a child.

Q And that's significant?

A Of course it's significant.

Q And why is that significant?

A Well, because, one, it's illegal to do that. Secondly, a child is not in a position to defend themselves as well as an adult might against the attempts at sexual abuse. Of course many times adults can't, either, such as rape and other experiences. Child sexual abuse has long-term, lifelong effects in almost anyone who's been abused. That means that as development goes forward, it interferes with the new developmental tasks that are arising. We'll jump to young adulthood, twenty to forty. There, it can interfere with issues relating to sexuality, intimacy, marriage, parenthood. I can think of a number of cases in which people refused to have children because they didn't feel they could protect them. It can lead to promiscuity or hypersexuality in an attempt to master the trauma; low self-esteem, low achievement in work.
In midlife, very often, it leads to divorces, people losing their religions. I've had a number of people in their sixties who were still having profound depression, anxiety, symptoms of posttraumatic stress disorder, despite having been abused fifty years before.

She doesn't wish to continue to focus on this powerful material about the lifelong effects of the sexual abuse.

Q Okay. Are there any other aspects of your diagnosis of sexual abuse of a child, focus on the victim that you intend to offer at the time of trial in the form of expert opinion that we haven't already discussed?

A Not that I can think of.

Q And I think you mentioned three historical diagnoses, one being bipolar, one being cannabis—

A Yes.

Q —and one being polysubstance?

A Right.

Q Were those the three additional diagnoses that you intend to offer at the time of trial?

A Well, they are diagnoses that others have made, so they are not based on my direct observation of him. They are based on the history obtained from Evan, his father, and the records of the treating therapists. So I will mention them. Yes.

Q Because they are relevant, why?

A Well, because they are relevant because they give us a full picture of him. But the focus of the lawsuit and the focus of my evaluation is primarily the sexual abuse and its effects.

Q But for purposes of testifying at trial, you are going to accept the historical diagnoses made by others, is that correct?

A I will mention that, that those diagnoses were made.

Q And you have no reason to question the qualifications of the psychologist who treated Evan?

A No, I do not.

Q And do you have any reason to question his diagnostic acumen as a psychologist?

A No, I do not.

Q And are you accepting the therapist's historical diagnosis of cannabis abuse, as well, for purposes of trial?

A Yes. But I also got that information from Evan himself.

Q What is your understanding of Evan's marijuana use? And just so the record is clear, cannabis means marijuana; is that correct?

A Yeah.

Q Okay.

A He told me that at age twelve he began using alcohol and marijuana. He had an incident of alcohol poisoning, and that's what sent him to rehab.

Q Did you consider ADHD as a potential diagnosis to explain Evan's symptoms?

A Which of his symptoms?

Q Any of his symptoms?

A I saw no evidence that he had ADHD.

Q Did you see any evidence that he was autistic?

A He is not autistic.

Q Did you see any evidence that he had Asperger's?

A There's no indication he has Asperger's.

Q Did you see any indication of an anxiety disorder?

A He has anxiety. I don't think that's the primary diagnosis. I think you can subsume his anxiety under the posttraumatic stress disorder.

Q Do you know Dr. L. [psychiatrist prescribing medication]?

A I might have met him a long time ago, but we have no relationship.

Q Do you have any reason to question his qualifications as a psychiatrist?

A No.

Q Do you have any reason to question his diagnostic acumen as a psychiatrist?

A I do not.

Q When we got started talking about Evan and your opinions, you briefly discussed your treatment recommendations for Evan?

A Yes.

Q And you recognize that Evan has multiple problems?

A I do.

Q And you indicated that you are providing opinions regarding future treatment of Evan that deal specifically with the sexual abuse by Mr. Z.; is that accurate?

A Yes.

Q Do you have any opinion on what future treatment Evan will require relating to his bipolar disorder?

A I have no specific opinions with regard to the treatment.

Q Do you have any opinion regarding the extent of future treatment Evan will require for his substance abuse?

A I'm not rendering any expert opinion on those matters.

I'm sticking to the issue of the case, sexual abuse, and not allowing her to drag me into other areas.

Q So the answer is no?

A The answer is no.

Q And with regard to the sexual abuse by Mr. Z., you indicated that you believed Evan will need individual psychotherapy twice weekly for three to four years.

A Correct?

Q And is that three- to four-year duration beginning now or from the time of the sexual abuse?

A From the time treatment starts.

Q So that three to four years does not take into account treatment he's had before today's date?

A It does not.

Q And then you mentioned, sometime in the future, he will need individualized psychotherapy one to two times weekly, for one to two years?

A I said sometime in the decade after the completion of the first course of treatment. Yes.

Q Which you estimated to be in his twenties or thirties.

A Yes. And I also said that he may well need treatment in the future, but that I'm not going to attempt to prognosticate that far into the future.

Q So your treatment recommendations at this point for purposes of this lawsuit, are that he will need two-times-weekly individual psychotherapy for three to four years and then, a decade later, will need individual psychotherapy one to two times weekly for an additional one to two years.

A Sometime in the decade after the completion of the first course.

Q And I'm not pinning you down to exactly what date or time or age he is going to need that. I'm just trying to understand the quantity of psychotherapy that you are recommending.

A Sure. Whoever is treating him will make that determination.

Q On the timing of the additional psychotherapy?

A Correct.

Q Understood. And what do you base your opinion that he will need twice-weekly psychotherapy to begin?

A On my assessment of his symptoms and his response to the abuse, on the nature of the abuse, meaning that there was actual masturbation there, and on my experience over decades with treating many victims of sexual abuse and evaluating approximately one hundred victims of child sexual abuse in lawsuits.

Q Is there any guidebook or a manual or—

A That is going to equate how much sexual abuse with how much treatment?

Q Is there anything that correlates those kinds of things to help you make that determination, I guess is my question?

A No.

Q So it is based upon your experience, your understanding of the severity of his response to the abuse, and also the nature and severity of the actual abuse?

A Well put.

Q Is that accurate?

A Yes.

Q And I assume the same is true with regard to the second round of future treatment. Is that also based upon your experience in treating this type of victim, the severity of his response to the abuse by Mr. Z., and the nature of the actual abuse.

A Yes. I will mention that there is a large body of knowledge about the fact that the effects of child sexual abuse last and continue to be detrimental throughout life. So the idea that more than one course of treatment is needed and that treatment may be needed at various points in the life cycle is very established. How much? No. That would depend on the individual case.

Q And Doctor, how can you separate out the treatment he needs specific to the sexual abuse from the treatment he will likely need ongoing for bipolar and cannabis and polysubstance abuse?

A Well, the same reasons we just talked about. Obviously, he is a whole individual, and those issues are there and will be there. But based on my understanding of the nature of the sexual abuse, based on my understanding of the severity of his response, and based on my experience, I can do that to a reasonable degree.

Q Is all of the treatment recommendation that we just discussed 100 percent attributable to Mr. Z.?

A Yes.

Q Did you prepare a report related to your diagnoses and opinions of Evan?

A Yes.

Q May I see that?

A Sure.

Q Did you write this report, Doctor?

A I did.

Q To the best of your knowledge, is the information contained in the report consistent with your deposition testimony today?

A Yes.

Q And in the historical section—strike that, did you actually type this report?

A I did.

She's looking for evidence that others may have influenced or changed my conclusions.

Q And does the content of this report reflect your—strike that, too. Is the content of this report entitled "Diagnostic Interview with Evan R.," essentially, a transcription of your notes from his conversation?

A A summation of them. Yes. Not word for word.

Q Is there anything you intentionally left out of the report that was contained in the note?

A No.

Q And in the "First Diagnostic Interview with Evan" section of your report, which, for the record was included in Exhib—

A 17.

Q —17, dated [date] with a cover sheet indicating that it totals eleven pages—is the information contained in the "First Diagnostic Interview with Evan" section of your report, essentially a transcription of your notes from that first interview?

A A summary of them.

Q Is there anything that you omitted from your notes when you drafted your report?

A Well, I didn't quote it word for word, so yes, things have been admitted.

Q Omitted?

A —Omitted, but only to make the report of a reasonable length, and the verbatim notes are here (indicating), in handwritten form.

Q Did you attempt to include everything relevant to your diagnoses and opinions in this report?

A I did try to.

Q And there was nothing intentionally left out—

Was I purposely leaving out material that might be damaging to the plaintiff case.

A No.

Q —of your conversation with Evan during the initial diagnostic interview when you transferred the information from your notes to the report?

A I did not intentionally leave anything out.

Q With regard to the "Second Diagnostic Interview" section of your report, is that intended to also be a summary of your in-person interview with Evan?

A Yes.

Q And did you intentionally leave anything out from the report that you had included in your notes from your conversations?

A No.

Q The "Review of Records" section of your report, dated [date]—do you have notes in your file about your review from records?

A I have notes that I took from reviewing the records.

Q And did you use those handwritten notes to transfer the information into the "Review of Records" section of your report?

A Yes.

Q Okay. And is the "Review of Records" section of your report intended to convey the information obtained through those records that's relevant to your diagnoses and opinions?

A Well, more for a sense of completeness, but—yes. Relevant information.

Q Are there any records you reviewed in formulating your opinions in this case that are not referenced in this "Review of Records" section?

A There may be. I summarized those that are particularly relevant to my diagnoses and recommendations.

Q Did you get any direction from Evan's attorneys with regard to preparing your report?

Obvious, but important to understand. The examining attorney was being thorough in determining if my testimony or report had been influenced by the plaintiff attorney.

A No.

Q With regard to the "Psychological Testing" section of your report—

A That was information that I took out of Dr. D.'s report.

Q Okay. And Dr. D. gave you an actual report of his psychological testing; is that true?

A He did.

Q And so you did not have to interpret the psychological testing data in order to get this information?

A I'm not qualified to interpret the psychological testing data.

Q So the answer is no?

A The answer is no.

Q And was your intention in drafting the "Psychological Testing" section of your report relating to Evan, to provide the information that was relevant to your opinions and diagnoses from Dr. D.'s testing report?

A To provide, basically, a summary of his testing report, with the understanding that his full report would accompany mine.

Q How did you pick out what to include in the "Psychological Testing" section of your report?

A I went through and tried to give a summary of his impressions and findings.

Q Did you receive any instruction or direction on what to include in the psychological testing aspect of your report?

A Just from me.

Q No one else?

A No one else.

Q And in the "Diagnoses" section of your report—is all the information contained in that section diagnoses that you reached based on the information in your possession?

A Yes.

Q Did you omit anything from your "Diagnoses" section when you drafted this report? That was a very poor question. Are there any diagnoses or opinions that you reached in this case that are not contained in the "Diagnoses section of this report?

A All the major ones are there.

Q Are there any additional, minor diagnoses that are not contained in the "Diagnoses" section of your report?

A There are no additional diagnoses. I'm just pointing out, again, that the purpose of the report is to convey in some kind of a legible and somewhat condensed way what my opinions are.

Q So we've, obviously, talked in much greater detail about your opinions in the course of this deposition, and as I understand it, you've provided me all the opinions you intend to offer at the time of trial with regard to Evan, is that correct?

She tries again to shut off other opinions that I might render at trial.

A I do with the exceptions, as we talked about, if there's additional information that comes out I'll review it, but I doubt that any information I'm going to get is going to change my opinions.

Q And with that, I suggest we take our lunch break.

PLAINTIFF ATTORNEY: Okay.

(The luncheon recess was taken at 12:01 p.m.)

Q Dr. Colarusso, may I remind you that you are still under oath?

A I understand.

Q Doctor, I just want to make sure we have covered everything that you are going to be discussing with regard to Evan. And I'm referring to the expert designation that plaintiffs have provided with regard to your anticipated testimony. It indicates that you will be testifying regarding the reasonableness and necessity of plaintiff's care and billings.

A Yes.

Q Have you made a determination with regard to the reasonableness of Evan's care to date?

A I will not be rendering any opinion on that.

Q And have we covered all of your opinions with regard to the causation of Evan's injuries?

A I think we have.

Q And have all of your opinions that you've provided thus far in your deposition been reached in your opinion within a reasonable medical/psychiatric certainty?

A Yes.

Q Doctor, would any of your opinions regarding the effect of Mr. Z. had on Evan change if there were evidence that shortly after the two encounters, Evan presented as happier, calmer, less depressed, less angry to his treating psychiatrist?

A No. You get a whole range of responses to—from children who have been sexually abused. Some actually appear to pull themselves together and to be better. Others fall apart. In this case in particular, it's such an embarrassing thing for a heterosexual adolescent, who is in the process of consolidating his sexual identity, to be sexually abused by a man—in other words, to have a homosexual experience—that I think Even did his best to cover it up, to pretend that it wasn't significant, and almost, even to defend the guy and say that what was happening wasn't important. And it's only later that he is able to see what actually happened, how illegal it was, and its effect on him.

Q Is same-sex or homosexual abuse more traumatic than heterosexual abuse?

A Well, that's a generalization and I can't make that.

Q I thought you assigned some significance on the fact that it was a man abusing a boy.

A Yes.

Q So the whole same-sex aspect of it—I thought I understood from your prior answer, which is why I was following up on that—

A Okay. But what I added was in a heterosexually oriented boy. In other words, you are heterosexual, you are adolescent, and you have an experience with another man, which goes completely counter to the grain of what you are trying to achieve sexually and how you are trying to consolidate your identity. So this is a very traumatic but terribly embarrassing experience.

Q Based on the fact that it was same-sex and not heterosexual?

Q Do you know for certain that Evan is heterosexual?

A Yes.

Q Did Evan tell you that he was heterosexual?

A He did.

Q Do heterosexual adolescents ever experiment with homosexuality in the course of developing their sexual identity?

A Yes, they do. The thing that is important is that when there is homosexual experimentation it's with chronological peers, as opposed to adults. And that makes it a totally different experience. For heterosexually oriented boys who do experiment sexually with peers, that usually drops out by mid-adolescence and doesn't occur after that.

Q When you say "sexual experimentation," does that imply that it is consensual?

A Between the two chronological peers?

Q Yes.

A Yes.

Q And if it's not consensual?

A I can think of a number of cases where it's characterized as sexual abuse. One was a case of a twelve-year-old boy who sodomized a five-year-old boy in a bathroom. That's sexual abuse, despite the fact that they are both minors.

Q In reaching your opinions regarding Evan, did you consider that Evan may have consented to the physical interaction with Mr. Z.?

A That's another one of these questions which gets me upset. And Dr.—your expert, again, said it was consensual sex. Legally, there can be no consensual sex between a minor and an adult, particularly an adult in authority.
Was this consensual sex? This boy was surprised, shocked, didn't know what to do and didn't know how to get out of the situation, which is, again absolutely typical when it comes, so—consensual? No. This is not consensual sex and to attempt to present it like that is a travesty.

Q The fact the Evan was surprised, shocked, and did not know how to respond—did that information come from your interview with Evan and his parents?

A Yes.

Q Any other source?

A No.

Q Did you understand that Evan was physically restrained by Mr. Z. during the two encounters?

A No.

Q Was Evan bound or tied by Mr. Z. during the encounters?

A No.

Q Was Evan locked in the room and unable to leave when the instances with Mr. Z. were occurring?

A No. He was not.

Q Are you aware that Evan was threatened by Mr. Z.?

A He was told not to tell and that they were good buddies. He felt threatened because he had no control of the situation.

Q Did he tell you when he felt threatened?

A He felt threatened as soon as Mr. Z. attempted to become sexually involved with him.

Q On the first time?

A Yes. Very definitely on the first time.

Q Are you aware of any evidence that Evan thought he was invincible at or around the time of his encounters with Mr. Z?

A No.

Q Are you aware of any evidence at all that would indicate that Evan was not really afraid of Mr. Z.

A Oh, there's lots of evidence that at first he was not afraid of him and, indeed, he liked him and—Z. did a perfect job of grooming. He was very nice to Evan, took him places, bought him things, so— No. At first, he was not afraid. The masturbation came out of the blue as he experienced it.

Q You brought up the term "grooming." What do you mean by that?

A Grooming is what a perpetrator does in order to gain confidence of a child and very often his family, and it consists of being nice, of forming a relationship with the parents so that he has access to the boy. It consists of becoming very involved in their lives in a very positive way. And with that foundation, he sets the stage for, one, opportunities to abuse the child—such as taking Evan out on his own—and, two, when he or she does begin to sexually abuse the child, that the child is confused and doesn't know how to respond, because it doesn't fit with the relationship up to that time.

Q So they develop a relationship of trust with the child and the parents and the people around them, in their environment, that then allows them access to perpetrate their crime; is that correct?

A Well said.

Q And is it just the kids and the parents that are groomed, or can it be caregivers and other people in their lives?

A That's possible that, you know, ancillary people could be groomed.

Q Has anyone from [the plaintiff law firm] told you what any of their strategies are for trial in this case?

A No. I asked if the case was going to go to trial. We do have a trial date. And the answer was, "We don't know. Most cases settle. This one may not." I knew that before.

Q Have you been paid on all the invoices that are in your file?

A I've been paid for everything that I billed.

My opinions are no being affected by the fact I had not been paid.

(Brief recess.)

Q Dr. Colarusso, for the final time, are there any additional opinions that you intend to offer at the time of trial that we have not discussed during your deposition today?

A For the final time, no. I don't recall anything. If I am asked anything, I might have more opinions, but you have all of my major opinions with regard to this boy in this lawsuit.

(The lawyer then rendered a check for hours spent at the deposition.)

Q I'm tendering a check to you at this time—

A Okay.

Q —receipt of which is acknowledged?

A Thank you. Yes. Receipt is acknowledged.

Q I don't think I have any further questions. (To the plaintiff attorney) Do you have any questions?

PLAINTIFF ATTORNEY: I have no questions.

Q I will offer the following stipulation: That other than preparing the transcript, we'll relieve the court reporter of her duties under the code. She will send the transcript directly to Dr. Colarusso at his office address, which is the location of the deposition and he will review the transcript within a week of receipt— Is that fair?

A That' fine.

Q —and return the executed and/or corrected edition of the transcript to my office—the court reporter will provide a self-addressed, stamped envelope addressed [to the defense law firm]—after review. We will notify counsel that it's been signed and notify her office of any changes within five days of receipt.

We will maintain the original at our office and make it available upon reasonable request. And if the original goes unsigned or is lost or otherwise unavailable, we'll stipulate that a certified copy can be used for all purposes, including trial.

PLAINTIFF LAWYER: Stipulated.

THE WITNESS: Would it be possible also to send a copy to [plaintiff attorney] so that she can then send me a copy to prepare for trial?

DEFENSE ATTORNEY: Well, she can order it.

PLAINTIFF ATTORNEY: We are going to be ordering a copy so we can do that.

DEFENSE ATTORNEY: So it will be possible for you.

THE WITNESS: Thank you.

(The deposition was concluded.)

In my opinion this was a very competent defense attorney who did a thorough, almost relentless job of attempting to understand my opinions in depth and to try to undermine them.

THE CASE OF EVAN DOE: DIRECT TESTIMONY OUTLINE

This direct testimony outline was never used because the case did not go to trial. However, the outline is presented as an example of preparing for trial with a child case. It was prepared by me and reviewed by the plaintiff attorney.

Q Dr. Colarusso, will you please outline your education from medical school to the present.

A I graduated from Jefferson Medical College in Philadelphia, Pa, in 1961. That was followed by a year of rotating internship at the York General Hospital in York, Pa, from 1961 to '62.

Q What training did you have in psychiatry?

A I completed a full-time, two-year adult psychiatric residency at the Eastern Pennsylvania Psychiatric Institute in Philadelphia from 1962 to '64. Then I completed a full-time, two-year residency in child psychiatry at the Albert Einstein Medical Center in Philadelphia from 1964 to '66.

Q Are you Board Certified in Adult and Child Psychiatry?

A Yes, I was Board Certified in adult psychiatry in 1969 and Board Certified in child psychiatry in 1972.

Q What did you have to do in order to become Board Certified?

A Complete two-year, full-time residencies in adult and child psychiatry as just described and take written and oral examinations by the American Board of Adult and Child Psychiatry.

Q Did you serve in the United States Armed Services?

A Yes, I served as an adult and child psychiatrist from 1966 to 1968.

Q Are you on the faculty of a university?

A Yes, I'm a Clinical Professor of Psychiatry at the University of California at San Diego.

Q Have you published any professional articles?

A Yes, I've published approximately fifty-five articles in professional journals and have published six books.

Q What does peer review mean?

A It means that the articles that I submitted were reviewed by peers who were on the publication board of professional journals and were deemed worthy of publication.

Q Are any of your publications on the subject of childhood sexual abuse?

A Yes, in 2010 I published a book entitled *The Long Shadow of Sexual Abuse: Developmental Effects across the Life Cycle*. New York: Jason Aronson.

Q What is the material in the book based on?

A My more than forty years of experience treating victims and perpetrators and my more than thirty years of experience as an expert witness in over one hundred cases of childhood sexual abuse.

Q Do you have a private practice?

A Yes, I have been in the private practice of adult and child psychiatry in San Diego since 1973.

Q Have you testified in court before?

A I've served as an expert witness in over 1,000 civil cases and appeared in court approximately 150 times.

Q Based on your experience as a clinician and an expert witness can you tell us about the psychological consequences of childhood sexual abuse?

A The consequences in most instances are lifelong and usually lead to new emotional problems as the individual moves into adulthood.

Q Please give some examples of what you mean.

A Women in their sixties, abused by priests as children, are still acutely suffering. Depression, alcoholism, refusal to have children, gambling, and broken or no marriages. Men in their forties and fifties who were abused by coaches or teachers as teenagers have sexual problems, depression, lack of achievement in the workplace, and broken marriages, etc.

Q What were you asked to do in this case?

A Do a thorough child psychiatric evaluation on Evan, and if indicated, makes diagnoses and treatment recommendations and determine future effects. I was also asked to comment on the conclusions of the defense psychiatric expert.

Q What did you do in order to evaluate Even?

A I conducted a 150-minute diagnostic interview with Evan's parents.
I saw Evan twice, once for 45 minutes and a second time for 95 minutes.
I ordered psychological testing performed by a forensic expert psychologist.
I reviewed the following records:

the trial reporter's transcript of Evan's testimony at Ben's trial
Evan's deposition
treatment records from his therapist
plaintiff's response to special interrogatories (set one)
the rehabilitation center's responses to form interrogatories (set one)

Q Why did you see Evan's father first?

A Because it is standard child psychiatric practice to see the parents of children and adolescents to gain an adult perspective on the issues involved in the case and to take a developmental history covering the child's life experience from birth to the chronological present.

Q What did you do during the 150-minute diagnostic interview with Evan's father?

A I gathered identifying information on the family members, asked about their knowledge of the sexual abuse by Ben and its effects on Evan, and took a developmental history.

Q Who are the members of Evan's family?

A His father is a businessman and his mother is a teacher. The couple married in 1987 and divorced seventeen years later. Evan, their only child, was born on August 14, 1995. He spends more than half of his time with mother but sees his father several times per week.

Q How did Evan get to know Ben?

A Evan returned to his mother's home late one evening when he was thirteen. He was very drunk. He was treated at the local emergency room and released. As a result, Evan was referred to an intensive outpatient program for substance abuse. A mandatory part of the program was attendance at AA meetings. A sponsor was required and Ben was suggested by a program administrator. Father asked what a forty-year-old man had in common with a thirteen-year-old boy. He was told that Ben attended the program and acted as a sponsor in order to remain sober. Father talked to other parents who described Ben as a great guy. Ben told mother that he was a gay man in a stable relationship.

Q How did the parents learn about the sexual abuse by Ben?

A They were told by the parents of Evan's friend. Evan had confided in his friend who told his parents.

Q Did Evan tell his parents about the details of the sexual abuse?

A No, they learned about the incidents of masturbation during Ben's trial.

Q Was there a change in Evan's behavior during the six months during which the abuse was occurring?

A Yes, during that time Evan was failing in school. Also, he was depressed and cut himself, resulting in an admission to a children's inpatient unit for several days.

Q Did the father describe other symptoms and effects of the sexual abuse on their son?

A Yes, they described Evan as becoming withdrawn and socially isolated. He had been diagnosed with Bi-Polar

Disorder in the past. These symptoms became more severe during and after the sexual molestation.
Evan felt more secure and experienced a sense of relief after Ben was incarcerated. He was fearful that Ben might make bail and come after him. Evan experienced nightmares.
"Evan is still the walking wounded. He has not begun to heal."

Q What did you learn from Evan's developmental history?

A Early development was within normal limits. Mother was the primary caretaker. There were no major separations from either parent throughout childhood. Evan was obviously bright and did well in school. He had friends and enjoyed sports. The parents were having marital difficulties during the elementary school years. When Evan was eight he began to act out and went into psychotherapy.
Puberty occurred when Evan was age twelve. He accepted the changes without difficulty. The sexual abuse by Ben began when Evan was thirteen.

Q Did you meet with Evan after your interview with his parents?

A Yes. I began by asking general questions about school to allow him time to become comfortable. He volunteered that he wanted to become a psychiatrist and treat drug abuse because he saw so many kids becoming addicted to drugs. We talked about his relationship with his mother and father. He described those relationships as "alright."
When asked about how he got to the rehabilitation center Evan spoke easily and without hesitation. He began using alcohol and marijuana at age twelve. After he developed alcohol poisoning and was in the hospital he was sent to the rehab program. He drank the alcohol to experiment.
Evan played Little League baseball for three or four years but wasn't very interested in sports now.

Q Did you have a second diagnostic interview with Evan?

A Yes, for 95 minutes. Early in the interview I asked why he got involved with alcohol and pot at age twelve. He explained that he was an outsider in elementary school and no one accepted him but the stoners. He struggled with the decision. "I had an angel and a devil on my shoulder." He did not see any relationship between his drug use and his parents' divorce.

I asked about his experience with his psychotherapist. Evan began therapy at age eight because of feeling about his parents' relationship with each other. He returned after the sexual abuse occurred.

Evan volunteered that he began to have trouble sleeping after his relationship with Ben began. Thoughts about the sexual abuse would keep him awake. Similar thoughts intruded into his masturbatory fantasies "a lot." Evan would think about a girl and "a thought about Ben would come into my head." Evan had intercourse for the first time during his sophomore year in high school. He was troubled by the thoughts of the sexual abuse that would intrude into his thoughts when having sex.

Q Did you ask about the sexual abuse by Ben?

A When Evan heard that Ben was gay, he wasn't concerned. He had no problems with gays. When Evan was taken to Ben's home Ben put on porno and gave the boy a cigarette. As they watched Ben asked if he could touch Evan's penis. Evan was shocked and scared and didn't know what to do or say. He mumbled OK. Ben unbuttoned Evan's pants, put his hand under the boy's underwear and masturbated him for fifteen minutes. "I didn't know what to think. I was scared." Then Ben pulled down Evan's pants and continued masturbating him. He asked if he could suck Evan's penis and kiss his butt. Ben told Evan not to tell anyone. "Dude, you're so cool. We're tight. You wouldn't do anything like that." After the abuse ended Evan cut himself in his upper thighs. "The physical pain distracted my mind from thoughts about the abuse."

Q Were there other sexual abuse experiences?

A Yes, there was one other that occurred soon after the first. As they rode in a car toward Ben's home he rubbed Evan's penis through his clothes. Once at his home Ben took Evan's pants off and masturbated him and performed oral sex. Evan was both anxious and depressed as he discussed the sexual abuse and its continuing effects on his life.

Q Did you get additional useful information from reviewing the record of Evan's trial testimony in the criminal trial of Ben and from Evan's deposition?

A Yes. In addition to describing the details of the sexual abuse Evan described his difficulty urinating in public toilets, becoming anxious when anyone touched him, feeling flat emotionally, and avoiding males. He felt shameful, regretful, and sad when engaging in sexual activity.

Q Did you review the records of his therapist?

A Yes. The therapist made a diagnosis of Posttraumatic Stress Disorder and rated Evan's symptoms in the severe range.

Q Did you obtain psychologist testing on Evan?

A Yes, a full battery of tests were administered.

Q What did the testing show?

A Evan was found to be anxious with constricted affect during the interview. He was cooperative and accurately reported his symptoms during the testing.
On the Wechsler Abbreviated Scale of Intelligence Evan achieved an overall IQ score of 120, placing him in the superior range of intelligence. There was no evidence of cognitive impairment on this or any other test.
On the Traumatic Symptom Check List for Children Evan demonstrated "clinically significant elevations on multiple scales, including those of anxiety, depression, posttraumatic stress, dissociation, and sexual concerns.
On the Personality Assessment Inventory for Adolescence the psychologist said "There is evidence of Posttraumatic stress in addition to significant symptoms of mood swings, anxiety, and depression. An unhappy and pessimistic individual, he has significant substance abuse problems as well."
The psychologist, who only did testing, suggested as diagnostic possibilities Posttraumatic Stress Disorder, Bipolar I Disorder, Cannabis Abuse, and a history of polysubstance abuse. He described the molestation by Ben in relationship to these diagnoses.

Q Did you make psychiatric diagnoses?

A Yes, using DSM-IV, the diagnostic nomenclature in use at the time, in my professional opinion Evan has the following diagnoses:

Sexual Abuse of a Child V61.21, Clinical focus on the victim 995.63
Posttraumatic Stress Disorder
Bipolar 1 Disorder, severe without psychotic features, most recent episode depressed. 296.53
History of Cannabis Abuse and Polysubstance Abuse.

At the time of the evaluation I rated Even's symptoms in the moderate range of severity.

Q Did you recommend treatment for Evan. *Did you recommend treatment for Evan?*

A I recommended individual psychotherapy, two times per week for three to four years to deal with the effects of the sexual abuse on his adolescent and young adult development.
At some point in the decade of the twenties and/or thirties, an additional course of individual psychotherapy, once per week, for one to two years is indicated to help Evan deal with the effects of the sexual abuse on the young adult developmental issues of intimacy, marriage, and parenthood.
Evan obviously has other problems that preceded the sexual abuse that also would benefit from psychotherapy and medication. I have attempted to separate the treatment required for these matters from the treatment required for the sexual abuse.
An experienced child and adolescent psychiatrist in San Diego would charge $250 per forty-five-minute session.

Q What is your prognosis for Evan if he receives the treatment that you have suggested?

A Child sexual abuse by an adult male, particularly during adolescence, has a profound negative effect on all aspects of adolescent development, but particularly on the emergence of a comfortable sense of masculinity. These effects tend to be lifelong and also affect self-esteem and later adult attitudes toward sexuality, marriage, and parenthood.
Coupled with the other significant mental and emotional problems that this young man is dealing with, the road ahead will be difficult but with personal and professional support the prognosis is fair to good.

Q Did you review the deposition and report of the defense mental health expert?

A Yes, I did.

Q What are your opinions in regard to his evaluation and conclusions?

Disagreeing with the defense psychiatrist in this case was not difficult because he was not trained to be a child psychiatrist, did not make the obvious diagnosis of child sexual abuse, and said that Evan consented to the sexual activity.

A The defense expert is not a Board Certified Child Psychiatrist. He did not take a child psychiatric residency. I question his ability to competently serve as an expert witness in this case.
In regard to his evaluation, he did not see the parents, standard procedure in a child psychiatric evaluation, and did not obtain psychological testing. Therefore, his evaluation is incomplete and inadequate.
He has very little experience with child sexual abuse. Experience and understanding of the manner in which perpetrators groom their victims and the devastating long-term effects are essential to understanding what happened to Evan.
Rather amazingly, since there is no question that Evan was sexually abused and the perpetrator has been convicted of the crime; he did not make a diagnosis of Child Sexual Abuse. This diagnosis is clearly stated in DSM-IV and DSM-V, as the diagnosis to be made when it is clear that child sexual abuse occurred. Further there is no indication in his report or deposition that he considered the criteria in DSM-IV or FV for the diagnosis of Posttraumatic Stress Disorder.
The defense expert essentially ignores the sexual abuse by Ben and says that Evan consented to the sex. Evan was pressured into the masturbation by a middle-aged adult who was in a position of authority over him. To suggest that Evan consented to the sexual abuse makes no sense psychologically or legally.
The defense expert blames Evan's symptoms on his preexisting problems. Clearly they were significant. That's why Evan went into rehabilitation in the first place. However, the sexual abuse stands by itself as a cause of the diagnosis of Child Sexual Abuse. It produced significant pathology and made preexisting problems worse.

NINE

A Survey of the Legal Literature

How Judges and Lawyers Think about the Role of Mental Health Professionals Involvement in the Legal System

After attempting to convey an understanding of how one adult and child psychiatrist understands what a mental health professional needs to know about the ins and outs of the legal system, it may be useful to consider how judges and lawyers think about mental health professionals. Not surprisingly, their thoughts are varied and complex and in a constant state of evolution. As our society changes, so do the way in which these two professions view and understand each other.

Courts are continually assessing the role of expert witnesses in the legal process. That assessment doesn't only apply to mental health professionals. For example, Galin (2012) proposes that courts disallow police officers from testifying as both experts and lay witnesses in federal drug prosecutions.

Another example of the dynamic, evolving nature of the legal process is the issue of restitution versus retribution. According to Reid and Collier (2012) restitution should be awarded to victims to compensate them for their losses, but excess retribution may be experienced as unfair retribution. Sentencing judges, prosecutors, and defense attorneys wrestle with this question as they try to instill a sense of fairness and justice in the issuance of an order to the defendant to pay the restitution.

Courts also struggle with the use and abuse of psychiatric evidence in rape trials (Ellison, 2009). Credibility barriers face rape complainants with a history of mental illness. The vulnerability of women with mental illness to sexual victimization is well documented but the same cannot be said of their treatment within the criminal justice system. When complainants fail to gain credibility at an early stage in the legal process, they frequently drop their suits. A recent survey of three hundred individuals with mental health problems, conducted by the charity Mind, found that a majority of victims had been victimized in the preceding two years and a sizeable number were facing ongoing bullying and harassment. Thirty percent of victims elected to tell no one. They feared that involvement in the criminal process would expose them to further discrimination and vulnerability. Sixty percent believed that their complaint was not taken seriously, in part, because of their psychiatric history. Ongoing change in all stages of the legal process is required to ensure that victims with mental illness have confidence in the criminal justice system and are treated with respect and dignity at every stage of the investigative, prosecutorial, and trial process. In a separate publication Ellison (2009) examined how psychiatric evidence is misused in rape trials and suggests more stringent limits on cross-examination to protect rape complainants against improper attacks on their credibility.

The ambivalence within the legal profession toward social science testimony is clearly evident in the following thoughts of Cunliffe (2006). Law is a discipline with its own rules and its own reasoning, but those rules and that reasoning are partial and culturally determined. To the extent that social science can encourage legal decision makers to glimpse that partiality and contingency, it should be embraced. However, it is difficult to discern the line between social science evidence that illuminates the partiality of common sense or the discriminatory effect of legal rules and evidence that tips the balance too far in favor of a particular interest group. To argue that social science evidence can perpetuate discriminatory reasoning within the law is not to say that all expert evidence should be admitted or excluded; rather a case-by-case determination of admissibility should pay explicit regard to the purposes for which the evidence is being adduced and the purposes for which the techniques and data underlying the evidence were produced. Principles of human dignity and equality that provide a means of controlling courts' engagement with other fields seem to offer the possibility of striking a right balance.

The legal concern about the use of psychiatric testimony is even more pronounced in the opinion of Showalter (1995). The differing nature of the theories of causality in generally accepted psychiatric theories, when considered along with the varying methodologies for obtaining psychiatric data through the process of psychiatric evaluation, and the diagnoses and treatment recommendations drawn therefrom; all create serious questions which are difficult enough to answer satisfactorily within psychiatry, and much more difficult to answer by a jurist who can only interpret the clinical psychiatric evidence from a lay perspective. The fact that the trial judge has a gatekeeping function in determining the threshold of admissibility of scientific evidence in the courtroom is clear enough but the law has not furnished a set of standards that can be taken seriously by the scientific community of forensically trained psychologists and psychiatrists.

Further, psychiatric testimony has caused consternation and confusion in both the court and the public in high profile cases (Braswell, 1987). For instance, consider the reaction of the public to the jury's not guilty by reason of insanity verdict in regard to presidential assassin John Hinckley Jr. As a result of that verdict Congress amended the Federal Rule of Evidence 704 in 1984. This led to courts prohibiting expert opinions on whether the accused was capable to judging between right and wrong and on whether the accused acted under an insane delusion or was impelled by an irrepressible impulse to commit the alleged crime. In Braswell's opinion concern about confusion does not justify keeping complex expert testimony from the jury, especially in an insanity defense case. Expert conclusions are particularly valuable at insanity defense trials where fact finders face enormous amounts of detailed evidence. When a psychiatrist testifies that a defendant has a mental illness that typically obscures the person's ability to tell right from wrong, the trial judge is in the difficult position of determining whether the testimony constitutes an opinion as to whether the defendant has the requisite mental state or is factual information concerning the defendant that the trier of fact can use to assess the insanity defense.

Concern about psychiatric testimony in the courtroom has been an issue for the law for a long time (Almy, 1984). Nearly fifty years ago Bernard Diamond, M.D., and David W. Louisell, Esq., noted that there had only been limited attempts to define the legitimate boundaries of psychiatric evidence and to develop broad general principles to direct the increasing use of psychiatric evidence into sound channels of legal process. Despite this obvious lack of legal definition and direction the courts permitted psychiatrists, psychologists, and other mental health professionals to testify at an ever-increasing rate. Little was done to control the circumstances under which their testimony could be introduced or to define its legitimate boundaries. As a consequence, psychiatric experts felt free to speculate on issues that often conclusively determined the outcome of a case. The issue was highly publicized after the successful use of the not guilty by reason of insanity defense by John Hinckley, the accused attempted assassin of President Reagan.

In this article Almy (1984) focuses on the use of psychiatric testimony in another area of the law, namely personal injury cases. The failure of the judicial system to define the appropriate limits for psychiatric testimony in personal injury cases is just as nebulous as in the criminal area but since these cases do not produce national headlines and public interest in reform little has been done, although the need is just as great. Almy gave an example from a case in the 1980s entitled *McCartney v. Lockheed* in which a six-year-old boy claimed brain damage and learning defects following an aircraft accident. A nonpracticing psychologist testified following a review of reports and case history documents, but without directly evaluating the child, who was then in first grade. The witness predicted that the child would hit a teacher sometime during high school and be expelled forcing the trial judge to try to cure this wild speculation by telling the jury to disregard what they had heard. That psychiatric testimony so ludicrous was still being offered illustrated Almy's belief that the judicial system had not come very far in defining the criteria for and the limits of psychiatric testimony.

Although I have not come across such "ludicrous" psychiatric testimony in more than three decades of serving as an expert witness, I am not aware of any widely recognized legal guidelines that provide a set of legal standards and expectations for psychiatric forensic experts.

Mental health professionals have a particularly important, clarifying role to play in personal injury cases and those which involve any other form of significant trauma (Goldstein, Whiteley, supplement text by LexisNexis J.D. authors). In such cases, mental health professional expert witnesses are essential to providing the jury with an analysis of a plaintiff's emotional injuries. The final determination of what is, or is not, emotional distress is left to the jury to decide.

The admissibility of a psychologist, as opposed to a psychiatrist, as an expert witness is a subject that has been discussed in the legal literature (Foster, 72 A.L.R. 5th 529). Physicians, especially those conversant with insanity or who have made a special study of mental diseases are widely recognized as being qualified to express expert opinion on the question of mental condition or competency. Foster addresses the question of whether a psychologist who is not a physician, but who has special training in the field of mental illness, is qualified to give such expert testimony. Courts have permitted psychologists to testify regarding mental condition or competence in a variety of areas including competency to stand trial, criminal responsibility, and the existence and etiology of many types of mental conditions or diseases. For example, in *Hutchison v. American Family Mut. Ins. Co.*, 514 N. W. 2d 882.72 A.L.R. 5th 785 (Iowa 1994), a neuropsychologist was properly permitted to testify that an insured's head injury was the result of an automobile accident in which she was involved.

It has not been my experience that courts hesitate to allow psychologists to serve as expert witnesses, particularly if it is recognized that psychologists have expertise that psychiatrists do not and that a psychiatrist and psychologist, working together, can provide the court with more comprehensive information on the issues at hand than either alone.

The subject of repressed memory in lawsuits is another area in which the court has grave concerns about mental health expert testimony while at the same time recognizing the valuable assistance that mental health professionals can contribute to a confusing and potentially very harmful accusations. According to Lazo (n/a) the main purpose of allowing expert testimony in repressed memory litigation is analogous to the rationale for using expert testimony in child sexual abuse prosecutions. Defendants argue that recovered memories of child sexual abuse are too unreliable to be admitted as evidence and that the current state of scientific knowledge about repressed memory is too contradictory and inconclusive to be a reliable basis for expert testimony. Many in the mental health profession, including this author, would agree with this view. However, the trier of fact needs the best opinion that the mental health field has to offer. Therefore, Lazo suggests that the expert witness in a repressed memory suit should be a licensed psychiatrist, psychologist, or clinical social worker with education, training, and experience in working with adult survivors of child sexual abuse. However, as most mental health professionals know, there is no agreement on this subject among the most experienced clinicians.

Doubts in the court system about whether or not to rely on the opinion of a psychiatric expert, alone, are described in an article by Burt and Philipsborn (1998). Some lawyers and judges support a position often taken in court by forensic mental health experts in which they propose that they are able to render full opinions on competence issues without resorting to other experts. Others in the legal profession prefer an enriched body of information developed for the trier of fact by a wider array of professionals. Judges differ in regard to their approach to mental health testimony but its usefulness is clear given the educational and professional differences between the functions that mental health professionals and lawyers perform in the court process.

CHILD CUSTODY ISSUES

Child custody is another area in which the court needs the help of child mental health professionals who have expert knowledge of child development and the role that parents play in a child's developmental progression through the first two decades of life. There is an extensive body of psychiatric studies dating back many decades that address every aspect of the relationship between parent and child in detail. Child psychiatrists and child psychologists who serve as expert witnesses in child custody cases must have the best interest of the child in mind as they attempt the courts with what are often gut wrenching decisions.

There is awareness of the mental health experts' ability to help the court focus on the best interest of the child. Take for instance the issue of whether to withhold visitation rights for failure to make alimony or support payment. (Raymond, 65 A.L.R. 4th 1155). Since the general rule is that visitation is to be denied only when in the best interest of the child, counsel for the custodial parent may wish to argue that denial of visitation by the noncustodial parent who has failed to make required support payments will foster the welfare of the child. A similar argument could be advanced where the noncustodial parent has failed to pay alimony, since the child's welfare could be adversely affected if the custodial parent were subjected to unnecessary economic worry. In opposition, evidence that visitation is in the best interest of the child should be presented. Psychiatrists, psychologists, pediatricians, and other professionals with knowledge of the child's situation may provide the court with essential information to make a decision that is truly in the best interests of the child.

It is my belief that almost all child psychiatrists and child psychologists would counsel that the best interests of the child are served by a continuous relationship with both parents unless one parent is considered to be severely mentally disabled or dangerous.

According to Becker (1996), judges eventually decide child custody cases on the basis of facts stated by ordinary witnesses and often on the basis of conclusions of expert witnesses. Therefore, the court must closely scrutinize the qualifications of experts and the relevance and reliability of the methodologies and theories underlying the experts' opinions must be subject to vigorous review.

Consider the issues faced by the court and any child mental health expert who had to advise the court or testify in the following case. A wife and mother informed her husband that she planned to move, with her children, to another state to live with her gay lover. When informed of this by his wife the husband presented his wife with two choices: she could fight to retain custody, knowing that the court might deny her any contact with the children due to her sexual orientation or she could stipulate to a reversal of the custody and visitation rights already established by the court. Father made allegations of sexual abuse. Mother and her partner facilitated the relationship between father and his children while father did the opposite.

The mental health expert suggested a physical examination of the children that showed no evidence of sexual abuse. The children were outgoing, healthy, and happy and showed none of the hypersensitivity to new people and environments indicative of sexually abused children; they did not suffer from PTSD. The masturbation of one of the children was presented as evidence of sexual abuse. The expert said that frequent masturbation is not a specific sexual abuse behavior, but it is common in children who are not getting their emotional needs met and feel isolated and lonely. Further, there was no evidence in the psychiatric literature that children of lesbian parents suffer psychological dysfunction or gender confusion. This case illustrates the complex issues involved for both the court and the mental health expert in difficult child custody cases, this one further complicated by the sexual orientation of the mother.

Mental health experts can be extremely helpful in child custody cases, not only by serving as experts at trial, but also by assisting counsel in assessing the case and in uncovering and defining factual issues (Gallagher and Dwyer, 2-34 NY Practice Guide). It has been my experience that a thorough psychiatric evaluation that includes a detailed developmental history of the individual from birth to the chronological present often brings to light information that the plaintiff or defense lawyer did not know and would not have discovered on their own. Often such information will significantly affect the lawyer's thinking and ultimate determination about how to present the case.

Helping lawyers gain knowledge about the various types of mental health professionals and how they may contribute to child custody cases is explored in an issue of *Family Advocate* (30 Fam, Adv. 4) by Richard Crane. He describes the various qualifications of the different types of custody expert witnesses, the required clinical experience, abilities, prestige, availability and, of course, the cost of paying for the expert. Crain explains the differences among psychiatrists, psychologists, and social workers in terms of their experience, education, and qualifications. Experts need to understand the workflow of the case, specific questions that may be asked by the judge, fine legal points in question and, of course, how to make a presentable and persuasive impression on the witness stand and in his or her report.

Bibliography

Almy, T. B. 1984. Psychiatric Testimony: Controlling the "ultimate wizardry" in personal injury actions. *19 Forum 233.*

American Psychiatric Association. 1973. *The Principles of Medical Ethics with Annotations Especially Applicable to Psychiatry*. Chicago: American Psychiatric Association.

American Psychiatric Association. 2013. *Desk Reference to the Diagnostic Criteria from DSM-5*. Washington, DC: American Psychiatric Publishing.

Braswell, A. L. 1987. Resurrection of the ultimate issue rule: Federal rule of evidence 704(b) and the insanity defense. *72 Cornell L Rev. 620.*

Brodsky, S. L. 1991. *Testifying in Court: Guidelines and Maxims for the Expert Witness.* Washington, DC: American Psychological Association.

Brodsky, S. L., and Heller, P. 2008. "Addressing the Perfect Phantom on the witness stand." *Journal of the American Academy of Psychiatry and the Law, 36*(December), 541–543.

Brodsky, S. L., Tese, M. S., Neal, Cramer, R. J., and Mitchell, H. Z. 2009. "Credibility in the courtroom: How likeable should an expert witness be?" *Journal of the American Academy of Psychiatry and the Law, 37*(December), 525–532.

Burt, M. N., and Philipsborn, J. T. 1998. Assessment of client competence: A suggested approach. *22 Champion 18.*

Caine, D., and Watson, J. 2000. "Neuropsychological and neuropathological sequelae of cerebral anoxia: A Critical Review." *Journal of the International Neuropsychological Society*, 86–99.

Clipson, C. 2012. Psychological testing evaluation of a plaintiff.

Colarusso, C. 1992. *Child and Adult Development*. New York: Plenum.

Colarusso, C. 2010. *The Long Shadow of Sexual Abuse: Developmental Effects across the Life Cycle*. New York: Aronson.

Colarusso, C., and Nemiroff, R. 1981. New York: Plenum.

Committee on Psychiatry and the Law, Group for the Advancement of Psychiatry. 1991. *The Mental Health Professional and the Legal System*. NewYork: Brunner/Mazel.

Cunliffe, E. 2006. "Without fear of favor? Trends and possibilities in the Canadian Approach to Expert Human Behavior Evidence." *IJEP 10 4 (280).*

Dasilva, W. H. Choosing the best custody expert witness. *30 Fam. Adv. 4.*

Ellison, L. 2009. "The Use and Abuse of Psychiatric Evidence in Rape Trials." *IJEP 13 1 (28).*

Ellison, L. 2009. "The Use and Abuse of Psychiatric Evidence in Rape Trials." *EvPro 13 1 (28).*

Fitzgerald, A., et al. 2007. "Anoxic brain injury: Clinical patterns and functional outcomes." *Brain Injury*, 1311–1323.

Foster, S. K. Qualification of nonmedical psychologists to testify as to mental condition or competency. *72 A.L.R. 5th 529.*

Gallin, B. R. 2012. To serve and protect? Officers as expert witnesses in federal drug prosecutions. *19 Geo. Mason L. Rev. 363.*

Gallagher, P., Dwyer, M. G. NY practice guide: Domestic relations 2 chapter 34 part C. *2-34 NY Practice Guide: Domestic Relations 34.20.*

Goldstein, J. A., and Whiteley, T. 11 Illinois jurisprudence personal injury and torts 6:27. *Illinois Jurisprudence 11-6 Chapter 6 II A.*

Gutheil, T. G. 2007. "The problem of evasive testimony: The expert 'waffle.'" *Journal of the American Academy of Psychiatry and the Law, 35*, 112–117.

Gutheil, T. G., Bursztajn, H., Hilliard, J. T., and Brodsky, A. 2004. "'Just say no': Experts' late withdrawal from cases to preserve independence and objectivity." *Journal of the American Academy of Psychiatry and the Law, 32*(December), 390–394.

Gutheil, T. G., Commons, M. I., and Miller, P. M. 2001. "Expert witness billing practices revisited: A pilot study of further data." *Journal of the American Academy of Psychiatry and the Law, 29*, 202–206.

Gutheil, T. G., and Simon, R. I. 1999. "Attorneys' pressures on the expert witness: Early warning signs of endangered honesty, objectivity, and fair compensation." *Journal of the American Academy of Psychiatry and the Law, 27*, 546–553.

Gutheil, T. G., and Simon, R. I. 2005. "Narcissistic dimensions of expert witness practice." *Journal of the American Academy of Psychiatry and the Law, 33*, 55–58.

Gutheil, T. G., Simon, R. T., and Simpson, S. 2006. "Attorney's request for complete tax records from opposing expert witnesses: Some approaches to the problem." *Journal of the American Academy of Psychiatry and the Law, 34*(December), 518–522.

Gutheil, T. G., Slater, F. E., Commons, M. L., and Goodheart, E. A. 1998. "Expert witness travel dilemmas: A pilot study of billing practices." *Journal of the American Academy of Psychiatry and the Law, 26*, 21–26.

Large, M., and Nielssen, O. 2008. "Factors associated with agreement between experts in evidence about psychiatric injury." *Journal of the American Academy of Psychiatry and the Law, 38*, 524–530.

Large, M., Nielssen, O., and Elliott, G. 2010. "The reliability of evidence about psychiatric diagnosis after serious crime: Part II: Agreement between experts and treating practitioners." *Journal of the American Academy of Psychiatry and the Law, 38*, 524–530.

Lazo, J. Comment: True or false: Expert testimony on repressed memory.

Macbeth, J. E., Wheeler, A. M., Sither, J. W., and Onek, J. N. 2005. *Legal and Risk Management Issues in the Practice of Psychiatry*. Washington, DC: Psychiatrists' Purchasing Group, Inc.

Melton, G. B., Petrile, J., Poythress, N. G., and Slobogin, C. 2007. *Psychological Evaluations for the Courts*. New York: Guilford Press.

Raymond E. L. Withholding visitation rights for failure to make alimony or support payments. *92 A.L.R. 3d 442*.

Reid, M., and Collier, C. L. 2012. When does restitution become retribution? *64 Okla. L. Rev. 653*.

Showalter, C. R. 1995. Distinguishing science from pseudo-science in psychiatry: Expert testimony in the post-Daubert era. *2 Va. J. Soc. Pol'y & l. 211*.

Slovenko, R. 2004. "Sequestration of lay witnesses and experts." *Journal of the American Academy of Psychiatry and the Law, 32*(December), 447–450.

Index

About the Author

Calvin A. Colarusso, M.D., is a clinical professor of psychiatry at the University of California at San Diego and training and supervising analyst in adult and child psychoanalysis at the San Diego Center for Psychoanalysis. In the private practice of adult and child psychiatry and psychoanalysis in San Diego since 1973, Dr. Colarusso is the author of more than fifty professional articles and six books on adult and child development, the long term effects of child sexual abuse, and various other clinical topics. For the past thirty-five years he has served as an expert witness in civil cases in California and throughout the United States.

www.ingramcontent.com/pod-product-compliance
Ingram Content Group UK Ltd.
Pitfield, Milton Keynes, MK11 3LW, UK
UKHW012035150926
475560UK00001B/29

9 781442 230392